The Apartme

By
Kate Good
Lisa Trosien
Mindy Williams
Jackie Ramstedt
Toni Blake
Pete Regules
Doug Chasick
Don Sanders
Heather Blume
Property Solutions

ISBN-10:0-9904769-0-1
ISBN-13:978-0-9904769-0-0
Copyright © 2014 by:
Kate Good
Lisa Trosien
Mindy Williams
Jackie Ramstedt
Toni Blake
Pete Regules
Don Sanders
Heather Blume
Property Solutions
Apartment Industry All Stars, LLC
All Rights Reserved
Printed in the United States of America
Edited by Kelly Treesh

The Apartment All Stars Complete Guide to Leasing Apartments

Table of Contents

Meet the Authors 1

Fair Housing Isn't Fair – It's EQUAL 3

Niche Marketing 13

Model Apartments 41

Maximized Rents & Economic Occupancy 60

Ring a Ling Leasing: The Phone Call Connection 85

The Psychology of Leasing 126

Competitive Selling: The Role "Value" Plays in the Pricing Game 146

Demonstrating for the Deposit 184

Overcoming Objections: Master This And Close More Sales! 219

The Art of Closing 239

You've Got Mail 273

iPad/Tablet Leasing 299

Fab-YOU-lous Fundamentals of Follow-up 315

Meet the Authors

Kate Good – As a speaker and author who is actively building, marketing and managing apartments, Kate Good brings real world experience into everything she does. Kate is Partner and Senior Vice President of Multifamily Development and Operations at Hunington Residential, and she is a founding member of the Apartment All Stars. Kate is an in demand speaker presenting to 15,000 apartment professionals each year.

Lisa Trosien is known for her meticulously researched presentations, high quality training and effective consultations. An industry expert, she is utilized by such publications as the Wall Street Journal, CBS MarketWatch, Chicago Tribune, Washington Post, National Public Radio and more.

Mindy Williams is the President of Rent & Retain Magazine and author of 10 books on property management. Mindy is THE guru when it comes to increasing occupancy with little or no money. Mindy lives with her amazing kids and husband in San Diego, California.

Jackie Ramstedt, CAM, CAPS, CAS from Austin, Texas is a requested repeat presenter and nationally renowned motivational keynote speaker, consultant, and performance coach who has more than 29 years experience in the multifamily housing industry. She is a veteran industry instructor teaching all National Apartment Association designation courses and core courses for the Texas Real Estate Commission.

Toni Blake is an award-winning speaker, consultant, author and comedienne inspiring multifamily apartment industry professionals every year. With over 30 years of training experience, her "laugh while you learn" approach has made Toni an industry favorite. As a published author, Toni's ideas have been published in dozens of trade magazines and blogs across the country.

Pete Regules has over 30 years experience in the Multifamily Industry working for CORT Business Services. He has Held leadership positions with The Apartment Association of Greater Orlando, Florida Apartment Association, and The National Apartment Association. Within these organization's Pete has been a motivational speaker, event emcee, and teacher. His passions include leadership, retention, and marketing.

Doug Chasick, CPM, CAPS, CAS is The Apartment Doctor, restoring rental health to Multifamily professionals for the past 38 years as a speaker, trainer, author, coach and gourmet chef.

Don Sanders has been a nationally recognized and recruited speaker within the multifamily industry for over two decades. He has held and continues to hold executive level positions with nationally recognized companies as their marketing and training expert. Over the years Don has guided both market rate and affordable companies to higher levels of success through his intense focus on employee development, elevated revenue generation and avid expense control.

Heather Blume is an author, speaker, trainer, & consultant for the multifamily housing industry who lives in the Seattle, Washington area. To learn more about her and read additional essays and articles, check out her website at www.btldconsulting.com, or www.behindtheleasingdesk.com

Chapter 1
Fair Housing Isn't Fair – It's EQUAL

By Doug Chasick

The essence of fair housing is an equal opportunity – which does not always look like "fair." In order to comply with federal, state and local fair housing laws, multifamily professionals must provide an equal opportunity for everyone to:

- Buy or lease the home of their choice, provided they qualify, and
- Have equal enjoyment of the home they have purchased or leased

While it's true that many fair housing classes tell us to "treat everyone the same," fair housing compliance is not always about "same treatment." Fair housing is always about "equal opportunity" and "consistent treatment for same circumstances." We'll take a closer look at how this distinction informs what we say and do, but first, some fine print:

- **We are not attorneys, and this information is not intended to be legal advice.**
- **This information is based on industry best practices and is offered as such. For legal advice, please consult an attorney who specializes in fair housing (which may not be the same attorney who is handling your landlord-tenant issues.)**
- **Make certain you are aware of any protected classes enacted by your state and local agencies; remember that any legislative body can create protected classes.**

- **Please do not change any of your policies and procedures without the specific permission of your supervisor.**

So what is this fair housing stuff all about and why should you care? Run an internet search for "fair housing laws" and start reading the search results that include "HUD" (which stands for the Department of Housing and Urban Development, the federal agency that, along with DOJ – the Department of Justice – enforces the federal fair housing laws.) You can also visit their websites (www.hud.gov and www.justice.gov) and start your search there. The Fair Housing Act (FHA) and the Fair Housing Amendments Act (FHAA – which explains the protected classes of Familial Status and Handicap) live there. You should also run a search using the words "fair housing" and the city, county and state where your community is located. Please remember that any legislative body can create fair housing protected classes, and it's important for you to know all of the protected classes that exist in your jurisdiction.

As Leasing Professionals, your job with regard to fair housing compliance is to treat everyone in an equal and consistent manner so that they feel welcome and are offered either the opportunity to lease an apartment home (if they are prospects) or the opportunity for equal enjoyment of their apartment home (if they are our residents.)

The most important thing to remember when interacting with your customers – prospects and residents – is to be consistent in your treatment of them based upon their situation and circumstances, not their personal attributes. We care about prospects meeting our qualifying standards and residents complying with our lease and house rules. We don't care about their personal attributes, such as race, color, religion, national origin, sex, familial status or handicap (which just happen to be the federally protected classes), or their age, sexual orientation, marital status, or creed (which are examples of some common state/local protected classes.) In other words, "Do you pay your rent on time and play well with others?"

In other chapters of this book, we will share about building rapport and establishing a relationship with your customers, and that is an essential element of any sales conversation. Fair housing compliance doesn't mean you can't talk about the fact that your customer recently moved to the US from some other country. Fair housing compliance requires us to evaluate the customer's application to lease based on our qualifying standards and not where they just moved from. If we deny their application because they don't meet one of our qualifying standards – income, credit or landlord history, etc – that is legal. If we deny their application because of where they moved from, that is illegal.

The "official" definition of discrimination, according to Dictionary.com, is: "Treatment or consideration of, or making a distinction in favor of or against, a person or thing based on the group, class, or category to which that person or thing belongs rather than on individual merit: racial and religious intolerance and discrimination."

To comply with fair housing, remember to treat each person as a unique individual and focus only on what they want and need in their new apartment home and whether they qualify for the home they want. While it is impossible to eliminate the possibility of being named in a fair housing complaint, it is possible to minimize the damage and this is the first step!

Also remember that discrimination is in the eye and ear of the beholder and that fair housing compliance is based upon <u>impact, not intention</u>. If someone feels like you are treating them in a discriminatory manner, they can file a complaint – even if you don't feel as though you treated them in a discriminatory manner. So if something you do or say is found to violate a federal, state, or local fair housing law, it doesn't matter whether you intended to violate the law; it only matters that you did violate the law. In case you were wondering: there are no do-overs, no "Oh, that's not what I meant!" If you said it, or did it, then you own it.

There is no way to guarantee that you will never be named in a fair housing complaint or lawsuit, even if you dot every "i" and cross every fair housing "t" because anyone can file a complaint, even if you "did everything right."

The best you can hope for is to minimize the damage, and the best way to do that is to proactively practice fair housing. In other words, don't focus on what you can and cannot say and do; focus on offering everyone who is qualified an equal opportunity to lease a home and offer every resident equal access and enjoyment.

Here are our suggested best practices, based on generally accepted fair housing compliance practices we've observed at many apartment communities across the country, heard in conversation with industry professionals, and seen in industry publications. Remember that "one size doesn't fit all." We are responsible for treating each person as an individual, and interacting with them based on situation and circumstance, not personal attributes that don't relate to whether or not they meet our qualifying standards.

For Prospects:

1. The initial contact:

- When asking about the number of occupants, ask about people, not adults and children (unless you are leasing at a Senior Living community.) Your occupancy standards are based on the number of people, not their ages.
- Don't discourage a visit, even if the prospect is not qualified. Once you have explained your qualifying standards to a prospect, it's up to them to decide if they want to visit your community, take a tour, and complete an application.

- When responding to information requests that come in by phone, email, or internet, make certain that you maintain consistency in the time frame and manner in which you respond. Check to see if your company has a policy about how much time you have to respond to a request and if you have templates for different types of inquiries that you can personalize to the customer.
- Remember that different cultures have different customs and a phrase or gesture (or lack of) might mean different things to different people. It is quite possible for someone to mistake our lack of knowledge about their customs as discrimination or disrespect, which is equally undesirable. Generally speaking, it is appropriate to rise when greeting customers, smile, make eye contact and inquire about the purpose of their visit.

2. The Tour:

- Do not discourage a tour (or an application), even if the prospect is not qualified. Once you have explained your qualifying standards to the prospect, it is up to them if they want to tour and/or submit an application. Have a defined tour route that you use for each prospect. If the prospect doesn't want to see something – the pool, tennis courts or whatever – make a note on the guest card and skip that part of the tour.
- Let the customer steer you – do not steer the prospect. It is a best practice to show the same apartments to each customer until the particular apartment is leased. For example, when you have a couple of market-ready two bedroom apartments, each customer who requests a two bedroom apartment should be shown these apartments until the apartment is leased.
    - If one of the apartments is on the first floor, and the other apartment is on the third floor in a non-

elevator building and the customer only wants to see first floor apartments, it's fine to show only the first floor apartment – that is an example of the customer steering you, which is legal.

- o If the customer is in a wheelchair and you decide to show only the first floor apartment, it could be seen as you steering the customer. Steering the customer is illegal.

- Show every prospect the same apartments within the style and size they requested. As shown in the example above, it is up to the customer, not us, to determine what they want to see in terms of size, view, floor, price, etc. Even seemingly helpful, benign advice could be misconstrued as steering. In the absence of a specific request from a customer about a particular floor, view, price, etc., show each customer the same apartment within the size/style requested.
- Document which apartments were shown on the prospect's guest card. Avoid using abbreviations or "codes" as they could be misconstrued; simply note which apartments were shown and also anything else that occurred on the tour regarding deviations from your tour route.

3. The Application:

- Don't discourage anyone from submitting an application, even if you're 100% certain that the application will be denied. The best way to offer an equal opportunity to lease is to give each prospect a copy of your qualifying standards and make certain that they read and understand the standards. After that, it is up to the prospect to determine if they want to submit an application to lease; we should not encourage or discourage them.

- Every applicant should be offered the same pricing, terms and conditions for each apartment home. If a price special is being offered, it should be a price special for a particular apartment, and not based on the person.

4. Follow-up:

> If your policy requires a follow-up phone call, post card or thank you note, follow-up with everyone and within a standard time period. If you place the follow-up phone call with everyone within 30 minutes of their visit, you should do that with everyone unless circumstances prevent it – in which case you should document what happened to delay the call.

For Residents:

- Remember that fair housing applies seven days a week, 24 hours a day, and 365 days a year. It's likely you will see your residents while you are both out and about, perhaps in the grocery store or at the mall. If you live at the apartment community where you work, chance meetings off-site are almost guaranteed! A best practice is to never say or do anything while in the presence of a resident off-site that you wouldn't say or do if both of you were in your office. Never assume you're "off the record" – you're not.
- Enforce all rules equally and consistently. "Equal treatment" means no preferences: everyone is given an equal opportunity to use and enjoyment of their apartment home, community amenities, and facilities, within the community rules you have established.
- Take all complaints seriously.

For Everyone:

- Attitude is everything. Disrespect (unintentional due to cultural ignorance or just not paying attention) can easily be mistaken for discrimination. Pay attention and be 100% committed to helping everyone you interact with.
- Do not make exceptions to any of your policies and procedures without the express permission of your supervisor.

Disability 101

The Federal Housing Administration tells us that everyone is entitled to equal enjoyment of their home and community, and the Fair Housing Amendments Act (FHAA) provides two ways to make that happen: accommodations and modifications.

Accommodations are changes in your rules, policies, and procedures. Modifications are physical changes to the apartment home, the common areas, amenity areas, etc. Each request must be evaluated to determine if it satisfies the definition of "reasonable" and if it is necessary due to the requestor's disability. The evaluation is typically made by a manager or compliance officer. Make certain you know what your company policy and procedure regarding requests for accommodations and modifications.

(NOTE: We can never inquire as to the nature of the person's disability. We can, under certain conditions, inquire about a person's need for a disability. If you are uncertain about your company policy governing this practice, ask your supervisor.)

It is of the utmost importance that you know and follow your company policies regarding disabled prospects and residents. At the time of this writing, almost half of all fair housing complaints filed – for the past five years – have alleged that the person was denied equal opportunity to lease a home and/or equal access and opportunity to enjoy their home.

For Prospects and Residents:

- If a resident or prospect appears to be disabled, do not ask them if they need an accommodation or modification. It is the responsibility of the disabled person to make a request, and we are not required to make the initial inquiry.
- The request for accommodation or modification may not sound obvious; for example, a prospect who requires an emotional support animal may casually mention that they have a cat. When you respond that you don't allow pets at your community, the prospect will respond with, "But he/she is not a pet." That constitutes a request!
- If a prospect or resident requests an accommodation or modification based on their disability, respond by saying "We'll be happy to consider your request; we'll just need to complete our request form." While you cannot force anyone to complete the request form, you should have a completed form for each request; if they won't complete the form, we suggest you complete it for them.
- Do not make any promises or offer any opinion about whether a request for an accommodation or modification will be approved, even if a number of seemingly similar requests have been approved. The law requires each request to be considered individually and treated as a unique request. The request should be approved or denied on that basis.
- The majority of accommodation requests are about parking spaces and assistance animals. Your job is to follow your company policy about documenting the request and completing a request form. Do not attempt to determine if the customer is disabled, if the animal is actually an assistive animal, or offer any opinion or statement about their request being approved or denied.

As Leasing Professionals, we are often the first contact person for the prospect and the most frequent contact person for the resident.

One very important part of our job is to collect information and pass it along to the final decision maker. The decision maker may be the manager who approves or denies leasing applications; the compliance officer who reviews and either approves or denies accommodation and modification requests; or any other team member who relies on accurate and timely information to make operational decisions. In this role, it's not our job to "vote" on a prospect's leasing application or a resident's modification request. Our job is to get as much accurate information and pass it along to the decision maker.

The most important aspect of our job – and the most expensive if mishandled – is interacting with our prospects and our residents. While it's important to know what the protected classes are in your jurisdiction, it's more important to remember that the essence of fair housing is equal opportunity and equal enjoyment. When you treat each person with respect, with genuine interest and with the goal of giving each person an equal opportunity to lease a home and enjoy living in that home, you greatly minimize the possibility of running afoul of the Fair Housing Act.

Chapter 2
Niche Marketing

By Heather Blume

Of the many hats worn by front office personnel at communities, the marketing hat always has the possibility of being the most fun. Marketing is one of those beautiful nexuses where the dreamer and the logician find common ground in our industry. If the attraction to the light of challenges and possibilities found in the realm of marketing are enough to draw our brightest creative and analytical minds, then it is the specialized challenges that keep these gifted moths fluttering close to the flame of innovation. One place you'll find a great marketing challenge is niche marketing.

Niche product presentation invites the marketing minded individual to delve deeply into a more limited subset of the customers that their product already serves. The eventual goal is to gain a higher share of business within that smaller, but more concentrated base of users, and attract additional customers from that group. Some examples of niche markets include student housing, military housing, artists, second chance housing, and strippers. That's right, I said strippers.

This chapter will teach you:

- How to identify those marketing niches that might exist in your current resident base
- How to get the information, analyze the numbers, and use that information to guide your marketing efforts
- The possible risks and rewards of embracing the niche market
- How to match your property's offerings with potentially untapped niche markets in your area

- Some of the challenges unique in this type of marketing with regard to following the federal fair housing guidelines

In addition to those topics, you'll also find ideas on how to extend your niche marketing efforts into both your resident retention efforts and as well your development and amenity offerings. Finally, we will round out this chapter with a few examples of niche marketing efforts by industry marketing masters that should help spark the fires of your own creativity!

Niche marketing isn't something you run as a "campaign." Niche marketing is about finding out who you are as a property in the market, and finding out what it is that you do better than anyone else. After all, renting to the masses is what everyone does – and to be an All Star, it's about knowing how to shine!

An Example with Frosting

For a moment, pretend that you work in a bakery. Your bakery produces cake, bread, cookies, and breakfast type bakery items. The types of cake your bakery sells are sheet cakes, wedding cakes, and cupcakes. You likewise sell different types of bread – loaf bread, quick breads, crackers, and scones. The types of cookies that you offer are sugar, oatmeal raisin, snicker doodles, and chocolate chip. And, finally, your assortment of breakfast items is made up of English muffins, donuts, muffins, and crumpets.

Now, while everything your bakery makes is excellent, when you ask people why they came to your bakery, the answer is often, "For the cupcakes!" Indeed, you seem to sell more cupcakes than anything else on your menu, and each day they're almost always sold out before 2pm.

When it comes to marketing your product, since you sell more cupcakes than, say, loaves of banana walnut bread, which is smarter: market the cupcakes and try to capitalize on that product since you know people love it. Or, rely on the fact that the cupcakes will always sell, so you put your marketing money into the lower selling items like cookies and banana walnut bread?

The answer is both. You know the cupcakes are going to sell, and you know that you have a reputation in the market for them. Clearly, putting your advertising dollars into pushing the cupcake sales is a wise choice. But if you also know that people are buying your crumpets or scones fairly regularly, then it would be folly not to market those as well, even if the section of the market isn't as large as the section of those who enjoy the cupcakes.

If you're going put all your marketing time and energy into simply chasing only the cupcake market, then it's time to stop baking the scones and crumpets. You've just become a cupcake shop – a boutique business. If you ignore the cupcakes in your marketing and focus exclusively on the products that are not selling as well, then you're giving up an excellent source of customer traffic and allowing a competitor a chance to come in and take that market share away from you while you're neglecting it. To remain a bakery with a variety, you have to pursue the three or four other quality submarkets that you service, as well as the "sure thing" cupcake market. You have to have a multi-pronged marketing offensive.

Being the smart marketer that you are, before you order a banner to promote your cupcakes or hire a skywriter to send out your delicious message over the city, you might first ask your customers WHY they love your cupcakes. Is it the recipe? The frosting? The cute little bakery where they're made? The customer service? Is it that your bakery is located close to their office? That you encourage moms to let their kids play in the corner of the store with a little play-land? What flavor is their favorite and why? It could be any number of things, and until you know why they're choosing your cupcakes, you can't promote that very valid justification as a reason for new cupcake craving customers to buy from you. Likewise, you have to ask the same questions of your other highest sellers. Are you the only place in the city that makes crumpets? Is it the crumpets your customers love and not only the homemade Nutella type spread that you use on them? Why do they buy your scones, and not the cheaper scones from the grocery store or the chain bakery type store down the road? No matter if we're talking about your best selling or your sub selling products, understanding why the money is flowing in for them is crucial.

Another question you might ask yourself is who exactly your customers are and what you know about them. After all, these people willingly give you their money. Shouldn't you know something about them besides the fact that they have wallets? What's the average age of the people who love your cupcakes? Are they female or male? Do they come in by themselves or in a group? Are they gay, straight, bisexual, etc.? Are they married, dating someone, or single? Sure, some of these things my seem like silly questions…right up until the moment that you discover your triple chocolate dream cupcakes, which have the super-secret ingredient of liquor, sell best to newly single people (most specifically women, but not only women) because it turns out that your treats offer more sweetness and are more satisfying than many romantic relationships out there.

If your data points about these cupcakes indicate that your shop provides the foundation of a break-up diet, then why not embrace it? Why not market to those who have already shown that they are most likely to use your product in an attempt to gain infamy among them, and more business from that group of people? It makes sense, doesn't it?

That's exactly what niche marketing is all about! But, instead of cupcakes, our product is apartments, and it's all about finding the right flavor in our advertising to sate the needs of our customers. The usual goal with niche marketing in the apartment world is not to become a boutique housing source (all though some properties do this very well), but to find areas in your customer base that you can best serve. It's not always about finding a single thing you do well, but a handful of sectors that you can send your message towards and get the best response. While niche marketing can seem intimidating to understand at the outset, if you're willing to put in the research and work behind understanding why people do business with you and what their common links are, you will never find a more satisfying source of new residents.

Marketing versus Niche Marketing

A Marketing plan – it's almost a certainty that your property has one. If you're not familiar with your property's marketing plan, it's time to take a look at it. Most marketing plans out there overlap with some basic components:

- **Analysis of the Current Situation** – How are things going today? What's our occupancy vs. economic occupancy? What are our weaknesses? What does our turnover rate look like? All of these questions (and more) are answered in this portion of the plan.
- **Goals** – What are we working toward? Whether it's an increase in occupancy, a specific percentage of NOI growth over the next year, a specific percentage goal to reduce turnover by, etc., this is where you clarify the direction that you want to move in the coming year.
- **Opportunity Assessment** – What else can we do? Frequently in property management, as in any industry, we get blinded by the glare of those sitting in the home stadium bleachers - whom we think our customers are. Through a quality assessment, we can attempt to seek out new fields to play ball on.
- **Target Markets** – Who's buying from us? This section is all about the demographics of your customers, and frequently by looking at these numbers and thinking creatively; we can find additional markets that share overlapping demographics with the customer base that we already serve.
- **Strategies** – How do we intend to achieve the goals we've laid out? Here is where you'll find strategies for everything from resident retention to ILS service usage, to Craigslist plans, to projected rent increases, to grassroots and social media strategies, to full marketing campaigns, and more.
- **Implementation Time Line** – When are we doing all of this? Knowing how the plan will be executed, and the approximate timeline for each component helps to ensure a

higher rate of success. It also helps us look at everything that has to be done and not be overwhelmed by the enormity of it all.
- **Budget** – How much can we spend? Understanding how much is a realistic amount of cash to shell out in order to drive traffic to your property can help you be more creative. Not only does is it important to not go over budget, but when our financial resources are tight, we have to think of more efficient and new ways to reach our customers.

Niche marketing isn't specifically laid out in any of these sections, nor does it have its own bullet point. This marketing approach isn't a step in itself -it is interlaced into each of these main areas. For instance, when you look for potential opportunities for gaining new customers, targeting markets, or for growth – that's got niche marketing written all over it! You have to have a strategy, timeline, and a goal to measure the success of your efforts, and you have to know how much money your property and company are willing to shell out in pursuit of a particular niche.

Niche marketing shouldn't be run as a campaign, or as a single-serving-sized effort. It's not a side project, or something that you include as part of your marketing plan. Quality niche marketing is the HEART of your marketing plan. It affects the demographics you focus on, the amenities and services you offer, the style of sales interchanges, and, especially, the marketing story that you send out to your customers. Knowing what your property does well and cornering the market on that is a recipe for success!

Marketing Research Begins at Home

It's an overused cliché to say "charity begins at home," but in our case, so does marketing research. Before you start looking for new residents, take the time to study the ones you've already got. Most companies track the demographics of their residents, many of them with the help of resident management software systems such as Yardi. Some of these basic demographics come from rental applications (age, income, occupation, etc.), but other information can be gathered at the time of the move in and from simple conversations that you have in an effort to build rapport and relationship with your resident. Depending on your local and state fair housing laws, what you can track may be limited. To simplify things for now, let's pretend that your property is located in an area where only the big 7 classes apply (Race, Color, Religion, National Origin, Gender, Familial Status, and Disability). Operating within the limitations of those restrictions, you could additionally gather statistical information on a number of other information points, such as:

- Marital Status
- Their Age/Generation
- Reason for Moving
- Local employer
- Make, year, and model of car
- Cable or ISP provider
- Referral source/Ad source
- Social Media usage - What platforms?
- Preferred method of communication - Social Media? Phone? Email? Text? Letters? In person?
- Hired a moving company vs. moved themselves
- Most frequently asked for features, floor plans, or floor levels.
- Why they rented with you
- White collar jobs vs. blue collar jobs
- Job industry
- What do they do for fun? Are they crafters, outdoorsmen, sports players, etc.
- Usual physical appearance – designer clothes? Dress clothes? Yoga pants and flip flops?
- Pets – cats? Dog? Hamsters? Snakes?
- Length of daily commute in miles
- Duration of daily commute in minutes

- Did they host parties/gatherings while in their tenancy with you? How many?
- Do they attend resident events regularly? Which ones?

Looking at this list, it's easy to be overwhelmed. After all, that's a daunting amount of data points to keep track of about our residents. It may seem odd to ask for or track some of these things, but the truth is that the more data points you are able to collect about the demographic that currently rents from you, the better your understanding of that demographic will be. As a comparison, consider the artistic style of pointillism, popularized by the French painter Georges Seurat. His painting, *A Sunday on La Grande Jatte (1884)* is one of the most frequently cited examples of pointillism. If you've seen Ferris Bueller's Day Off, this is the painting that Ferris, Cameron, and Sloane spend time staring at while they're at the Art Institute, which features a group of people on a hill in the park and is comprised completely of tiny little dots of paint. With only a few dots, a painting like this wouldn't be much to look at, but once you add in enough dots, they grant the image depth and create a complete picture of the people on the hill. This is our goal with gathering all of these resident data points – to create a complete picture of the people who rent from us in an effort to better understand them and reach them with our marketing messages.

If the thought of asking for this information seems a bit too forward to you, then take a moment and think of a single building or floor at the property where you work. Do you know all the residents who live in that space? Odds are you do. Make a list of those residents right now. Next, by the name of each of those residents, list as many of these data points that you can remember. You'll be surprised how much you already know about the residents at the community where you work if you just take a moment to think about it. This exercise makes a great teamwork assignment, and it can be fun to compete over who in the office knows the most about the residents on your property. Invite your maintenance staff to join in – remember, they're on the front line. We deal with residents in the office, but they deal with residents in their homes, so it's likely that they know even more information about what our sub-demographics are than even we do! This activity is great when you're first looking for the niche markets that you can serve, but it can also come in handy during your renewal process. Add to the questions about your residents a list of all the interactions that you've had with them in the months leading up to their renewal and a speculation as to the possibility of the resident signing their renewal. Regional Manager Kris Buker at Equity Residential says that this practice is part of the renewal process at their apartment homes and that their team finds the exercise to be useful in building and keeping resident relationships.

Factor in Additional Data Points

Data from your residents is essential to your research, but what they provide are not the only data points that matter when it comes to identifying possible niche markets for your property to serve. The local area around you can factor greatly in exactly the demographic that would see your property as a viable option for a home. Below is an exercise that your leasing team can do together, or that you can do on your own, to help identify and find information that can help lead you to the discovery of possible niche markets that your property can excel. You'll find the worksheets for these lists at the end of this chapter, or you feel free to make your own.

- First, pull up your property on a Google Map. Open the map so that the radius shown around your property is five to seven miles.
- Make a list of every business in that area. Classify them into categories such as retail, restaurants, grocery stores, services, industrial, etc.
- List the 10 top reasons why people would "drive by" your property. This could be that you're located on the main road, that you're down the street from the library that your property is near a state park or another recreation source, etc.

- Next, make a list of the top five employers in your area. Then make a list of the top five employers of your residents. These lists might match, and they might not.
- Finally, list 10 additional points of interest near your property. Here you'll list things like state parks, historical sites, parks, climbing gyms, or other attractions that wouldn't be found around every property – just yours!

With these lists, you will be able to see a bird's eye view of everything industry or lifestyle-wise that could drive someone to rent at your property. Add to this list any research that you can find about industries in your area that may be getting ready to bring an influx of workers to the area. Also, take a look at the economic forecast in your region for the current year. You can often get this forecast from online sources or your local apartment association. Many of the associations have a yearly economic forecast session that discusses things like hiring trends, buying vs. renting trends, and occupancy stability possibilities in your region.

While the bird's eye view is great for starters when it comes to learning the area around your property, the case for actually getting out and experiencing the community around you cannot be overstated. You might tell people how great the library three blocks down is, or how fantastic the pizza at Ralph's is, but if you've never experienced either, how can you really sell them? That would be like trying to rent someone an apartment at a community that you've never been to, seen, and, therefore, have no reason to be vested. When you haven't taken the time find out for yourself first hand and have your own impressions about what you're discussing, then all you're selling are rumors. Your credibility as a sales professional is worth more than that!

Compare and Contrast with your Comps

Knowing everything you can about your direct competitor properties will be a huge assist in helping you find your niche. Identifying "comps" for some properties can be challenging because, while you have several properties within a 3-5 mile radius of you, they might not have the same style of product as your property.

Start by creating a list five to seven properties that are close to you – ideally, they will offer a similar product to you, but if that is not an option then list the properties that come closest to what you offer. These five to seven properties are your "geographical comps," meaning that they are close to your property in location, but not necessarily in what they offer to residents.

Next, either make a list from your own knowledge or check back through your guest cards for other properties that potential residents have mentioned they're looking at as well as your property. Some of these properties may be in your geographical comps list, but odds are some of them aren't. For example, years ago when I was onsite, I worked at a B+/A- property in the area of Bellevue, Washington, known as "Eastgate." While we had several properties around us that offered comparable product, frequently we would be on a prospect's tour list next to properties in Issaquah (7 miles away), downtown Bellevue (8 miles away), Kirkland (15 miles away), and Redmond (15 miles away). These properties would have been easy to discount as comps because they weren't located very close to us at all, but we stole more than a few leases away from these other housing options, so they definitely counted as "Product Comps." They offered accommodations very similar to ours and matched up with us on amenities and rent costs closely. Because of the close matching on product offerings, their resident demographics also correlated closely to the demographics that our property most frequently served.

Usually, our market survey covers the weekly updates in offerings for our top five comps. This analysis is going to be cover more properties, and will go a bit deeper. Also, unlike our standard market survey, we will only do this one every 12-24 months, or when new lease ups/rehabs enter the market around us. While we will make use of the information that we've gathered on their amenities and average rents, as well as the floor plans that they offer, we're more looking for the niche markets that our competitors serve.

Since it's not likely that they will just come out and tell you their niches in a telephone call, it's up to you to survey their listings on Craigslist, ApartmentGuide.com or Rent.com, and their reviews on Yelp and Apartment Ratings. From these sources, you can not only get a feel for whom they're targeting (Are they pushing one bedroom or two bedrooms? Are they pushing for bigger households or studio residents?), but you can deduce the education levels and professional levels of the residents who have left reviews. That will also allow you to find out what needs they're satisfying for their residents, and, more importantly, what needs they're not, giving you a chance to corner the market of folks who are most likely to be looking for a new home where their needs can be better met – BY YOU!

<u>Make it Mean Something</u>

Now that you've taken the time to analyze your own residents, the external area where your property is located, and your comps, it's time to do something with the information you've gathered. All the data in the world is useless if you don't apply it to a situation and find the advantages that it reveals!

When looking at a spreadsheet of numbers in search of connections, it's sometimes easy to get causation and correlation mixed up. In the world of data analysis and statistics, a phrase often used is "correlation does not imply causation." This simply means that just because two points of data may have similar changes or actions, it does not necessarily mean that one of these data points causes a change in the other. For example, every human being on the planet drinks water and every human eventually dies. Does this mean that the water causes the death of humans? When you start looking at the data in front of you, keep this principle in mind. Occasionally a coincidence is really just a coincidence.

So, what are you looking for and how do you draw conclusions? Let's start with the broad demographics in your resident base. For now, supposing that you're disregarding certain data points for fair housing purposes and that you're in an area that only has protections for the "Big 7" classes; look at the data gathered for marital status. Do you have more single, married, cohabitating, or divorced people on your property? For the purposes of example, we shall suppose that in running the numbers, we find our property has about a 60% population rate of divorced people. The question is why. There could be any number of reasons:

- The price point for your property falls in the average area where a formerly two income household, when reduced to a single income, can comfortably afford.
- Current residents provide an excellent source of referrals
- Maybe, in the cases of a bad divorce, your property has inside hallways or excellent security that helps curb the easy access to stalking that a garden style apartment may provide.
- Your property has garages or additional storage that can accommodate the downsizing from a larger home to a smaller apartment
- Your property offers the only three bedroom apartments in the area and in the price range that would be optimal for this demographic

Besides these potential reasons, there could also be external causes/correlations. This is where those lists about the area surrounding your property will come in handy. Are you close to schools with excellent reputations? That is a factor that might attract parents or single parents. Are you near a major employer that would be considered "stressful" or "demanding" workplace? That could potentially be a factor in making marriages more difficult. Are you near a community college, social help center, or some other place that a person might be drawn to when going through a life re-launch? All of these factors, or none of them, could be connected to the divorced population for which you're providing housing.

Finally, look at that divorced demographic and contrast the needs of those people against the offerings of your comps. Are you scooping up the market share in your area because you offer the cheapest studios? Do they flock to your property because there are reviews of other communities in your area that say the office staff is rude to single parents? There could be any number of reasons, and while you don't have to identify each and every one of them, it is important to at least know some of them so that you can better aim your marketing to grab more of this demographic.

While we used the potential demographic of divorced folks as an example, this same analysis process works for pretty much any demographic that you can deduce from the numbers whether it's marital status, employment locations, outdoor sportsmen, etc. For each niche that you discover in your data, it is important for you not only to discover that the niche exists, but to also search and find out why it exists, and why it rents from you. Only then can you find a way in and really leverage your marketing.

Finding a Way In

A hallmark of superior marketing is having an excellent sense of targeting as well as a direct delivery system for our message, and when we talk about niche marketing it becomes even more important. It isn't enough to just identify potential new groups of customers – you have to find a way get your message to where your customers are at. Because we are focusing on a smaller group of demographic of customers, wide media messages such as hiring a skywriter or launching a television campaign, are not the wisest investment of our advertising dollars or marketing time.

Let's go back to the hypothetical assessment where we came up with that niche market of divorced people. In the step above, you've already extrapolated the data and made some conjectures as to why, for some reason, your property is divorcee central. Now it's time to figure out how to get more of them!

If we look at the market of divorced people, and we decided that we want our property to make this demographic a core of our business, then we need to know where to find more potential customers. You might start with divorce lawyers in the area and ask them for referrals. But if you knew that people often lived in your apartments because they were returning to the community college to finish their education or because they were receiving social help from a local provider, those would also be places to pursue referrals from or advertising space within.

What if your property wants to cater to the outdoor sportsmen – people who are like living action figures with their rock climbing, kayaking, or marathon running? Sure, you might have already put a rotating climbing wall in your gym as well as updating the equipment for your fitness center, but why not spend some of your advertising efforts at a local rock climbing gym? The people who have memberships to that kind of specialized gym are exactly the demographic that you're pursuing, so it makes sense to find a concentration of them and put your message there.

Claire Collins with Princeton Properties in the Boston area runs marketing on an asset their property manages that serves this type of niche. The story goes that when the property was being designed and built, one of the developers had a hobby that he really enjoyed – Kayaking. Since the property was located on the water, he pressed for the property to have superior outdoor supplies for the residents, including kayak storage! This turned out to be a smart gamble because a lot of people into these types of sports belong to clubs or groups that get together, so by offering a very unique amenity that couldn't be found at any apartment complex, this community corners the market on these "action figure folks" from word of mouth marketing and referrals.

Holli Beckman with WC Smith in the Washington D.C. market embraced the niche market of Americans who love pets... but maybe don't have time to have one of their own. Enter Emmy, the 2M Street Resident Puppy. Residents can pick her up from the office and take her to the dog park, take her out for walks, or even just stop by the leasing office to give her belly rubs! Not only is 2M Street pet friendly, but they've taken the extra step to provide unconditional love to their residents in the form of this little English bulldog. Because of Emmy, 2M Street can go to bark parks and pass out treats or toys to other pet owners as a great grassroots marketing campaign that targets their demographic perfectly. They employ Emmy as their way in…because the marketing message she shares in her language of belly rubs and ear scratches is one that their prospective residents gravitate to! (If you'd like to take a peek at the cuteness that is Emmy, check her out at http://2mstreet.com/emmy-2mpup/)

Risk vs. Reward

Did you ever notice how even really great things in this world can be a little complicated? Ice cream is fantastic, but when you eat it too fast, the delicious taste is dimmed by a headache which punishes you for being gifted with hands that move too quickly. Likewise, in niche marketing, as positive as it is, we can be exposed to a bit of risk, but the rewards can also be great.

Risk vs. Reward is an equation that we run with every marketing/business choice we make, and it's an important part of an informed decision making process. Very little in this world is risk free, so the trick is to explore what the real risks to your bottom line are and to figure out if those risks can at least be mitigated by thinking ahead.

Laurel Zacher of Weidner discussed a practice she did with a former company when she was working as a manager, where her property became THE PLACE where traveling performers stayed. Now, if you know anything about tour performers, you know that they are usually in a city for 6-12 weeks, maximum. Usually, our companies aren't all that thrilled with the prospect of us signing a 3 month long lease, and this was years ago, before the advent of rent optimization software. Why would she take such a risk with her occupancy? Laurel mitigated some of the risks by taking a look at the calendar and the times of the year that these performers were coming through.

We know that apartments don't move very quickly from late October to early March, so if they were looking for a lease during this time and she had the openings to accommodate them, she saw the situation as win-win. It was better to have those units occupied and not losing rent, even on a shorter lease, during the winter months, than to have them sit vacant until the moving season started up again. Putting the cost of loss rent side by side with the cost of the turn made it easy to see that the real risk was in allowing her competition to grab up this lucrative demographic.

Another great example of this risk vs. reward scenario in the multifamily housing industry can be seen in the area of military housing. Regional Manager Kris Buker with Equity Residential discussed a portfolio of properties that she managed near Joint Base Lewis-McChord.

The portfolio near the military base, as one might expect, had a high contingent of military personnel living on them, whether the properties chose to market to the troops or not. These off post properties went above and beyond the usual behavior of a usual property when it came to accommodating the housing needs of military personnel. In response to these efforts, her properties were reputed to have up to an 80% resident base of military connected households.

The risks in running a conventional property with high military population, she explained, were that when deployments happened or transfers happened, the "law of the lease" was nonexistent. Once a soldier gets "orders" to a new location, he or she can break their lease and go without any sort of penalty fee whatsoever. Was the risk worth the reward in occupancy? Kris said that the answer to that question depended on the political climate at the time it was asked. During peacetime when troop turnover and deployments are somewhat predictable, the rewards were fantastic, however, during wartime, the effect could have been devastating. Given that the people who lived mostly in the area where these properties were located most likely were attached to the base in some way, or another, it would have potentially been very difficult to retain a high occupancy on those properties without embracing the military base on their doorstep.

An interesting perspective on the risk vs. reward situation with niche placement in the market can come from servicing so-called "negative" niches. Some perceived negative niches are demographics like people with large dogs, strippers, student housing and military housing, but there are other "negative niches" to consider, with a bit of creativity. For example, as popular as non-smoking apartments have become in the last decade, it begs the question – Where will all the smokers live? Indeed, on the west coast in many areas non-smoking apartments have become so prevalent that people who engage in smoking as a habit are having difficulty finding a place that they can call home. While it might be an obnoxious situation to live next to or above someone who "smokes like a chimney," the truth remains that everyone deserves a place to live. If your property is the only property in one of these enthusiastic non-smoking regions that still allows residents to smoke in their homes without penalty, then you have a niche – and one that people will probably pay a bit extra for. Better yet if you're the only community in town where smokers are welcome! You can market through local smoke shops, ask gas stations to put up one of your "Smoke? Live Here!" flyers on the outside of their sales cases, or any other number of places where smokers pick up their cigarettes, and that's just the visibility campaign.

The word-of-mouth and resident referrals will send folks streaming into your "negative" niche. Now, yes, you will need to budget the cost to offset the additional work needed for turns, but when you're considering this, you should also remember that if you're the ONLY place a smoker can rent from within the community rental market in your area, how high are the chances that a person will be moving out at the end of their lease?

Aaron Stright, Vice President of HNN Associates, shared that his company not only services the potential "negative" niches in their western Washington market but that they actively pursue them. HNN Associates have branded their tag line to be, "Life is better here!" and, more than just a line of marketing; they have made it a way of business. HNN works with several landlord liaison type programs, ranging from non-profits that assist in finding stable housing for single, middle-aged women who have mental disorders, to programs that assist young adults transitioning out of the foster care system that are heading to school and living on their own for the first time. The programs that they partner with are numerous, but they all drive to the same place – a chance for a better life for their residents. Partnering with these government programs and non-profit organizations eliminates some of the risks that can be associated with second chance housing situations and gives the employees who work for this company a feeling like the jobs that they're doing make a difference in the world. HNN has embraced the negative niche and remade it into a cornerstone of positivity in their company.

Take a moment with your team at a staff meeting and see how many potential "negative" niches you can come up with for your market. You'll find a place to list these in the worksheet pages at the end of this chapter.

Once you've listed the risky niches, work as a group to come up with three ways to overcome the risks of each niche that you've put together. Even if this exercise is simply for academic purposes at this point, it's a great way to get the creativity flowing and put yourself into a problem solving frame of mind!

Fair Housing Challenges with Niche Marketing

Fair housing laws can be intimidating if you don't know exactly what you can and cannot do, and with the recent rulings on disparate impact, it has become even more complicated. A lot of people think about shying away from niche marketing because they think fair housing laws will prohibit them from doing so effectively.

While fair housing does give us some constraints to work within, it doesn't stop us from using niche marketing philosophies and techniques, as long as we remain mindful of the protected classes in our area.

Since fair housing strictly forbids us from directly targeting or discriminating against any of the protected classes in our region, how can we market to our chosen niche while still following the law? Take this hypothetical situation:

Your property is in the middle income section of the city. The major demographics at your property are families whose adult members are part of the latter half of Generation X. Of these families, over 60% of them are first generation immigrants from Somalia. How do you possibly market to this niche without violating the law? Here are some possible solutions to explore:

- Where do your residents go? What businesses and services in the immediate area do they use? By developing a practice of reciprocal recommendation with these businesses, you'll be able to drive word-of-mouth while being non-discriminatory.
- What kind of activities do your residents enjoy? Why not do community wide activities and open them up for the public to attend? You might spend a bit extra, but all you have to get is 1-2 leases from an event, and you've most likely more than covered the additional cost.
- Is the culture that you're attempting to target an insular one? Indian, Pilipino, Somali, and other cultures world-wide are known for keeping their social connections within their own racial circles. While we cannot directly target a demographic by race, we can rely on word of mouth marketing and resident referrals. Offer a compounding referral bonus to your residents over the year as they bring you your new leases. Not only are you getting more of the residents that you best know how to serve, but, as the adage

goes, no one moves out of a community where all their friends live!

As always, when it comes to niche marketing, please remain very aware that the rules of steering and blockbusting are always in effect. Even if your property's niche is contract workers from India, who are employed at Microsoft, and they ask you to put them in buildings where other Indian families live, you cannot consciously do this – even if the customer requests it directly.

The rules of fair housing change from state to state, county to county, and city to city. Make sure that you are well acquainted with what the protected classes are where you work, on every level from federal to city. For more information on the fair housing laws, please go to:

- http://portal.hud.gov/hudportal/HUD?src=/program_offices/fair_housing_equal_opp/FHLaws

Let it Flow: Extending your Niche Marketing Message Through Your Policies, Events, Development Choices, Amenities & Service Offerings

By this time, you've already identified and defined what your niche in the market is. You know what you're good at, and you've been actively chasing that slice of the customer base. If your marketing is really targeting them, you just might get these residents to move in, but remember that in the world of occupancy, the first sale isn't the benchmark of success – it's the renewal at the end of the lease that we're really chasing! This is why your niche marketing choices need to be carried through your policies, events, development choices, amenities, and service offerings.

If we promise a perfect home to pet lovers, it won't make sense to charge a pet deposit that is twice as much as the one that our competitor charges. To attract a resident based on a niche marketing message for a lifestyle we don't support with our business choices will amount to bait and switch in the minds of your customer.

Policy can be one of the hardest things on the property to modify, but it's worth taking a look at if you're chasing a niche that would be directly affected by certain policies. For example, like I mentioned above, a larger pet deposit on a "pet friendly" property will raise some eyebrows, much like a policy of requiring "pet rent" if that isn't a common policy in your market. Likewise, if you're targeting divorced people, high credit ratings and a super clean credit history don't make sense as something to require since we know that a divorce can often negatively affect one's credit score. It is important to note that you shouldn't reduce these requirements for just that demographic but that it should be a broad policy change for everyone. It's about fitting your requirements to meet the needs of the niche you're looking to attract.

Events can also be aimed to meet the needs of your niche residents. If your niche is student housing, then hosting in-house tutoring makes sense, as does holding a finals week "decompression session" party for those that live there. Remember that visible resident retention is ALWAYS good marketing, and often times if you're holding an event that people in that niche demographic of residents would attend, they're also willing to bring friends if you allow them to do so. And if you don't have a cabana type space to use, you can still design events for your niche residents by better understanding their likes. A good example of this is a property that is built near bike trails organizing a resident biking group that meets at different times during the week. This requires no amenities on your property besides perhaps a bulletin board on which to post a flyer advertising the group.

Likewise, the services that our property offers need to support our marketing efforts. If you're aiming to get the local market of insanely busy business professionals to live in your studio apartments, then it makes sense to offer services that appeal the most to them, like dry cleaning drop off, package delivery, dog walking, discount clubs like Purqz, and concierge services. If you're trying to corner the market on pet owners, then providing dog walking is a great service, but so is arranging for a mobile dog groomer to come through your property once a week, or bringing in a dog trainer to assist in addressing the noise issues from barking dogs. If you don't know what services would be most useful to the niche markets of residents that you're attempting to attract, ask those that already live with you what services you could offer that would make their lives easier.

Choices that we make when in the development process of a new property often steer the niches our leasing teams will pursue, but so do the decisions on amenities that we update or replace down the line. A property on a lake may design boat slips as part of their offerings or may build a private beach for their residents. A developer in an area overrun with conventional floor plans might choose to build a series of lofts, or to transform the inside of an old factory or warehouse into a funky living space with an industrial feel. Properties built in the metro area might design their buildings with a wine bar on the roof, or a boutique grocery store on the ground floor. Developers looking for a low cost amenity choice to add to their property could put in an off-leash dog park, a corn-hole pit, or even a community garden.

Each of these development choices makes a statement about the people who would choose to live in these apartment homes because each one targets different submarkets like people in their 20's, students, pet owners, singles, and even community minded hippies.

Wrap Up with Some Resources

While by no means comprehensive, this chapter has given you a good overview of the concept of niche marketing. You've learned what niche marketing is, and how to look at your own existing resident base to find some of the niches you're already serving. We've covered how to gather data and how to analyze what's there and make conjectures about how that data may relate to our marketing efforts. You've learned how to find a way into the market that you're pursuing, and how to weigh the possible risks against the potential rewards of different niche markets, as well as how to mitigate some of those risks or how to remove them completely.

We've discussed a few of the fair housing challenges, and finally, we talked about how to extend your niche marketing messages into the areas of policy development, amenities and services, and even development choices.

Complementing this fairly basic overview, here are a couple of resources with regard to niche marketing:

Rent & Retain Magazine – www.rentandretain.com – This periodical is packed full of great ideas, many of them specifically for niche markets. It also has great springboards to help you develop your own ideas and get your creative juices flowing.

Multifamily Insiders – www.multifamilyinsiders.com – MFI is like Facebook for the multifamily professional. Here you'll not only find blogs and articles written by great industry experts, but you'll also gain access to all of the discussion forums where you can get input and advice from your peers and colleagues. Why struggle your way through a problem if someone else is willing to share their already tested solutions with you?! MFI is also home to the Webinar Wednesday series of education that is in partnership with the Apartment All Stars and NAAEI. The classes are offered at an exceptionally reasonable rate, and everything else on the site is FREE!

Numerous Industry Blogs:

- www.naahq.org/blog
- www.propertymanagementinsider.com
- www.leasingcafe.com
- www.behindtheleasingdesk.com
- www.markjuleen.com
- www.mbrewergroup.com

These are just a few of my favorite resources, and there are many more out there, as well.

Worksheets

Tables and list sheets for the gathering of external data points

Hyper-local Business Listing and Categorizing Table (Feel free to make copies as needed):

Business Name	Category

Top 10 Reasons for Drive-By Traffic
1.
2.
3.
4.
5.
6.
7.
8.
9.
10.

Employer Table

Top 5 Employers in Your Area	Top 5 Employers of Your Residents
1.	1.
2.	2.
3.	3.
4.	4.
5.	5.

List 10 additional points of interest that are near your property:
1.
2.
3.
4.
5.
6.
7.
8.
9.
10.

COMPS Niche Tables

Geographical Comps	Main Niche	Sub Niches
1.		
2.		
3.		
4.		
5.		

Product Comps	Main Niche	Sub Niches
1.		
2.		
3.		
4.		
5.		

Negative Niches Work Table

Niche and Risks	Mitigation Strategy 1	Mitigation Strategy 2	Mitigation Strategy 3

Special Thanks

This chapter was written with input from several amazing multifamily housing professionals. Special thanks go to Laurel Zacher at Weidner Apartment Homes, Holli Beckman at WC Smith, Claire Collins at Princeton Properties, Jill McNeish at FPI Management, Aaron Stright at HNN Associates, and Kris Buker at Equity Residential.

Chapter 3
Model Apartments

By Pete Regules

If you were to visit each and every apartment community in the U.S., how many would have models? I'll give you a hint: most of them. For the span of history, a hinging factor of multifamily success has been the psychology and "salesology" of model apartments. The multifamily industry is not alone as new single family home communities rely on beautiful model homes to showcase the possibilities of what your future home can look like! Existing home sales have a greater level of success when properly staged. Everyone wants to be able to see themselves living in the place you want them to call home, and it all comes down to lifestyle.

In this chapter we will discuss:

- Why models are set up the way they are.
- How your model relates to your marketplace.
- The types of models apartment communities use.
- Some of the common challenges faced when creating a model.
- The importance of training to use the model.
- Using the model to close more leases.

Lifestyle, or the way in which a person or group lives, is the most important factor to consider when it comes to the sale of any type of real estate. Due to the close-quarters environment that multifamily living provides lifestyle is especially important. Potential renters need to be able to envision themselves living in the spaces your particular community offers. It isn't just about the walls and the finishes. A model apartment should represent the culture of the community. A model gives a touring prospect a sense of what life is like at your community and the opportunity to imagine the things they will do during their time living there. The model has the power to inspire a renter and can potentially be your ultimate sales tool.

Why is Our Model Designed This Way?

In most cases, no two models are the same. However, some management companies want their models to be consistent for branding purposes. Still, due to each community being a unique product, every model has its own unique feel and vibe. One of the most important factors in how your model should be designed is the community you offer. For example, a student housing community is going to have a much different model than an age-restricted community. Just remember to do your research and make certain that your model will appeal to the demographics of the area and the qualified prospects you wish to attract!

Your model design should also take into consideration the structural design of your property. Is your community a garden-style in a rural setting? Is your community a downtown high-rise? Maybe your property is located in a town-center development with lots of loft space. The most effective models are the ones that appeal to the people looking for the lifestyle that the subject community's setting provides.

The actual location of your community also matters! City dwellers, suburbanites, and people seeking small communities and rural areas all have different wants, needs, and desires. The furniture and decorations placed in the model to showcase the benefits of living in each of these area types is vastly different. Also, regions of the country, state, city, or even what is close in your neighborhood most certainly play an important factor. What works for an apartment community in south Florida is different than what works for a community in upstate Washington.

An important consideration when designing your model is to keep in mind your target audience. Each generation has key elements that drive it culturally as well as esthetically. Picture a model that is toured by four groups of prospective residents. Each group is looking for the same basic amenities, and they all have a similar household income. What is different about each group is their age. The way a Baby Boomer (those born between 1946 and 1964), a Gen X (those born between 1965 and 1984), a Gen Y (those born between 1975 and the mid-2000s), and a Millennial (those born from 1982 to 2005) looks at the model are all vastly different.

Another contributing factor is the prospective resident's socio-economic status. Executives, white collar workers, blue collar workers, families scraping by on minimum wage, and families needing government assistance all see the world differently and, as a result, will view your model differently. Even gender can sometimes play a role in how your model and your community's lifestyle is perceived.

My Model, My Market

Millions of dollars are spent by management companies each and every year in the pursuit of better models for their communities. For existing communities, models are constantly updated, spruced up, renovated, and redesigned to keep up with the demands of an ever-evolving resident and prospect base. As money is spent on capital improvements to the community (i.e., new cabinets throughout, new paint schemes) models are often redesigned to compliment these changes. Many communities change minor things seasonally or yearly to try and keep a fresh look. Many times this is done not only to benefit the tour for prospective residents but also to invigorate a leasing staff that has to show the same model apartment day in and day out. From a few fresh items to a complete overhaul, new energy is derived from each piece of an ever-evolving model.

Newly constructed communities are sometimes at an advantage in the model game. After tireless hours of meeting with ownership, conducting market research, and studying new and future trends, designers are able to create a model that best represents the community and the lifestyle of the target demographic. Because of budget flexibility, these communities will often show the latest and greatest features that complement whom they see as the perfect renter. Rapidly progressing technology is giving new and innovative tools to not only interact with residents in the model, but to aid in the sales and follow-up process. So what model should your community have?

Types of Models

Every community is different, and that means every model should be different too. The overall theme should complement the lifestyle of the people living at your community and excite the prospect about the potential of moving in! Please keep in mind that there is no perfect model but there are several types of models we should discuss.

"The Museum Model"
A museum model may appear more like a museum than a home. This model is meticulously designed with great detail, and each and every item is strategically placed to enhance the overall visual experience. Each morning a team member enters that model, ensuring that everything is perfect and ready for that day's tours. There is not a speck of dust and not one thread of carpet out of place. It is perfectly manicured in every way.

Benefits
The museum model is there to tell a story. Often utilized by "A" communities, this model shows luxury, style, and sophistication. It is an impression piece designed to not only put the best foot forward, but to create a "Wow" factor and be memorable.

Challenges
The museum model does not usually look "lived-in." The fact that the model looks so prestigious; it may misrepresent the lifestyle of the community. All too often, there are so many 'things' in the apartment that the finishes get lost in the experience. It becomes less about sales and more about statement.

The "Lived-In Look" Model

The most common model type has a "lived-in" look. Everything is not 100% perfect but still shows style, form, and function. This model is strategic and deliberate in selling to a targeted demographic, as well as a general audience. Just because it looks "lived-in" does not make it messy. The design should create a notion of "this is how a person who lives here actually lives." Items like open magazines, slippers by the bed, and a plate in the sink can create an emotional connection during a tour.

Benefits
The "lived-in" look is exceptionally diverse and adaptable to a variety of sales demographics. It is easy to swap out just a few pieces to freshen the look and is often driven by a connection on a cultural level. You can tell when someone instantly connects with your model apartment when you hear them sigh in relief as to say they have found their new home.

Challenges
If all the competitor apartment communities are also selling to a similar lifestyle and demographic, it is easy for your model to get lost in the shuffle. Also, for communities that have an established resident base, "lived-in" models get dated quickly. American consumers' tastes are transforming faster than ever before. It is important to stay on top of this evolution, or your model will become out-of-date.

Mini and Flash Models

Do you have a floor plan or an individual apartment that is hard to rent? Are you finding that there is something missing in the connection between your prospect and an empty apartment? A short term, mini or flash model, may be just the thing you need to capture a new move-in quickly. Mini or flash models are often favorites of income-restricted communities due to their ability to be flexible and moveable. Sometimes it takes just a few pieces to make a memorable statement.

Benefits
It is difficult for some customers to envision themselves in an empty apartment. Where will my sofa go? Will my bed fit? Is there enough storage? All are questions that a prospect considers when touring an empty apartment. Having a few items placed in the apartment will allow for a more open dialogue about the resident's needs and concerns. Also, the cost flexibility is a wonderful benefit. Why spend a lot of money and take up space in a rentable unit, when all you need is just a couple of items?

Challenges
Sometimes, a little is not enough. Some communities that struggle with occupancy concerns and budget shortfalls don't have the desire to spend the money for an enhanced sales tool. The mini-model has to suffice. When volume rental is key, a few pieces of furniture or accessories in a unit often fail to create an emotional connection to a touring prospect. Also, if your competitors have a model that is more engaging, the minimalism of a flash model in one room is quickly forgotten.

Some Things to Consider About Your Model
Great models are about the little details. However, there is a risk-reward value in any model that you have. Fair Housing standards, design aesthetics, and informational propaganda can all create barriers to your creation of an unbelievable model tour experience. These challenges are often met with creative solutions and practical substitutions that bring a model that is ordinary to extraordinary.

Photos on the Wall
Fair Housing lawyers and educators across the nation love to beat down the desire to have photography on the walls of a model apartment. They love to create a fear of misrepresentation and discrimination against protected classes. While there is a need to be cautious, you do not have to let fear deter your ability to have photographs that show lifestyle and connect to people on a personal level.

Touring prospects love to see photos on the walls. The more realistic the photos are the better. Prospects would rather see real photos rather than purchased stock photos. Another factor to consider when choosing art is diversity. Just like your apartment community is diverse in its resident base, your model can benefit from offering a diversity of photos and images. Be sure to represent as much diversity as possible while having the people in the photographs taking part in as many lifestyle-related activities as possible.

Another great opportunity to connect with your prospect is to frame art drawn by staff and residents! Framed art drawn by staff and residents is a great opportunity to not only create a memorable model piece, but to have a fun resident retention event as well. If you are a community that accepts pets, make sure to have photos of your furry residents in the model to build that connection to pet owners.

Accessibility and ADA

Another common concern is the accessibility of your model and compliance with the Americans with Disabilities Act of 1990. There is a great debate amongst property management and legal entities as to what is and is not allowed. Often, the letter of the law and the spirit of the measure are in conflict. There are some general guidelines you should follow that not only protect your property legally but will benefit the entire model experience for anyone who tours your property.

Models, except in certain circumstances, need to be accessible to everyone. Communities that are multiple levels that do not have an elevator should have the model(s) on the ground floor so that anyone can tour them.

Communities that have multiple models will sometimes have only one of the models on the ground floor. This is acceptable as long as you are (let's say it all together now) consistent with your tours and do not show any discrimination on your explanations of your community's policies when it comes to tours.

Also, once inside the apartment be certain that a wheelchair can make it through the tour with no barriers? In the event something does get in the way of a wheelchair, immediately offer to move the item out the way to accommodate the wheelchair. As long as you are providing reasonable accommodation and are adhering to a consistent policy, there should never be any problems. However, if your model is so filled with items that a wheelchair cannot make it through a tour unscathed, you might want to make sure that your space is not overly crowded.

Too Many Tchotchkes
Is your model filled with stuff? I mean lots and lots of stuff? Things here, thinks there, knick-knacks, novelties, miscellaneous brick-a-brack everywhere? The abundance of things is staggering. Having decorations in the model can add personality and connect to certain demographics. But, too many things can create a hodge-podge of items that distract from the overall benefits that the model is designed for. It is important that the finishes and the functional elements of the apartment are not only seen, but accentuated. Strategic placement of decorations should be used to draw the eye to certain specific features that the apartment offers. The decorations should complement the lifestyle of the target demographic and not detract from the overall lifestyle that the community offers. An apartment model should look functional.

Paint
Whether just an accent wall or the entire unit, paint can create anything from a statement to a subdued psychological advantage for sales. A bright accent wall can show a lifestyle of fun and energy. Bold colors attract kids and can be made beautiful and classy. More subdued tones can create an environment of dignity and calm and often attracts a more diverse cross-section of society. Also, neutral colors have a much longer span where they remain relevant vs. a color that is trendy or outside the box.

Different hues of color can have a major impact on the moods of the people touring the model. Reds are seen as ways to ignite passion and elicit a bold response whereas blue tend to have a calming effect. Greens have a great soothing effect that is perfect for urban apartments that are hoping to connect back to nature. Oranges are extremely popular because they have been known to create enthusiasm.

Whatever color(s) you choose make sure that you are able to tell the touring prospect not only what color it is, but where they can find the same color for their apartment. Try not to use paint colors in your models that residents are not permitted to use in their apartment homes!

How Often to Update

Trends evolve; fads go in and out of style, and what is poplar today is gone tomorrow. In our fast paced world of technology, it is often hard to try and keep up with what is "IN." Many times what works for one generation may fail to catch the eye of the next. Be ready to make necessary changes when your model has reached its expiration date. Models that appeal to a broad spectrum of society and contain a neutral color pattern will have a longer shelf life than those that are hip to the current trends or fads. Utilize subtle changes over a long period to get the most out of every dollar spent. A small seasonal or yearly change just to "freshen" the feel is all that is usually needed to make an improvement. In most circumstances, models will last five to eight years before they start losing their luster and relevance.

Some communities want their model to stand out and pop when a prospect walks in. The power to amaze, surprise, and artistically engage customers is perfect for certain community demographics, most notably would be communities with a downtown or urban feel. Beware; because what was in style today is not necessarily what is stylish tomorrow. Models that are designed around a modern trend will usually last less than five years and sometimes as few as two years.

Is Rental the Answer?

Renting, rather than purchasing, model furniture is a viable option for the ever-changing needs of an apartment community. Today's furniture rental companies have design professionals on staff to assist property management professionals in creating fabulous models that will compliment the marketing goals of the property.

Determining whether or not to rent or buy model furniture would depend on how long you anticipate the model staying intact. If planning on keeping the model for three years or less, it would be a wise decision to rent furniture rather than purchase

Having models that are flexible means the look, and practical applications can easily be changed. With a few quick furniture changes, what was once a two bedroom model can quickly become a one bedroom with an office or den. Switching out a few rental items can easily change a model that appeals to roommates to a model that will accommodate families with kids.

What Community Take-a-Ways Should Be in the Model?

Sit with them at the table or on the sofa. Ask them the things they like and did not like and make sure to take great notes. Have a copy of their floor plan ready so that you can note what those things for you, and them to remember. If the floor plan they prefer is different from the model, take the time to show how the model they are in relates to the layout of their future apartment. Once you get back to the clubhouse, it may be too late, and there may be too many distractions. Take the time to connect with your customer in a meaningful way and provide them the take-a-ways when they are the most relevant.

Would You Pay More?

Do you think that the only thing that matters to your customer is price? If so, you are wrong. Even the most frugal customer has more than the price on their mind. Take advantage of the time you have with the prospect in the model and sell the features and benefits that make paying more worth the price.

Up to 85% of people will pay more for a product if it means better customer service. If your community has a higher review score than your competitors, the model can be a great place to remind potential customers of your superior standing. Great reviews are often a sign of outstanding customer service. While in the model take the opportunity to review the must-have features and benefits of your apartment. Whether it is the technology, location, or ability to save on utility bills, it is important to know what your customer's "must have" items are and how your model can help address those needs. Let the prospect know how the layout can be customized for their lifestyle. Take a photo of the prospect in the model and send it to them as a follow-up effort. Anything that you can do to make yourself, along with the model itself, more memorable will help them come back to you when it is time to decide where their new home is.

Most importantly, your prospects are renting from YOU so be certain to make great efforts to personally connect with them.

Using Psychological Selling

During your visit to the model, there are many subtle things you can do to "sell" without "selling." Determine what activities your current residents enjoy and tailor your model to include items that will appeal to your target market. For example, if many of your residents are interested in sports, have copies of Sports Illustrated, Men's Health, and Self magazines on counters and coffee tables. If showing a prospect a vacant apartment that is already rented, post an 8.5 x 11 piece of paper with "ON HOLD" printed on it and use magnets to place the paper on the refrigerator of a unit with a mini-model. By doing so, you will increase the urgency that this apartment is not available, so the prospect should hurry to rent a similar floor plan if interested. Also, leave to-go menus of the local eateries strategically placed in the model. Again, you are giving the prospect an idea of the lifestyle of the people that live in the community. Small details like this will often be the difference between a good model and a great model.

Training

Whether you are a twenty-year apartment industry veteran or have only been at your community twenty days, training is an ongoing process. Each day that we strive to be just 1% better is a day that we get closer to meeting our overall goals. Unfortunately, once all of the benefits of the community are learned, and the leasing process is understood, we often slow down on the training and focus more on the daily needs of our on-site lives. A great loss happens when we do not adequately train and learn how we can use our model apartment as a tool that not only increases our occupancy, but tells the story of our community.

From our training and research we know the features and benefits of our competitors. We know what is in their models and how they conduct their tours. But are we using this information to our advantage? Most prospective residents will tour not only our community but most of our direct competitors as well. Does our model stand out against them and create a unique a memorable presence in the marketplace? Do we have opportunities within our models to provide a response to a need that our competitors do not have? Even if our community may not be as new, or have as many "bells and whistles" as our competitors, are we using our time in the model to sell the things we do best? Are we convinced the "our model sells itself" or are we taking the opportunity to make a meaningful connection to our future resident and to leverage our time in the model to create a sense of home?

Models are About Lifestyle

It does not matter if your model is full of the latest and greatest furniture and artwork. Who your model speaks to is more important that what your model is. Remember, a model's purpose is to tell a story and to explain the lifestyle that your customer will experience when they transition from prospect to resident.

Here are some things for you to consider.

- Which rooms are the most important to your customer? If they are into cooking, how can the kitchen be a palace of deliciousness for them? If they love to host their friends, how can they use the common areas to create a more welcoming place to visit? If they are seeking a place to create peace and tranquility how can their space be designed to enjoy a good book, or sip a glass of wine as the sun goes down? Connecting to the living desires of your customers help build an emotional picture of what their lives will be once they move into their new apartment home!
- How is their furniture going to fit in their new home? Models are arranged to show how furniture will optimally fit into an apartment. But, every person's furniture is different. By taking the time to learn what items they possess and to understand the things that are important to them, you can help them begin to develop a mental picture of how their apartment will actually look. When they can envision themselves living there, then they will have a hard timing looking anywhere else.
- How can the loves they have when they are away from their apartment be remembered when they return home? When people leave the confines of your community what awaits them in the nearby community? Have you taken the time to understand the places that your residents take advantage of when they are out and about? Where are the schools, jobs, daycares, and recreational items that people who live in your community prefer? Does your model create a sense in what lies beyond and how the surrounding community benefits your residents?

Focus on the Finishes, Not the Model Itself

Many times, leasing agents spend too much time pointing out how amazing the model is only to have people not remember anything but how pretty the apartment was that they just visited. When the furniture and decorations have taken away from the vision of the benefits that the apartment offers, your model becomes lost in a sea of design.

The finishes in the apartment are very important! It is crucial that models not only highlight impactful finishes but that the leasing team is trained about the finishes and why they are of benefit to a resident's lifestyle. Why does your community offer large garden bathtubs, tile back-splashes in the kitchen, or USB plug-ins on all outlets? By pointing out these features and giving their reasons, rather than covering them up with a bunch of decoration, you will add value to the model tour.

Selling Against Your Competitors

What does your community offer that your competitors do not? What are the things that your community offers that are truly one of a kind? You and the rest of the community staff are unique to your community! Place photos of the community staff in the model and introduce your future resident to them as part of the model tour. Just as you would have photos of family and friends on the walls of your own apartment, your model's walls can show off your community's family.

Consider ways to highlight the existing residents of the community. Have a coffee table book that highlights all the jobs and careers that have employees living at your community. If you are pet friendly, have photos of all of the furry residents that live at your community. These simple tools can create a connection between your future residents and the people that live there.

What can you place in the model that creates an impression of your surrounding area? Remember those photos of your community staff? Take your staff out into the surrounding community and take photos of your staff enjoying the local restaurants or having fun at a local park. What a great way to show how your community interacts as part of the neighborhood!

Selling Your Model

The model isn't just another tool in your toolbox for increasing the occupancy at your community! It is a place to express the uniqueness of your community and why a person should want to call your apartment community home. Unfortunately, once the model has been erected, and the occupancy goals are reached, often times the model becomes just another facet of the day-to-day lives of the leasing team. Each visit to the model should be treated as a new experience just like each day is an opportunity to help someone find a new home. It all begins at the start of your tour.

The Tour

The journey you take each time you leave the confines of your desk to tour a prospective resident is often known as the "Golden path." Have you become bored with the same tour day in and day out? When you get to the model do you just open the door, step in with your customers and let them look around only to ask, "What do you think?" It is time to stop the madness! Albert Einstein once said that the definition of insanity is "Doing the same thing over and over again and expecting different results." When you get to the model do something different. Have the prospect sit in the bathtub to see how big it really is. Don't just tell them that the closet is big; tell them that it holds 250 pairs of shoes. The important thing is to do something different to personalize your tour each and every time.

Sensory Marketing

Most people that tour your model get to "see" how beautiful it is. Seeing how beautiful your model is only activates one of the five senses! What are you doing to engage the other 4 senses? Marketing managers and researchers have spent millions of dollars, and thousands of hours developing marketing techniques that will engage all five senses thus creating a sensory experience! If a sensory experience is accomplished while your prospects tour the community, a more memorable experience will be achieved!

Sight – People love to see themselves enjoying an experience; thus the reason why "selfies" are so popular. Be sure to place mirrors throughout the model so that your customers have the opportunity to see themselves enjoying their future home.

Sound – Music is a great way to create emotion. The music you play in your model apartment is as important as any other decoration. Ambient sounds, like a bubbling brook or ocean surf, are a great way to connect to a resident in a relaxing, indirect method. For urban spaces, a more modern beat may drive home a great sense of city life.

Touch – Have your resident engage with the model. Ask them to turn on the water to see how quickly the water becomes hot. If they love to cook, ask them to open the stove and the cabinets. If their apartment will have a balcony, have them go outside and feel the air. Even children can be engaged with touch by having an activity that draws their attention inside the model.

Taste – Snacks in the model are an opportunity to get your customers to sit with you longer and to relax during the sales process. Each morning have someone from the leasing staff bake fresh cookies in the model and put them on a plate for all visitors to enjoy.

Smell – This is the sense that is closest attached to memory. Using a trend that originated in the hotel industry, many management companies have developed a trademark scent so that they can keep the smell experience consistent throughout each of their communities. We just mentioned the cookie trick, but some other popular smells you can take advantage of are: coffee, bread and vanilla.

Memorability

Is your model memorable? For someone looking for an apartment that has toured 10 communities in one day, will yours be remembered? Of course, terrific follow up is one great way to be remembered and get a lease, but we need to be memorable throughout the entire model experience. Below are some tips that you may like to try to create a memorable experience.

Mini-Model Top 5

- Put clear balloons, Styrofoam peanuts, or bubble wrap in the bathtub. Add a shower curtain and bath mat, and you'll make this small space more inviting.
- Cover the floor of the entire apartment with balloons.
- Need help explaining how furniture can be laid out in an empty apartment? Use blue painter's tape and trace where each item goes. You can even take it a step further by putting crime scene tape up and saying that the only crime here is that no one has moved into this apartment yet.
- Flowers increase a favorable impression by 35% so put a wreath on the doors of vacant apartments.
- Mini models do not have to be expensive. Have a contest with your sister communities to see who can create the best mini model (or the one that closes sales the fastest) for under $25.

Take your Model from Drab to Fab

- Put live people in your models. Dress them up in fun costumes (or ones that go with your marketing theme) and watch the reactions from prospects. This definitely separates you from the crowd. Hire high school kids for minimum wage or student actors from your community theater. They may have access to great costumes too!. To save money, arrange for the live models to be present during your heaviest traffic times – normally, weekends from 11am-3pm.
- "Power Lunches" in models with prospects help them see, feel and taste (so to speak) the apartment. This will help take away that sterile feeling many of our models have. It

may be a chore to clean up afterwards, but when prospects "test drive" the apartment, sales are closed faster.
- Teddy bears (yes, you heard me), lots and lots of teddy bears. A suburban Chicago apartment community needed something, anything, to bring their models to life. But with no money and rising vacancies, they had to be clever and thrifty. Thus, the teddy bear model was born. Teddy bears were placed throughout the models. There were teddy bears playing backgammon, sleeping in the bed, eating at the table in the kitchen area - even taking a bubble bath! Did it pay off? Leasing consultants began to notice their "be-backs" saying things like, "You're the teddy bear apartments, right?" as their occupancy increased. To make certain their prospects don't forget who the teddy bear apartments are, they even added a teddy bear to their business cards.
- The "WOW" fridge. Stock the fridge in the model until it is bursting at the seams with every imaginable soda, juice boxes, candy bar, snacks, and treats. Load the freeze with ice cream, freezer pops, and a bevy of other frozen delicacies. Put a sign on the outside of the fridge that says, "Open if you dare!" Let every prospect take one food and one beverage item with them when they leave.
- Mannequins in the apartment. Dress them up and have them ready to pose for photos with your future resident. Rent model furniture for a day and set it up outside, near the front of your community. Set it up and decorate it just like it was inside an apartment. Then, have members from your leasing team, "live" in the model for a day. Place a very visible sign that says "Waiting to move in." This is a great way to grab some quick drive by traffic!

Let Follow-up Work for You

The Power of Video: Invite your prospect to video their model tour with a small camera that you provide. Upload the video and email it to them as part of your follow-up. Vine and Instagram are also great tools to use and connect to your resident on Social Media.

Remember Me in Pictures: Take a picture of your resident enjoying the model apartment. Whether it is drooling over the "WOW" fridge or laughing at the 'bubble bath' in the tub, sending them a photo of their tour will help you stand out.

Great Resources for Model Ideas and Gifts

Decoration:
www.etsy.com
www.fab.com

Food Props:
www.justdoughit.com
www.fake-food.com
www.faxfoods.com

Liven up your space and save $$$:
www.Shindigz.com
www.oriental.com

Design ideas and Rental options:
www.cort.com

Chapter 4
Maximized Rents & Economic Occupancy

By Toni Blake

How to READ & LEAD the Market

I drove by a property in a small western city 18 months after a market cycle had changed and saw a banner hanging on the building screaming in all caps 'TWO MONTHS FREE RENT." I thought to myself, "Do they not have a computer or TV? They obviously have not paid attention to the market and are losing money and reputation by lagging behind with the wrong market approach."

What you don't know can hurt you. Knowing how to read and lead the market maximizes your rent potential and improves your value position. There are plenty of experts that evaluate details such as job growth and consumer confidence. You simply need to know whom to watch and what to look for when planning your marketing strategy. Kenny Rogers hit song The Gambler said "You got to know when to hold'em, know when to fold'em, know when to walk away and know when to run." We need to add, "know when to raise'em."

In this chapter, I will connect you to my best resources, show you how to read and lead the market and then apply the right techniques and tools to confidently increase your rent potential and value position. This chapter will focus on confidently negotiating rent increases and value positioning. You must understand and know how to confidently discuss the economics of apartments and the values of renting versus owning.

Frequently when a resident gets a rent increase, the first thing they do is turn in a service request. Your technician is about to be the first to have to answer the question, "Why did you raise my rent?"

In this chapter, I will give you and your team the tools, strategies, techniques and negotiation tactics you need to succeed in moving your property toward financial success.

Apartment marketing is not just about being full! It is about what you are full of. Economic occupancy has to do with maximizing the rent potential on each of your apartment homes. Increasing revenue requires knowing how to watch the market and lead the move toward higher rents. A simple understanding of market supply and demand will help you to identify trends. Too many customers and not enough supply will lead to an increase in the cost of goods. Conversely, too much product gives the consumer the "upper hand" in negotiations, and you will then begin to see properties offering concessions.

Here's a great example for you. Recreational marijuana was recently legalized in Colorado. I heard a caller into a radio show complain to the Governor that the retail price of marijuana in a "store" was more expensive than buying it at the park at the "street rate." It was an interesting moment to hear the Governor of Colorado talk about how local marijuana growers would soon establish a better understanding for market demand. He indicated that as soon as there was a clear understanding of supply and demand, the retail price of marijuana would become lower. Both knowledge of market demand and having the correct pricing structure are key elements to selling any product to the public.

We experience the same issues with apartment leasing. When the need for apartments outnumbers the apartments available, rents will increase. Our market has cycles influenced by job growth, favorable lending for multifamily projects, and the formation of new households.

I'm sure you have heard the old saying, "Give a man a fish, feed him for a day. Teach a man to fish, feed him for a lifetime." I want to show you how to read and lead the market and connect you to key resources to make sure you have a constant flow of accurate decision-making data.

Monday management reports keep you on track with important information that you need to manage your individual community. However, managing your asset for optimal financial results requires both local and national data. Understanding where to look outside your Monday management reports and knowing what economic indicators to review will assist you in monitoring important economic cycles. Once you have this valuable information, you can use it to lead the market. I will show you how to base your marketing strategies on reliable information supplied by key reports and resources. You need to think like an owner, regional and executive when planning your properties future. You must establish a habit of following the market and knowing when to increase your rents and change your marketing approach.

Below you will find some great resources:

Market Data Resources

It's good to know what is happening on the national scene. Start your marketing research by following the national marketing trends for multifamily housing. The most watched number here is the national vacancy rate. This data was provided by REIS, a well-respected New York research firm.

The National Homebuilders Association tracks both single family and multifamily starts along with completions and net absorption. The graph shows developers when to slow down or stop building. As long as the new units are being absorbed more building permits will be issued. You can see where the construction and absorption tops out and then begins to slow.

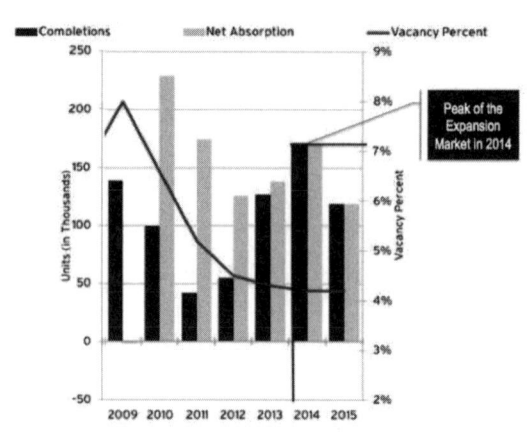

Both are great resources to watch, and they provide easy to read graphs and charts.

Below are some additional resources:

- www.conference-board.org/data/consumerdata.cfm
(Monitors ongoing data on consumer confidence.)
- www.econsources.com/index.htm
(Provides links to census data and resources.)
- www.econlib.org/library/sourcesUS.html
(Library of Economics and Liberty)
- www.zillow.com/local-info/
(Zillow's local provides real estate marketing reports and home value index plus mortgage rates.)
- www.realtor.com/local/
(Allows you to search for local data including overviews, home prices, lifestyle and rental prices.)
- www.city-data.com
(One of the most thorough data sites for housing professionals.)

An Attitude of Increase

I like to say that when I take over a property it is like a big girl getting in the pool – everything goes up! Occupancy goes up! Closing percentages goes up! Motivation goes up! Even attendance at the parties goes up! I have an attitude of increase! I like to measure a direct correlation between my presence and increased success on the property. I have heard of site teams who ask for rents to be lowered, or a concession added. This is in direct conflict with your primary goal, which is to produce financial results for a real estate asset.

Did you know that you are a fiduciary? I learned that from Jennifer Nevitt, Chief Executive Officer at Forty-Two, LLC Apartment Management Company. A fiduciary is a person entrusted with the value of a real estate asset. You are responsible for increasing the value of your property.

A great onsite team provides valuable advice to upper management. Being observant and paying attention to trends, keeping track of the competition and understanding your product will allow you to more effectively market and manage your property.

My goal has always been to collect more rent than was projected by demonstrating an attitude of increase. Budgets are established on the potential rent that can be collected. If you see the potential to rent above the recommended rate, you'll find yourself at the head of the class in property management.

I was hired, as a leasing consultant, in August of 1978 on a property in Dallas called The Settlements Apartments. I shopped my competition and found our apartments to be larger and older. Plus, we had THREE pools, which I found extraordinary. I was so impressed I decided I could get more money than was listed on the vacancy sheet. I saw other communities around us charging more for what I perceived as less product. I didn't think they should get more money than us when we were (in my opinion) better. Some would see the age, scars and old landscape as less valuable. My fresh eyes saw it was NEW! It was new to me, and I loved it! I loved the pools, the huge rooms and found I could do 3 cartwheels through our largest living room! I was 19 and used to be a cheerleader. Nothings say BIG like seeing the leasing agent practice acrobatics through the living room (although I don't suggest that you do that!)

Prior to becoming a leasing consultant, I sold antiques with my Dad. In the antique business, the value of the item was set based on the "story." Where it had come from, who had owned it, where it had been found and how it was made.

I decided to add a story to my apartments and raise the rents. I began leasing every apartment at increased rents. When I turned in the paperwork to the assistant manager she said, "This apartment doesn't rent for this amount." "It does now," I replied. Apparently, leasing consultants were not allowed to adjust the rent, and she quickly reported me to the manager. However, when the manager saw that I had charged MORE rent, she was thrilled. We had a quick conversation about what I thought I could get for new market rents and never looked back. Many Property Managers and Leasing Consultants hear "it's not in the budget." That's because the property underperformed and did not bank the rent that had been budgeted. In this chapter, I want to show you how to raise rents without raising eyebrows and keep your rents higher than all of your competition.

Good Money

One of the most expensive lessons in property management is that people, who pay less seem to care less and cost more! Have you ever shopped at Ross's Dress for Less or TJ Max? You can buy a name brand shirt on clearance for less than a Subway sub sandwich. Have you ever read the label on your new shirt only to find it is dry clean only? What do you do? Do you take the shirt to the dry cleaner and pay more to have it cleaned than you paid for the shirt in the first place? Do you put it in your washing machine and just see what happens? Sometimes it says, "hand wash!" When you pay less for a discounted item, it's easier to ignore the instructions on how to take care of it! Are you guilty as charged? Nothing establishes value more than the price. We take better care of things when we pay "good money." If you want to attract quality people to your community, you're going to need them to pay "good money."

When rents are lowered to the bottom of the market, your product becomes 'discounted.' By discounting the rent, you run the risk of attracting bargain hunters (who only care about getting the lowest price) who may not appreciate or take care of their home properly. There is not as much value in the apartment that is leased on a discount. When you charge "good money" people appreciate their home and your community. All rents are not created equal and in the chapter I am going to talk to you about value perception and price positioning.

Value Positioning Your Apartment

What is Value Pricing? Value-based pricing (also value optimized pricing) is a pricing strategy, which sets prices primarily on the value, perceived or estimated, to the customer. Based on how important the purchase is to their quality of life, pricing must relate to not just market value, but also the customer's willingness to pay. Generally, finding a home is on top of most lists

If people are consistently complaining that prices are too high, it may be necessary to evaluate your pricing structure. Conversely, if nobody is complaining about your price, then it's likely too low. A great apartment should be priced to make the customer pause before saying, "Yes!"

Value Positioning with Lists – Premium Package
When presenting your price it is important for people to understand everything that is included. Automobile salespeople go to great lengths to produce a long list of what is included in each package.

When creating brochures or marketing material, listing features that are offered in the apartment homes will increase the perceived value of the apartment! Because numbers add value and bring a concept into focus, be sure to list the number of cabinets and drawers in the kitchens and bathrooms. Additionally, list the cubic feet of all storage space, the number of square feet of living space, the lineal feet of the closet by inches, and the number of hangers that are accommodated in the vertical hanging space. (A good rule of thumb is two hangers per inch of hanging space).Have you created a comprehensive list of the many features offered in your apartment homes?

Define Your Community Services
Have you defined your services? Are you doing a good job of communicating and showing value in your community services? Spend time with your team building a list of services at your community that you can market to prospects and residents.

Examples of services are:
- Package Delivery Service: The resident signs a waiver of liability and gives staff members permission to enter their apartment to deliver packages. This service could be valued at approximately $15.00 per month but will be included in the premium package when they rent
- Emergency Services: Staff will be available to turn off an iron or a stove accidentally left on or check for running water.
- Seasonal Flowers, Pool Maintenance and Landscape Care: Are all things a local homeowner would have to either do or pay for someone else to do. These are all included in the services we provide the residents of our community.

Community Amenities and Tournaments
Increase the value of your community amenities with easily added services. Take a new look at your property and determine how you can capitalize on existing amenities by being creative and adding further value! Here are a few ideas for you to try:

- Your Community Fitness Center: The value of a Fitness Center is approximately $29, per month. However, as part of the Premium Resident Package, there is no additional monthly charge for membership to the community fitness center.
- Community Fitness Director: Ask around and find a local "Certified Trainer" who is willing to adopt your fitness center. Create a non-revenue barter agreement that allows for the trainer to gain new clients and you to gain services! Have the trainer conduct two classes per month that can be videotaped and added to your Youtube channel. Residents who do not attend can watch the training on their mobile phone and increase their workout intensity. Each quarter ask the trainer to create a new workout using the equipment in your fitness center.
- Photo Trainer: Laminate and post images of the trainer in the proper stance using each piece of the fitness equipment. These are easy to take, copy and display. During tours with prospects be sure to introduce the Community Fitness Director!
- Fitness Director: Print business cards for the Fitness Director and include in all of your move-in packages. Simple business cards have a way of "making it real" for a new resident.
- Fun and Games: How can you increase the value of your pool and other areas of your community? During the summer, I love to share 3 fabulous lawn or pool games with sister properties. Each property should purchase a game for the lawn or pool; -Pool golf, pool ping-pong (my all time favorite) and bocce ball are always a big hit with residents. At the end of each month, trade the games with your sister properties. Give the residents all month to practice and sign up, then have a tournament the last weekend before the property changes games. Purchase an affordable engraved trophy online and the residents will go all out to win

Don't Be the Coupon

During a recession, a large percentage of consumers take great pride frequently using coupons and finding discounts. During better financial times, people still clip coupons with the intention of using them but often forget to take the coupons along as they shop.

I remember when my husband was looking for a Lasik surgery center, and he found a coupon that offered "One Eye Free." We both laughed and thought "no way"! We value his vision too much to choose a discounted place for the procedure. A few weeks later my daughter called to tell us she was going skydiving, and they had a discount on Wednesdays. My first reaction was to offer to pay the difference for her to go on any day but Wednesday. What made Wednesday cheaper? Was it a new guy who wasn't sure where to drop people? I didn't know, but I didn't want my daughter to find out the hard way!

Value is found in more than just the physical product. We find value in skill, expertise, service, location and many other attributes. For example, maintenance is rated high on consumer lists of "what matters" when searching for an apartment. People will pay "good money" to ensure their daily life experience is enjoyable, and service is reliable.

When selling your product, make sure you clearly point out not only the features of the apartments and the community but their associated benefits! Value is important and for a prospect to understand true value, it is your job to show them the "big picture" which includes the benefits of those amazing features that are offered within your community.

I don't like coupons. I strongly advise against using a price reduction as an incentive when leasing. It is very important for the future resident to agree to pay "good money." However; it might be appropriate and appreciated to assist them with some of their moving costs as a thoughtful 'housewarming gift." I always advise against rent concessions.

Sometimes a rent concession allows a resident to write their initial rent check at a lower rent amount. The problem with this is that the resident then mentally sets the value of their apartment at that lower rent. Then, every month after that when they write the rent check, it feels like an increased payment on a lower value product.

Value positioning demonstrates high value and gives the perception of "a great price." We must strive to establish the rent as "good money" with a high value. When the rent amount is the main reason a resident selected to live at your community, they are more likely move out for a discount near-by and will be reluctant to pay a rent increase at renewal time.

I like to position my community as "high value" and I believe that a "coupon" or rent discount is a trap that the prospect could regret the next YEAR of their life. I also tell them, "This is a decision you have to live with for a year. If you want to save money shop at Wal-Mart, but move here and enjoy a community full of value and top-notch service. There are plenty of ways to save a buck, but compromising your address is simply a bad idea."

Toni 's Five Simple Rules for Raising Rents Without Raising Eyebrows

Standard Pricing Strategy
There are many books available that explain why certain pricing strategies work. Many of the strategies are unknown to the consumer yet are very simple to implement.

The minor changes in your pricing structure will not deter anyone from looking or renting but will have a very positive impact on your economic occupancy! It is easy and it works!

Below are a few suggestions:

Use Standard Price Points
$05 becomes $19
$20 becomes $29
$35 becomes $49
$55 becomes $79

Example: If you have a rent that is $805.00 per month, change it to $819.00 per month.

Always end with a 9
The University of Chicago and MIT tested 3 prices for a woman's dress; $34, $39 and $44. There were more sales at $39 than any other price. Some researchers explain that prices ending in "9" are viewed subconsciously by shoppers to have been discounted. Shoppers view a price ending in "9" as a good deal!

The final digit in rent is often inconsequential to the decision. From the customer's perspective, $756, $755, $759 all look similar!

Now, for a quick pricing lesson on the impact of adding a 9 to your rents. $9 does not seem that significant on one month rent, however, when multiplied by 12 months and 250 units it equals revenue growth of $27,000. Also, if you consider the value of your apartments and you could potentially add $27,000 in cash flow to your business, while also increasing the value of the asset. I always end my rents in a 9!

Never use a ZERO
It simply gets you NOTHING!!! Avoid using a zero when setting a rent amount. Replace the zero with a one instead.

<u>Never go above $79</u>
People searching online will be shown products based on price range by the $100's. If you set rent at $799, it will be shown to people searching with a $700 budget. If the shopper needs to stay on the lower end of the $700 range, $799 may seem way too high. If using $779 as your price, you may attract people who would be willing to stretch to $779. The customer looking with an $800 budget will not even see it. Once you feel you can go above $779 go ahead and jump to $819. This will bring in a whole new customer and increase your resident profile and economic occupancy.

The Economic Anatomy of a Rent Increase

Watch the market for signs of rent increases. You want to lead the market! 100% occupancy is a sure sign that your rents are too low. Never be proud of 100% occupancy as it is a sure sign you have left money on the table.

Each new available apartment should be evaluated for a potential rent increase. It is important to understand the economic anatomy of a rent increase. Watch for opportunities to adjust rent in two ways. First, adjust the rent to cover inflation. Increasing rents for inflation is not profit. When a resident signs a year lease, we must forecast the income required to pay for any increase in the cost of managing our community for the next year. If the insurance, utilities, equipment, taxes or any other cost increases throughout the year; we must be prepared to cover that cost. The second way we increase the rent is to move rents toward market rent. Market rent is simply the 'going rate' for similar apartments in your specific market. Determine the cost per square foot of what you are charging for rent and then compare it to that of your competitors. If your competitors are getting much more per square foot, you will most likely be able to increase your rents.

Let's explore how to understand and confidently discuss each opportunity to adjust rent.

COBA – The Cost of Business Adjustment

Each year the social security administration announces the COLA (Cost of Living Adjustment) made to the social security payments. The COLA is considered a key indicator of the cost of inflation. It is a national statistic, widely recognized and respected.

As discussed earlier, the first part of any rent increase should be implemented to adjust for inflation. By increasing your rent by the same percentage as the COLA, you will be taking into account an increase to cover the cost of doing business. Trying to successfully operate your property on last year's budget, without an adjustment for inflation, is not a good business practice. Always include a COBA (Cost of Business Adjustment) when raising rents.

The Cost of Business Adjustment is reasonable and easy to explain, don't you think? I must admit a very important point – I MADE IT UP!!! Someone made up the COLA, so I just followed that with COBA! However, I have many clients who use a COBA as it is simply a smart business practice. In order to increase actual profit, you must, first and foremost, adjust rent to match inflation. Then, and only then, can you work on increasing profit.

Regardless of the cost of inflation, never renew a lease at the same price. If you do, you will be paying the cost of inflation. Adjusting rents to match the cost of living adjustment, established by the social security administration, is an easy position to defend and a powerful principle for maximizing rents.

Leasing at Market Rate

Once I have established the Cost of Business Adjustment, it is time to evaluate the market rent. This is where the quick "supply and demand" lesson is important for the residents. They may have moved in during a "special" and now in recovery mode, you are beginning to raise rents. It is important to have market research available to share with your residents. By researching and showing the residents rents and cost per square foot in your area, you will be able to justify the increase in your rent.

Also, explaining that, "Your increase of $50, includes $29 that is simply an adjustment for inflation, designed to cover the increased cost of doing business next year. We have only asked for a $31 market rate adjustment. The cost of moving is estimated at $1500 or $125 per month over a year. You save a minimum of $70 by staying and all your stuff is already neatly tucked away, plugged in and hanging! The $50 increase is fair and reasonable, based on the current rate of inflation and market conditions"

During the recession rents were reduced, and revenue lost. Renters were moved in with concessions and will expect the same when they renew. The market has turned, and, you will need to recapture market rate. The new market might be able to bear a higher increase.

Shoppers have stopped clipping coupons, and consumer confidence is up. They are back in the malls, stores and restaurants. Make list of the services you provide, benefits of renting, and area lifestyle advantages. Build a leasing portfolio with pages of positive reviews, floor plan design ideas, area entertainment, parks & rec, drive times and community services. This is the time to step up leasing, resident services, and customer service. People are going to want to know why they have to pay more for the same apartment. Step up to the challenge with value marketing.

When the market gets rough, don't follow the "free rent" crowd off a fiscal cliff. Stay calm, be creative, but do not give free rent.

In lieu of free rent, offer residents a cruise, custom paint, or lighting upgrades. Maintain the maximum possible rent, the market, will allow. Have a plan and be creative, because you do not have to give away rent. Begin by committing to avoid "free rent thinking"! Stop, think, research, create and implement a plan that will keep the money in YOUR bank! Everything you do from flags to flowers impacts the image and value. One misguided move like hanging a "free rent" banner can devalue your market position. When you lower the rent, it not only reduces your bank deposits, it also reduces the perceived value of your product in the market.

Your reaction to a soft market should not decrease the value, but increase it! It is best for the customer to see your community as the best choice, not the cheapest choice. One of my favorite closing lines is, "Choose your next home because of what you get, not because of what you get free."

People want a good deal, so give them one! Do not feel obligated to keep up the "FREE RENT" game. It is a dangerous game and the industry loses every time it's played.

22 Confident Negotiation Statements for Increasing Rent

It's important to know how to negotiate a rent increase. I like to think of it as raising rents without raising eyebrows. This means your team, including maintenance; need to know how to confidently address the reasons for renting. Below you will find 22 renewal negotiation statements that will assist you in raising rents without raising eyebrows!

1. Hold up! Are You Covered?
Most car insurance plans do not cover rented moving vehicles, and your homeowner's policy may not cover your goods in transit. Rental truck insurance only covers damage to the vehicle, not the contents. Purchasing an insurance rider is yet another hidden cost of moving. Don't get left holding the bag, just STAY!

2. Economic Recovery!
Reflecting the rate of inflation on goods and service, the Social Security Administration calculates the Cost of Living Adjustment (COLA) each year. In 2009, the COLA was one of the highest on record, 6.2%. During this time, our rent and revenue was going

down. Now the market has turned, and it's time for economic recovery.

3. Saving a Few Bucks Could Cost You BIG!
When you move you most likely end up making many unintended purchases such as drapes, rugs, dishtowels, shower curtains, furniture, plants and items that suit your new living space. Instead of the pain of moving, enjoy the pleasure of staying. With the money you saved from not buying new stuff, you can afford a luxurious day at your favorite spa and still have money left over!

4. The Hits Keep on Coming!
Credit scores have dropped, and even considering another place to live can affect your score when they run your credit. At the same time, credit is harder to obtain. Instead of risking additional hits to your credit score, renew your lease here. We've already approved you and you're building a solid rental history. Save your credit for when you really need it and STAY!

5. It's No Picnic!
Taking time off from work to pack, load and drive the moving truck may mean a loss of salary, sick days, or vacation time, that may prove even more costly than hiring professionals. In addition, if you use up your vacation days or sick days moving, you can't get sick or go on vacation! Save your days off for that vacation in the sun, you've been talking about. Just STAY!

6. The Devil is in the Details!
Along with the details of packing, moving means spending hours updating your records. You'll need to change your address and contact information with the utility company, cell phone company, banks, doctors, lawyers, accountants, insurance, schools, credit card companies, church, family and friends. Why not just STAY!

7. It All Stacks Up!
For four rooms, you will need approximately 50 boxes ranging in size from small to extra large as well as wardrobe boxes. Moving is expensive; you will need, box-sealing tape, furniture dollies, moving labels, twine, mattress covers, markers, packing paper and other moving accessories. In all, these items can total hundreds of dollars added to your final moving costs. Loaded to full capacity, a 26-foot U-Haul truck will average 8 miles per gallon of gas and your need to rent furniture pads to protect your items from damage in transport! Those moving cost really add up! Just STAY!

8. You'll Get a Charge Out of Moving!
Whenever you start up services, you'll find you have to pay a connection or administrative fee. Utility companies charge large deposits to set up service. Don't forget the time and effort of moving your home entertainment system, and getting all those wires, plugs or even satellite dish in the right spot. Everything is connected now – why undo it all? Stay!!!

9. Things are Looking UP!
The increase in rent is both a market rate adjustment to our new residents and a cost of living adjustment for inflation to our current residents. Economic expansion has enabled housing prices to rise across the nation, and there is a high demand for apartments. If you give notice on your apartment, it may be re-leased quickly at a higher rate and force you to move. This would mean not only an increase in rent but also the cost and stress of moving. Please be sure to confirm the new location before giving notice on your apartment. We are dedicated to maintaining your high standard of living and appreciate the opportunity to serve you for the next year.

10. National Turn Around!
The National Association of Realtor and the National Association of Home Builders are reporting increases in occupancy and rents in apartments for the coming year. It's not just us. Apartment rents are rebounding all over the country; a sign that things are turning around and we are heading for better days!

11. In-come & Out-Go!
Just like you, this community's financial health depends upon our ability to grow our income to match the rate of inflation, which has risen on an average of over 3% per year over the past 10 years. Growing our income to match inflation is not profit and much of your increase in rent will simply allow us to continue to provide excellent service and the quality of life you and your neighbors enjoy.

12. Bad For Us – Good for you!
In the last few years during the recession rents not only did not maintain growth to cover inflation, in some cases they were reduced and even were accompanied by special incentives. The amount of money you saved during the slower economy, multiplied by 12 for each year is an astounding amount of money.

13. Just Stay!
The average cost of moving is $1500 which is equal to a $125 increase in your monthly cost of living for the next year. Stay where you are and save the time, money, heartaches, headaches, backaches, days off work, damage to your goods and complaints from your friends and family for helping you move! The only paperwork you'll need to sign is your lease! STAY!!!

14. Renting ROCKS!
We keep your community groomed, blooming, manicured and maintained. We provide well trained maintenance technicians and cover the cost of repairs, taxes and waste management. According to Money magazine, homeowners have unexpected annual costs that equal 1% of the value of their home. We will continue to cover the cost of ownership, and you simply enjoy the benefits of renting! Renting ROCKS!

15. Just ONE thing!
How about if we pay the street usage fees, property taxes, school taxes, pool maintenance, lawn care, parking lot repair, roof repair,

plumbing, electrical, lighting, landscape sprinklers, waste management, sewer, service technicians, on-site management team and all the other costs involved in your home – you just pay ONE thing – the rent! While we deal with the variables of changing cost – your rent stays the same! Renting ROCKS!

16. Cleaning Knee-ded!
Moving means cleaning wall-to-wall, behind, underneath, on top of and in-between – a real workout for your knees! You'll need to clean your old place before you leave, and you'll want to clean your new place when you arrive. You can do this yourself, or you can use a cleaning company. Either way it requires your money or your time.

17. Cleaning: A Dirty Word Indeed!
Let us not forget this shopping list: Laundry soap, dish soap, Windex, 409, trash bags, paper towels and light bulbs. Add all this up, and it sounds like you're the one being taken to the cleaners. Why not stay and relax in your place? Spend your money on a great bottle of wine and toast to another year here!

18. A Chilling Thought!
Take a look in your freezer! Moving the contents in your freezer can be difficult, if not impossible. You could eat it all yourself, or have a few parties, but why? Wasting that food would add one more cost to moving, or could be one more savings for staying! Freeze your plans to move and eat your food when you want it!!

19. Not-so-sweet Sorry!
Leaving the area may also mean losing your established services. Who will cut your hair, make your Starbuck's drink, dry clean your clothes and provide all the other services you have come to enjoy? You are relocating more than your sofa! Moving means shopping for a new hairdresser, dry cleaner, bank, school, doctor, etc. Take a deep breath and count your blessing! STAY!

20. Breakups are Painful!
Hired packers, or even your friends, may have a tendency to rush and, therefore, be neglectful with your possessions. Items that require assembly are at serious risk during both the disassembly and reassembly of being lost or misplaced. Don't take the risk with your stuff – just them be and STAY!

21. Haste Makes Waste!
Moving means packing up a lifetime of memories. Deciding what to keep, sell, give away and trash! This can be very time consuming as we stroll down memory lane in each drawer, closet and box. Often treasured memories can get lost in the shuffle and thrown out with the massive amount of trash generated by the move. For heaven sakes –keep your keepsakes and STAY!

22. This is HOME!
The grass is usually not greener on the other side, and good service is difficult to find. Why risk your happiness and quality of life on an unknown place? If you are unhappy where you move, you are stuck with a 12-month lease and the cost of potentially moving twice in a year. Our small cost of business adjustment for the services you've come to expect is a small price to pay for staying within the comfort of the place that has become your home. We hope you will stay!

Important Reasons Why Renting is Better Than Owning!

Today owning is NOT seen as the best economic option. Financial advisors are suggesting renting as a better option to home ownership and are providing alternative investment opportunity. Housing is not long a fluid investment. On average, a person must stay for approximately seven years before a return on investment can be realized.

Development in multifamily housing lead our nation into the last economic recovery and renting will go on record as the BEST choice for Americans between 2014 - 2017. Unfortunately, you would never know that if you Google renting versus owning. The realtors have out posted, out tweeted and outright published more data for their cause than multifamily.

While many people own their own homes in today's society, this wasn't always the case. Historically, families either needed to build their own homes or rent a home from someone else. While both renting and buying have their own sets of financial advantages, renting does appear to have an edge when the economy is poor. There are tremendous financial benefits to renting as opposed to buying a house of your own. Here is a look at eight reasons why renters have the better financial deal over homeowners.

Simplicity
For those who prefer a simple life, rent a great living space with many of the hidden cost of owning included in the rent! Additionally, renting a place cheaper than the maximum amount simplifies financial aspects as well.

The Issue of the Paperwork
It begins with the agreement of sale, home inspection and termite inspection, closing documents for the loan and one for the house, truth in lending statement, itemization for the amount financed, and the proceeds distribution. It continues with anything the lender will pay to others on your behalf, like prepaid finance charges, cost of origination of mortgage, monthly payment letter with itemized components of that check, or automatic deduction from your checking account. Also, papers to sign that outlines the principal and interest, escrow of taxes and insurance, the promissory note, and the penalties and lender renege. In addition, the lien on your property, disclosure settlement statement or HUD-1, proration agreement, deed, name affidavit, title search abstract, utility receipts, and the

acknowledgment that you have seen all the reports for the property. After all of this, you are stuck at one address with the neighbors.

There is The Money Required Upfront

Another area where renters have the better financial deal is upon signing. You do not have to have a huge down payment saved up to move into a rental property. While the exact amount you need to move in varies from case to case, the total amount is significantly less than you would need to buy a house.

According to a graph released by the New York Times, many landlords require a rental deposit equal to the amount of one month's rent while a down payment for a house is much higher. For example, with a 5% deposit on a house that has a market value of $175,000 your move-in costs start at $8,750, which is much more than the average one-month rent rate. Also, those buying will want to save up much more than 5% for their initial down payment because the bigger the down payment, the better. By renting, you can avoid the high initial down payment costs.

Property Taxes Are Included in Your Rent

Homeowners are responsible for a variety of federal, state, local and school taxes. Real estate taxes can be a hefty burden for homeowners and vary by county. If you have never had a mortgage, be aware that your monthly bill won't simply reflect the loan amount plus interest. It will also reflect property taxes and premiums for homeowner insurance, which all mortgage borrowers are required to obtain.

Federal Tax -The IRS imposes a capital gains tax on the sale of real estate. Generally, homeowners who sell their homes must pay tax on net gains exceeding $250,000. Homeowners may be exempt, however, depending on whether they achieved a net gain and the amount of the net gain. Another factor is the duration the homeowner has lived in the home.

State Tax - Homeowners pay state tax. States determine their budgets based on payroll for state employees and state-sponsored programs. One way states fund their budgets is through real estate tax. States determine a rate that each homeowner will pay to fund the state's budget. States task local assessors to collect the monies taxed to homeowners for state budgets. Homeowners pay a portion of the state's budget when they pay their local real estate tax bills.

Local Tax - Counties and municipalities typically charge a "mill rate," or "mill levy" for real estate. A "mill" equals 1/10 of 1 cent, or $0.001. The mill rate is the amount a homeowner is taxed per $1,000 of assessed real estate value. Depending on the budget needed and the total number of real estate owners in the area, each municipality may assign a different mill rate. Mill levies pay for streets, police and fire protection, and city and county administration and operations.

School Tax - Regardless of whether homeowners have children in school, their county property taxes also help pay for local school districts. The tax pays for all aspects of public education, such as school land and buildings, teachers' salaries, textbooks and school administration expenses. Homeowners may also pay taxes to fund community colleges.

Maintenance Costs and Repairs Are Included in Your Rent.
One of the key benefits to renting is that the rent includes all of the maintenance cost and repairs. When your apartment is professionally managed, it includes professionally trained service technicians. If an appliance stops working or your roof starts to leak, you do not have any financial responsibility to have these things fixed. Homeowners, on the other hand, are responsible for all of their own repair, maintenance and renovation costs.

The 1 Percent Rule - One popular rule of thumb is that one percent of the purchase price of your home should be set aside each year for ongoing maintenance. For example, if your home cost $300,000, you should budget $3,000 per year for maintenance.

Amenities Are Included in Your Rent.
Apartment residents enjoy wonderful amenity packages with no cost of construction, repair and upkeep. These amenities would be a huge expense to any homeowner. Luxuries such as an in-ground pool or fitness center come standard at many midscale to upscale apartment communities with no additional charge to residents. If a homeowner wants to match these amenities, he or she can expect to pay thousands of dollars in installation and maintenance costs.

Flexibility to Relocate
In today's economy, many people struggle to make ends meet. By renting, citizens have the option to downgrade into a more affordable living space at the end of their lease. When you are a homeowner, it is much more difficult to break free of an expensive house because of the fees involved with buying and selling a home.

Mobility
Don't buy a home that you are planning on living in for less than five years. Renting offers the ability to move around. Buying a home leaves no room for mobility.

Chapter 5
Ring a Ling Leasing: The Phone Call Connection

By Kate Good and Jackie Ramstedt

Even in our technologically advanced society, the phone can still be a powerful tool in leasing apartments. By learning some simple techniques such as putting aside distractions, learning how to truly listen to your caller, and selling your property with an effective verbal tour, you can increase your traffic and your leasing power over the phone. Making a personal connection with a prospective resident over the phone will give you a professional advantage over other properties not utilizing the phone to its full advantage. Learn how to correctly and appropriately handle difficult callers and questions while building a relationship with your future residents at the same time.

It is doubtful that Alexander Graham Bell ever anticipated all the uses of the telephone. He didn't foresee the smartphone, and while he probably anticipated some form of texting, as the telegraph was a similar function, he was probably clueless that the phone would one day occupy 90% of all free time of teenagers.

Kate distinctly remembers her father giving her career advice when she was 15 years old. He said that she should strongly consider a career in telemarketing because she did not mind having a phone next to her ear for the majority of the evening hours. But for us multifamily folks, the phone is a business tool, and just like any tool - now more than ever - it demands a special skill set and proper use to ensure a more effective outcome.

A telephone call is the prospect's first opportunity to speak with a "live person." Up to this point all contact has been made through either technology communication or advertisement to get them inspired to make this call. So how important is it? VERY! That first impression sets the tone for all future encounters with your prospective resident.

If we don't make the experience warm, inviting, friendly, informative, and "memorable," the prospect will just move on to the next apartment community phone number in the area. They will never know just how wonderful your community is or discover all it has to offer because you have failed to "connect" with exactly what the prospect needs.

We understand the importance of making that connection has on the overall success of the sales as a whole. It may look like a lot of information to discuss on the telephone with your prospect, but the best conversations last about 5 to 10 minutes tops. It gives BOTH you, the leasing consultant, and the prospect enough time to gain important information about each other and still make a great beginning relationship.

Nobody calls each other anymore. We all can relate to entire weekends when the phone did not ring at all. Texts and emails may come in non-stop, but it often seems rare to receive a call. As for making a call, we find that we only call when we don't understand an email or text and want to get to the bottom of it. It is for these reasons that people feel very special when the phone rings. When someone takes action to pick up the phone, it is important to them. In the world of leasing apartments, this is a very good thing. Someone has picked up the phone and called **you**. You now have an advantage over all your competitors to earn this lease.

Does your company have a marketing department? The designated person who is responsible for marketing your property? Even if your property has hired a Madison Avenue advertising agency, never think that generating traffic is not your job - it is. Marketing is a big part of being a Leasing Consultant. The top people in our field know this fact, and they know that this is what makes them more successful than most. They create their own traffic. When the phone rings and the caller is interested in leasing an apartment, you have your next leasing appointment opportunity right in front of you. Work it, my friend - and add "telephone master" to your growing list of talents.

Many marketing professionals and trainers will tell you that your most important job on the call is to set an appointment. While this is, in fact, a vital part of the leasing process, you must consider your absolute most important task is to get the caller's name. Before you run off and tell your boss that Kate and Jackie say I just need a name, let us explain. We don't expect you to just get the caller's name, we expect you to understand that by focusing on getting someone's name, you are reaffirming that the caller and their needs are where your focus should be – on them. Think of getting the caller's name as having the same impact on the conversation as being aware of "body language" does in person. It helps to connect both you and the caller in "seeing and visualizing" what each other is talking about. We'll get into that more in just a bit, but let's start with some practical information for having a good call.

Preparation for the Call: "Thoughts, Attitude, Actions and Tools"

Preparation is crucial, so do your homework first. If you prepare well before you pick up a phone call, you will have the knowledge and tools needed to make your calls go smoothly and allow you to make appointments and lease over the phone.

Routinely call other communities - not just properties in your market area, but ANY property - and listen to how those leasing consultants handle your call. Did they seem friendly? Did they treat you as if you were an interruption? Did they answer the price question with the price?

By calling your competition, you will hear what your prospects will hear if they call that property. Getting in your prospect's mindset will help you to overcome deficiencies other communities might have in their phone conversations. This gives you the "sales edge" knowing you already know what your prospect had heard before they called you.

Gather your tools for the conversation, beginning with knowing your company or property Guest Card (either paper or electronic) well. Update your Guest Cards with appropriate "open-ended" questions, not just the typical "yes or no" questions. You need to find out so much more than just "what size of apartment?" or "how many people will be living with you?"

Have an iPad or tablet with a Leasing App or your desktop computer set up to take all of your caller's information. In addition, have your marketing and leasing notebook available that contains information about your general area, shopping, conveniences for your residents, utility phone numbers and all aspects of the interior and exterior amenities of your community. Also have your own community web site address, your company's corporate website, all sites where you advertise, and anything else that would be a "benefit" to living at your community, listed with all details. You will find that you'll refer to these more often than you think.

Walk all your current vacant units while using the Unit Marketability Checklist that Jackie has provided as a sample included at the end of this chapter. Take notes about each unit's differences, interior amenities, exterior locations, etc., to be able to "mentally" walk through the details with the prospect while on the phone. Use the unit's unique selling points and advantages while filling out the "Feature, Benefit, and Emotional Appeal" section of the checklist.

- For Example: If the **feature is the fireplace**, the **"benefit"** is the option to use the fireplace on cold days without having to necessarily turn on the heat, or at least not having to turn the heat on as high which saves the utility cost. The **"emotional appeal"** would be the coziness and warmth a fireplace brings, evoking happy memories of family and friends.

Accuracy of availability of all apartments available to lease or pre-lease from those on "Notice to Vacate" is VERY important! Create a "Target" or a "Hot" list of specific units that are currently ready to show and that can be leased today. Those vacant apartments that are ready to show but NOT leased yet should be the immediate focus. This gives you the ability to describe a particular apartment that meets your prospect's needs and wants, not just the model apartment or the "generic" version of that size. For "Notice to Vacate" apartments and their availability dates that are not pre-leased, give maintenance time to walk these units ahead of time and "estimate" when they will be ready to show after current resident moves out. Model apartments are great for comparison if you have nothing else to show currently, but make sure to let the prospect know the differences between them and the ones coming available to lease.

Having a "Telephone Conversation Script" to guide your conversation with your prospect helps you learn to gain a good "flow" of the conversation and shows examples of how to ask those important questions in a positive way. Jackie has provided a sample of a generic conversation script at the end of the chapter.

Before You say Hello, You Must Learn to Say Goodbye.

Kate once had a boyfriend who was obsessed with internet checkers. If she happened to call him in the evening and he was relaxing at home, he was usually on his computer playing checkers. How did she know? She could hear the click of the mouse in addition to noticing he was distracted from their conversation, and it did not make her feel good. She started to grow more and more upset with him over the thought that his internet checkers were more important than their relationship. Always remember that the caller can tell when you are not listening, making them feel less important. Our customers (and your boyfriend or girlfriend for that matter) should never feel like they do not have your full attention.

Changing "mental hats" from whatever you are currently doing at the time the telephone rings to focus on the call and really listen to the caller is paramount. Some essential points to remember:

- The caller isn't an interruption in our workday; they are the reason we are in business!
- Your initial response and greeting will make all the difference between the professional YOU and the competition!
- Understand that a great telephone call can result in a prospect ready to lease and put down money now!

The resident or future resident should feel like you are interested in what they have to say, and their business is important to you. Pull away from distractions and make this important caller the center of your attention. It might be the needed behavior for setting an appointment with the future resident, letting an existing resident know we appreciate their business, or for your girlfriend to know she is important to you.

Set Your Call Up For Success: Attitude

Great first impressions on a phone call are significantly harder to make than when greeting a prospective renter in person. On the phone you have only a few talents to use to make that great impact - your tone, your word choice and your attitude. These are all important, but we're really big fans of making sure your attitude is positive and upbeat. How many times have you bought something from someone or done business with a person who perhaps wasn't the best salesperson or may have even messed up a bit in their presentation, yet their attitude brought it across the finish line? Attitude can be heard in your breath, your cadence and, of course, in your words and tone. So more importantly, attitude can make up for errors, ignorance, and inexperience. Prior to answering the phone, check yourself. Am I in a positive state of mind? Am I excited to share information with the caller? No matter what else you do, have a great attitude when you pick up the phone.

Now, unless you're moonlighting at the Psychic Friends Network, you are most likely not going to know who is calling or why they are calling as the phone rings, so you need to be prepared for every call to be a resident or prospect. For the purpose of this book, we're focusing on phone techniques when dealing with prospects, but keep the etiquette tips and other ideas in mind when dealing with residents, too. Offices with caller ID displays on their phones should most certainly utilize that tool, but be advised to NOT assume you know who it is on the other line because caller ID says so.

Here is a lesson in how wrong caller ID assumptions can go: Several people were in a manager's office noodling over some ideas for a resident function when the phone rang. The caller id displayed "Angela Curtain." The leasing manager, a phenom in leasing, speaks up, "I've got this - it's my cousin." The leasing manager grabs the phone and answers with a screechy morning-after-a-great-party voice calling her "cousin" a name that starts with B and ends with an H, with a couple extra vowels in the middle. Turns out, "Angela Curtain" is not that unique a name. In fact, if you were to do a quick search on Facebook or Google, you'd be shocked at how many exist. The leasing manager didn't bother to notice the phone number wasn't her cousin's. Thankfully, being a phenom and having a great attitude, the leasing manager recovered and was able to provide Angela with information and set an appointment. But the moral of the story is clearly to treat every call in a professional manner.

So what do we have so far? Great attitude - and expect every call to be a prospect or resident. What does expecting the call to be a prospect look like? It means being prepared with your thoughts, attitude, actions, and tools and making sure you aren't distracted. Now you're ready to pick up the phone.

That Powerful First Impression: Greeting the Prospect

Answering the phone doesn't need to be a Broadway production; no cute jingles or rhyming phrases are necessary. Be professional, identify your community and yourself, and ask how you can help the caller. It was popular for many years to do fun little greetings such as, "Crossing Brook has a new look." Thankfully, that trend died with the Macarena. So keep it simple, professional, and short.

There are some easy ways to make a powerful first impression over the phone:

- Answer the telephone by the third ring.
- Take a deep breath, and SMILE (the caller will actually be able to hear it in your voice!).
- Have a short but pleasant greeting prepared thanking them for taking time from their busy schedule to call: "Thank you for calling (your property name), this is (leasing consultant's name), how may I help you today?"

If you want the customer to like you, it is important to be believable. Keep in mind that we buy from people we like. In order for someone to like you, there has to be a realistic first impression. If you open the call with an "over the top" bubbly voice that sounds like you just drank an entire case of a very strong energy drink, you may be perceived as fake. In the same respect, you don't want to sound like you are bored or have no care or concern for the person who is calling.

As a good start, **be nice before you know who is calling**. Many years ago Kate held a position in a national REIT, and her title was Director of People Success. This basically meant that she was the head cheerleader at the company. She "planned the fun," created team spirit, trained and encouraged people to be in the top 1%, and set an example of the power of a good attitude. She had a lot of contact with their sites and is proud to say that she knew all 1475 team members by name. One afternoon, she called a property in Roswell, GA. The Leasing Consultant answered the phone, and Kate thought she just woke her up, based on the Leasing Consultant's monotone greeting and fading voice. Kate responded and said, "Hi, this is Kate Good." Instantly, she could hear that a smile now covered the consultant's face, and she suddenly had life in her voice. In fact, it sounded like she stood up at her desk and started jumping up and down! This Leasing Consultant was so proud to tell Kate that she closed 7 leases in the last two days. However, it appeared that she had to determine it was someone whom she wanted to impress on the phone **before** she projected a positive attitude. From that day on, Kate placed signs on all property phones that said, "Be nice before you know who is calling."

Phone etiquette should be observed at all times and includes the following must dos:

- **Choose your words wisely.** You should never use slang and avoid curse words, even the soft ones such as "dang," "shoot," or "crap."
- **Listen before you speak.** Always remember your focus should be on the caller and their needs.
- **Be cognizant of your prospect's time.** Directly ask your prospect if they have a few minutes to discuss their needs.
- **Speak clearly and slowly.** Enunciate and never take a call with any gum or mints in your mouth.

Attempt to get the caller's name in the first minute or two. You can do this while bridging the conversation from the greeting to getting the caller's needs. Let's look at an example:

Leasing:	Thank you for calling Summit Place. This is Kate, how may I help you?
Prospect:	Hi, I'm looking for a two bedroom apartment.
Leasing:	I'm so glad you called - we have several wonderful two bedroom floor plans to choose from. Can I get your name and a little more information so I can help you?
Prospect:	Sure... My name is Lisa..

After you get their name, it is a good idea to see if you can find out how they found out about you. If the call didn't come in on a tracked number, you will want to see if you can get info about what marketing efforts brought them to you. Prior to the internet and social media, it was simple to figure out how someone found out about a community, but in today's connected world people will often learn about a community through multiple channels prior to calling. It is still important to learn what prompted them to call, so ask the question, "May I ask how you learned about us? What prompted you to call today?" This will give you powerful data and will help you spend time, talent, and treasure on the right marketing efforts.

Now you're ready to find out what your prospective resident really wants and needs by putting on your leasing hat and asking qualifying questions. "Qualifying questions" does not mean questions about whether or not they can afford the rent - it means figuring out what their needs are.

Lose the Script

Though there is a sample "Telephone Conversation Script" included at the end of this chapter to help new leasing consultants learn how to ask important questions that are designed to help open up a true conversation, our advice is; lose the script! The customer can sense when you are using a script, and that will seem very impersonal. You want to have a conversation that will get you to the lease faster than any script - if you do it right!

Diane Keaton was once interviewed as part of a lecture series, walking out on stage in a black hat, leather jacket and polka dotted circle skirt. Her outfit was sassy; the actress was in great form, and those in attendance were sure her interview would provide them with some of that wit that only Diane Keaton can deliver. The interviewer had a pile of blue cards that seemed to have a question on each of them. One question after another fired out of his mouth, and the cards dropped one by one to the floor. In the end, while he got through all of his questions, he did not get to the heart of Diane Keaton. He only asked the questions on his cards, and she stayed on the surface with her answers, only answering his questions.

That's the difference between a script and a conversation: had the interviewer actually listened to Diane Keaton's responses to his questions and asked other questions based on her responses, he would have taken the interview with her deeper. A conversation would have ensued, and it really would have gotten interesting. The audience could have heard about decades of Hollywood drama and details about a life well lived, instead of hearing short answers to a list of pre-determined questions.

Do not interrogate the caller! A Leasing Consultant in Tempe shared about a customer who walked into the leasing office to see an apartment. She pulled out her guest card and pen and asked her first question. The guest handed her a return address label and said he would save her the time of filling it out. You see, the customer was expecting an interrogation, but he just wanted to learn about the apartments. We must remember it's not about just filling in a guest card in the order the card is written; we need to ask the questions in a "flow of information" that is comfortable for the prospect to give. Work on your ability to develop a conversation with callers and guests and you will see your closing ratio improve because you are able to know your customer a little better through a productive conversation.

Use the included sample script as a starting place for your calls, but allow it to open a true conversation instead of sticking solely to the questions in front of you. It can be used as a reference point, but it should never run your calls – listen to your caller, asking questions to lead your conversation, and begin building a relationship with your future resident. A great opening question to begin that relationship might be, "If you could describe your perfect apartment home, what would it look like?"

Learning Needs and Qualifying

If your caller has indicated they have time, you can spend a good amount of time helping the prospect and listening to their needs. Utilize open-ended questions to allow the prospective resident to really tell you about their needs. If the question can be answered with one word, "yes" or "no," then you just asked a closed ended question. Open ended questions also get the conversation started and will extend the amount of time and interest the caller will give you. Examples of open-ended questions could be:

- Tell me about what you would like in an apartment home.
- What do you consider the ideal apartment?
- What are your top three "must-haves" in an apartment home?
- What do you have in your current home that you would like to see in your future home?
- What is the most important room in your home?
- Tell me about any special furniture you need to fit in your home.
- Do you have any special housing needs? (Although this question was originally designed for helping people with disabilities in special modification or accommodation request needs, it has evolved to just finding out more specific information of any prospect's needs.)
- May I ask why you have decided to move? (This question helps you to determine the back story of what the prospect actually liked or didn't like about where they live now.)
- Any of these questions will get your caller to lower their guard while giving you all their hot buttons for closing the lease. It will also allow you to build a natural rapport with the caller, helping you sell without doing a hard sell. It is important to build trust with the caller, and the easiest way to get there is for them to feel like they are talking to a friend on the phone, not a salesperson.

Leasing has always been and will always be a form of sales, yet a strong leasing consultant understands that being "salesy" will never get the job done. You must see your job as helping someone find a home and use that desire to help them drive your presentation on the phone. Be genuine and be happy about helping them, and the prospect will trust you and want to find out more about your community.

Caution: if you answer every one of their responses to your questions with information about your apartment community, you will sound like a sales-pitch. Hold on to those replies until you are finished with your information gathering stage. Use the caller's own words to help with your responses. It shows you were listening and understand what they really want.

In Today's World, People Do Not Want To Be Sold. People Want To Be Served.

Have you ever walked into a store and been approached by a sales person who asks if they can help you? Typically, you respond, "No thank you, I am just looking." If that same salesperson approaches you in the shoe department, sees you holding a shoe and asks to get your size, is your response different? Of course, it is (you know Kate loves her shoes!) Why did you say "no" to the first question but "yes" to the second? Here's why; because the second question serves your needs. The first question was a sales strike because you did not yet have a need. But once that awesome pair of shoes caught your eye, you were ready to be served. The customer appreciates sales people who are focused on serving their needs versus trying to sell them something they do not yet know they want.

Once you have gathered your information, match the prospect's need requests to your community's availability listing and begin selling them on the benefits of fulfilling those needs using specific examples such as...

- "You mentioned a washer and dryer connection as one of your important needs. We have full size washer and dryer connections in every apartment at our community! We even have washers and dryers you may rent as well."
- "I understand that parking locations are always of concern for everyone. The good news is this particular apartment's parking is right outside your front door."
- "You said you definitely needed two complete bathrooms. Totally understand you need your own space. This particular floor plan has two identical size bathrooms including bathtubs."

Use the information you gathered during your conversation, and serve your future resident with solutions to their own needs.

Dealing With the Pushy Caller

If your caller is in a rush, you have to alter your approach. You know the people who call and demand the prices right off the bat, making it crystal clear they have no interest in staying on the phone with you. These callers are challenging, but you can work with them to find their needs. You just can't use an open-ended question approach or the call will likely end abruptly. Use closed-ended questions to get the most pertinent information. A closed-ended question generates an absolute answer and does not require the prospect to elaborate. Here are some examples of closed-ended questions to help move the leasing process forward without taking up too much time:

- When would you like to move?
- What size apartment home would you like?
- Are you interested in coming to tour our community?

You also want to be polite and understand their time is limited. If the caller is obviously in a serious rush, help them get what they need.

To build rapport and trust with this type of caller, immediately acknowledge that their time is valuable. Do this by asking for their contact information and recommend that you talk when they have more time.

Here is an example of how that conversation may go:

Prospect:	How much are your two bedrooms?
Leasing:	We have several floor plans available and I'm happy to help you. May I get a bit more information from you to help figure out which one would best fit your needs?
Prospect:	I just want the price range – how much are they?
Leasing:	Okay, I can tell you that they begin at $850, but since you're in a hurry; may I quickly get your name and contact info? I can call you back when you have time or even just email you. I would love to tell about why you'd want to live here and give you more information.
Prospect:	Great thanks and sure, it's Bob. You can email me at BobHurried@gmail.com.
Leasing:	Thank you Bob. I will email you more information after we hang up and hope you have a great day!

Introducing the Rental Price

Though we just discussed "pushy callers" and those who need to be addressed with closed-ended questions, we recommend that you never give out the price right up front in the conversation, as it doesn't add any "value" to the dollar amount. You must show the value through all the benefits of living in your community. If the prospect DOES ask just for prices, give a price range and verify that these prices are in the prospect's budget range. Immediately get back to controlling the conversation with your open-ended questions. Draw more information out of them so you can show them the true value of your community.

Hold back on giving out "specials" or "discounts" over the telephone; it sounds desperate and lowers the value of your other rental prices. If you do want to use the "specials" information, use it at the very end as a "pleasant surprise" and give the timeframes for that particular special.

Try not to sound like a "laundry list" of figures when discussing financial details:

> "The security deposit is $300 for a 2 bedroom and $200 for a 1 bedroom; the application fee is $50 per application and $75 if you have a joint application; the admin fee is $175; there is an "upgrade charge" of $50 for 1st floor views; the washer and dryers are $100 per month; the garages are $175 per month; the carports are $100 per month; door to door trash pickup is $25 extra per month."

…and on and on and on and on!!!! Imagine how your caller will feel after hearing that – you've just reduced the relationship you've been trying to build from future-resident-and-caring-consultant to consumer-and-money-hungry-provider.

For questions about Section 8 Communities, ask your corporate attorney for guidance on how to properly respond.

As for Tax Credit Communities, which were built or created to accept people who could not qualify at a regular conventional community because they don't make enough money, you can explain it correctly when someone asks by saying, "We are on an "income sensitive" program as part of our qualification process. What that means is our residents may only qualify if they make between (certain amounts.)"

Fair Housing

Before we move on to your phone presentation and verbal tour, we really should talk more about the law.

The Fair Housing Act prohibits discrimination in the sale, rental, and financing of dwellings, and in other housing-related transactions based on race, color, national origin, religion, sex, familial status (including children under the age of 18 living with parents or legal custodians, pregnant women, and people securing custody of children under the age of 18), and disability.

Fair housing cases involving phone calls are more common than you might think. It is critical that you understand the law and ensure each and every phone call abides by the law. This means you cannot ask prospects if they have children, or suggest they come and tour a downstairs apartment because they are older and use a cane. In addition, you can't tell someone you don't accept pets when they ask about their emotional support animal. This chapter is not about fair housing, but we advise everyone to get in the know about federal, state and local fair housing laws. If you are unfamiliar in the slightest, get on the phone with your supervisor right now and tell them you need training in this area. This book also contains a chapter on Fair Housing, which we strongly suggest you read first and continue on with the rest of the book.

Most of the time, while on the phone, you cannot tell if the caller is a member of a protected class, so you always assume everyone is. However, the hearing impaired are easily identified as they will use a trained operator or special device for the deaf to communicate over the phone. Text Telephones (TTY), also known as Telecommunications Device for the Deaf (TDD) help hearing impaired, deaf, and individuals with speech impairments to communicate. All site personnel should be trained to expect calls from TTY operators and know how to properly handle the call. Generally speaking, you should treat these calls as you would any other call. You are in violation of the Americans with Disabilities

Act and can be charged with discrimination under the Fair Housing Act if you ignore or hang up on TTY calls. This is a serious matter and the law, so be ready.

So while we're discussing the law, if you are on a HUD community or participate in any HUD programs, you are obligated under an Executive Order to provide interpretation services for individuals with Limited English Proficiency. So if this topic sounds like we're speaking a foreign language to you, get on the phone again and ask for more help in this area.

Verbal Tour

We've checked our attitude, we've asked a few qualifying questions, we've built rapport, and we've done it all while maintaining compliance with fair housing laws. Whew, I'm beat, but we're just getting started. Now you have to lease! Yes, LEASE on the phone!

The real reason many consultants don't convert calls to appointments is because they are so busy worrying about getting an appointment that they don't focus on the caller and lease to them while they are on the phone. The prospect is on the phone with you because they need to rent an apartment, and they like your community enough already to pick up the phone and call. In today's world, we find that the majority of callers have also checked out your Website or an Internet Listing Service (ILS), such as ApartmentGuide.com or Rent.com, where they started their search and narrowed their choices. The call is to gather more information and qualify their choices. They are looking for a reason to keep you on their list. They WANT you to lease to them. So do it!

Most of the things we buy we do so because there was an emotion tied to it. You really want something because it means something to you. Your emotions tell you that you want this. Do you have anything hanging in your closet that still has the tag on it? If you have never worn it, why did you buy it in the first place? Our educated guess is that you really wanted it because the clothing tapped into something important to you. Possibly, when you were trying it on, someone told you how great you looked, and the feeling that it was good enough for a compliment meant it needed to be in your closet. We make decisions based on our emotions. When you are conducting the verbal tour, you want to link items at your property and features in your apartments to the caller's needs and wants.

Conducting a tour verbally on the phone is a bit of an art form. If you can get a caller in front of a computer and have them pull up your website with pictures, you can use those tools to help you show off your community. If they have already checked out your website, explain to them that you want to point out some interesting features that meet their needs they may have overlooked. Hopefully, you've listened to the prospect and have a good understanding of their furniture and can show them images and demonstrate placing special pieces. Use the information you've gathered to focus your verbal tour on their hot buttons.

If you can't get them in front of a computer, you can still show them your community with your fab verbal leasing skills! Remember to use what they've told you so far. For example, if they told you they absolutely must have a community with a fitness center and your community has a gym Jillian Michaels would be envious of, start there. Describe your community and the apartments in detail with adjectives that bring life to the words and allow the prospect to visualize what you are describing DO NOT say, "We have a 24 hour fitness center…" Instead try, "Our fully equipped fitness gym and yoga studio provides even die-hards with the tools to work out and get fit. We've got all the latest equipment and multiple of each apparatus, so no waiting for machines. You can work out anytime day or night as it is always open for residents." You never want to rattle off a list of amenities. Take the time to describe each amenity and use the information you have learned about this specific customer in that description. At this point, you are making a strong connection between their needs and your apartment community.

At this point, start to use assumptive language. This means that the way you describe the apartment and community are to use words that make it sound like they have already rented. A few examples are:

- Your new home will feature…..
- When you move in, you will enjoy….
- Spend your day off taking advantage of your new….
- Your dog will meet lots of buddies at the….
- Invite your friends to the clubroom and….

Conduct your phone tour as you would in person – paint a picture of your community and apartments for them and entice them to come out and see it in person. You don't need to describe every amenity and every aspect of your apartment homes in painstaking detail, but try to dial in on their wants and always cover their needs. At this point, you are ready to ask for action.

Remember this:
- A need must be satisfied.
- A want is a sale maker.
- A wish contributes to earning the sale.

Listen for the language your customer uses when describing themselves and their needs. Even if they use the word "need," try to find out where that item is on their priority list. For example, if the customer says they want a washer and dryer, is that a need, want or a wish? Sorry - that was a bit of a trick question, because, at this point, you don't know enough about the customer. Soon, the customer volunteers that they are a single mom with two children under the age of six. Now you know this customer has a lot of laundry! A washer and dryer may be at the top of their list. If you are ever in doubt about a need they mentioned, simply ask them where they place this item on their list of priorities.

If it's appropriate, extend your verbal tour to include discussions of your company and the general market area. Considering the caller's needs, wants, and wishes, think about sharing stats about your company like; who the national management company is, or if it's privately owned or has a smaller management company, etc. and the "benefits" of living at your community. If you've bonded over your love for great shoes (the caller needs space for her extensive collection in your generously-sized closets, remember?), discuss the local shopping areas. Kids? Talk about the school districts.

Other things to share in your verbal tour are:

- Local attractions: zoos, ball parks, recreational attractions, lakes, rivers, event centers
- Transportation: Metro lines, shuttle routes, light rails trains, etc.
- Local shops and restaurants within walking distance
- Lifestyle activities: jogging trails, gyms, swimming, etc.
- School districts: all levels of educational opportunities, including community colleges and trade schools.

Dealing With Difficult Questions: "Who will my neighbors be?"

Sometimes prospects have had a difficult time with a particular group of people that causes them to have concerns about your property. It's understandable, and in some cases, it may be the very reason they have decided to move. But the questions that they might ask may have discrimination implications, and we need to be able to answer them correctly and appropriately.

We respond with the same verbiage that we do with safety concerns: "We lease to everyone who meets our resident selection or qualification guidelines, and we are compliant with the Fair Housing laws." Below are some of the questions you may hear from prospects that require you to use the statement previously mentioned.

- "Do you have children on the property?" Some people have raised their children and just don't want to live in an area of the property with lots of children. It's not that they don't like children; they just want to be in more quiet location, without all the noise - OR - the prospect has children and wants to know if there will be other children to play with on the property.

- "Do you have students living on the property?" Students generally have a "certain perceived behavior" based again on noise, loud music, and lots of "coming and going," etc. This may be why they are concerned about the student population. Assure the caller that you do monitor noise levels from all the residents and guests and take actions accordingly to maintain a good property environment.
- "What kind of people lives at this property? This question can have some "negative undertones." The words "kind of people" typically refers to racial mixes, criminals, and "general bad people." To help with this response, remind them that everyone who applies goes through a criminal background check as part of their qualification process. You also do a credit check which eliminates individuals who are not credit-worthy to live at the property; therefore, qualification guidelines must be strictly adhered to.
- "Who will be my neighbors?" Living in proximity to many people is not for everyone. Some people have come from individual homes and are most concerned about who will be sharing the building with them. Our best suggestions are to tell your caller, "Since everyone goes through the same qualification process once you move in, introduce yourself to your neighbors. You will see that our residents are as concerned about you as you are about them. They want good neighbors too." Again, please ask your company or

corporate attorney how they would prefer that you answer these questions.

Dealing With Difficult Questions: "Is this a safe place to live?"

We are inundated daily through social media, television, newspapers, and radio with stories about the horrors that people do to one another. Unfortunately, crime is on the rise everywhere, and, as we say, "crime has no address."

When asked specifically about the safety of a particular community, we are trained to answer, "We lease to everyone that meets our resident selection or qualification guidelines and are compliant with the Fair Housing laws." However, that response doesn't seem to satisfy everyone. So we encourage the prospect to either call the local police using a "311" type phone number or general information line, or go onto the internet to obtain statistics of the zip code area. CAUTION: Make sure you have seen these statistics and are able to interpret them accordingly. Some police may use the property's address when stopping cars on the main street in front of the property to log activity, so that shows up on the report too.

Even if you are leasing at a gated community, we never want to give them the impression that we are responsible for residents' safety. Use of the word 'safe' or 'secure' can imply that you are guaranteeing all of your residents' safety. This is impossible to do, so never tell your residents or prospects that you have a 'safe' or 'secure' community.

If you tell the caller your community is safe and that the caller becomes a resident who experiences a crime while living there, they could blame you for this unfortunate incident and expect responsibly and restitution on the part of you and the owner. It is important that all people, no matter if they are on the property or off, should take safety into their own hands and always be aware that crime can happen anywhere.

"Uh, oh! We had a break in! Do I need to tell them?"

When discussing issues such as crime specifics, we cannot lie to the prospect. "Knowingly and willingly or failure to disclose" are legal terms that most attorneys use when looking for negligence of reporting criminal activity in your area or on your property. With that being said, when a caller asks specifically about this activity we must tell them, even if it means losing the sale.

We can also let the caller know about the systems we do have in place to help deter crime in the area (if you have such a system), such as:

- Resident Notification Binder or File: The property keeps a record of those alleged events and notifies the residents via a system of letters on the residents' doors, text or email blasts, or postings by common areas such as mailbox or laundry areas.
- Neighborhood Watch meetings held in your clubhouse on a regular basis are always a great way to keep all the residents informed.
- CAUTION: Many of our personnel live at the property where they work. Using phrases such as, "Well, I live here, and I haven't had any problems," or "No, this is a very quiet property with no problems that I know of," can actually open the door to a possible discrimination issue if, in fact, the prospect moves into the community, and they experience a "false sense of security" and then their apartment gets broken into.

Finally, remember that by answering the caller's concerns but not overdoing the explanation, you can still keep the interest level positive and continue with your call. Once they come to visit the property, you can reassure them by showing the positive aspects of your community.

Closing the Caller

While leasing in person, your job is ABC, Always Be Closing. On the phone, you want to never hang up without AFA – **Asking For Action.** Yes, even on a call you want to perform the closing action. This typically occurs at the end of the call and should almost always include asking for an appointment – however, sometimes it is asking for the lease. Every Leasing Consultant should consider generating their own traffic as part of their job. This is your chance. Set an appointment and your next piece of traffic will be walking through the door. Here are some action questions to employ:

- May we set an appointment for you to come out and tour in the next day or two?
- Are you available to come by and look at the apartment home we just discussed?
- Are you ready to make a decision - can I hold apartment #123 for you?

You can often move right into using assumptive language and move to appointment setting by saying:

- "I would love to show you your new home – are you available to come over now?" (You have them on the phone, why not have them come out right away?)
- "We are open until 6:00 pm; I would like to show you the apartment I have available for you. Can you come at 2:30 pm or 4:45 pm?"

Notice how we set a specific time and choices of those times? This is an important technique. Setting a specific time says to the customer that you are busy, there is demand for your apartment community, and you are a professional. In addition, consider setting an appointment at a time other than at the top of the hour. If you set an appointment for 10:00 am; they may stroll in at 10:30 am.

Using specific time feels like a more formal action, and they are more likely to keep an appointment.

Look at your schedule to see when you would have the most time to show them. Remember, it is better to have an appointment during your "less busy" times than to have them show up during those extremely insane times between 3:00 pm and close of day!

Never just give out the office hours – they could walk in when you're not there! Don't set appointments if you will not be available at that time, unless there are no other times for the prospect to visit the community. We are also busy, and we want people to come in when we have the best time to show them and an opportunity to close them!

If you get push back on your action question, you can use urgency to help influence the prospect into agreeing to an appointment. Now, DO NOT lie about availability - ever. Honesty is the best way to stay out of trouble with fair housing and also helps you remain genuine. Adding a personal testimony or even a third party validation coupled with the urgency will also help drive interest. If you've got multiple vacancies of the same floor plan, find another aspect of a particular unit to stress the urgency and add a personal touch – yours or someone else's - to validate the greatness of the apartment. For instance, you could do this by saying, "I'd love for you to find time to stop by and tour #1202. It is the only two bedroom left in that building, and it has my favorite view of the woods behind the community… it is so peaceful." Alternatively, maybe this is more your style, "I really want you to see this apartment before someone else does and snags it. Our manager, Ann, had someone trying to change their work schedule to come and look at it tomorrow afternoon. Any chance you can come earlier?" Remember, urgency closes are ineffective and dishonest if they are not true. Never 'make up' urgency to entice a prospect to lease.

Always discuss a specific apartment. This act will further build the trust bond between the caller, your community, and you. Some

Leasing Consultants may be worried that the apartment may lease before the customer gets out to the property to look and lease. However, this excuse is very short-sighted. Think about it - if the caller arrives for their appointment and the apartment is on hold or leased, they will see that apartments are leasing fast, and if you have another apartment that meets their needs, they should take it off the market. Again, do not lie about your availability. Always be professional.

Jackie remembers having a saying at her properties and even had it framed on the wall in the leasing offices: "The apartment you looked at today, and want to think about until tomorrow, maybe the same apartment someone else looked at yesterday and wants to lease today!" Urgency was not just based on having only "one apartment left," but on the fact that it would be the only apartment that would meet the caller's specific needs.

Once you set an appointment, do not just thank them and hang up the phone. You need to do a bit of housekeeping. First, be sure to ask how they prefer to be contacted. Some options include:

- Email: Send eBrochures, qualification standards for Tax Credit properties, direction links, etc.
- Cell phone/Text
- Mailing Address: Sometimes people still like to have "paper" brochures in different market areas of the country. Know your resident and prospect profile and their preferences in communication.

Make sure they have your community address and know how to get there. If your leasing office isn't really easy to find, tell them how to find you when they get onsite, also. Today, many people use their GPS applications and devices to locate their destination. We strongly suggest you test various apps and devices to make sure your address routes the customer to the proper location. If they need directions, have a Word document ready to email to the

prospect, or have the "link" to text to their telephone for the page on your website with the directions on it.
Share some final details:

- "Make sure to bring (whoever will be living there with the prospect - roommates, spouses, etc.)," or even family members or friends that are "helping in the decision" with them.
- "Don't forget to bring a valid photo ID for everyone wanting to look at your new home and, of course, your checkbook!" If your property doesn't accept personal checks for that initial deposit, remind the caller of a local store location where they can get a money order instead. NOTE: This isn't pushing; it is a positive way to make sure there are no roadblocks to showing AND closing this prospect when they come to your community.

Finally, confirm the time again and remind them to call if they have any problems. Now you can thank them and prepare for their visit.

Texting

Today's renters use smart phones to surf and text more than they use them to place phone calls. So even though we covered proper phone techniques, we'd be remiss if we didn't touch on texting.

Texting residents are fairly commonplace today, but with prospective residents you need be more cautious. Follow these rules when it comes to texting prospective residents:

- Never text without explicit permission from the prospective resident.
- Just because you have permission doesn't mean you can text until they respond – text and wait for a response before texting again.

- Keep it professional - never have personal conversations with a prospective resident via text or otherwise.
- Text pictures and short video clips to show off features and the community.
- Never text from your personal phone unless this allowed by your management company or owner.

Follow up for Phone

If more than 24 hours exist between the call and visit, there is an opportunity to perform follow-up and further confirmation with the prospect and prepare for their visit. This will tell the customer that you are excited for their visit, and they are a priority for you. Prepare yourself by walking that unit you described to the prospect, and let other office staff know about your appointment time. Prepare all information for their visit (floor plans, even a "small gift.")

Send your eBrochure and a personal note which is written based on the customer's needs. Making a "Reminder Contact" the day before the appointment confirms the prospect's time and enables you to ONCE AGAIN get them excited about the visit. Be prepared to CLOSE them!

It's All in the Details

All the while we've been discussing phone technique, and how you can build rapport and convert your call to an appointment, we have not mentioned documentation. Just as you document, follow up, and collect data with your in-person leasing efforts, you must do the same with your calls. Immediately record the traffic information – don't wait! Depending on your company's methods, document the call details on paper or in your computer and start your lead follow-up schedule. Whether on-line or with a paper guest card, the purpose of documenting your call is to record your prospect's information to refer to during their onsite visit. Just remember those fair housing laws and do not put down anything that indicates someone is a member of a protected class.

Since we're talking details, it is vital to know your own statistics and details. If you don't keep an eye on your conversion rate (the percentage of calls that set appointments with you), you really need to start now. *Compare* your stats within your office and company if possible – it will help you understand how you're doing and hopefully encourage you to always be improving your phone technique.

More Things to Consider

To find out just how effective leasing teams are, most companies hire an outside company to "shop" their communities to see if their employees are professional and convincing. The goal of the shop is to gain a "snapshot" of time that can then be used as a training tool for improving the leasing consultant's skill levels. Most companies shop their onsite personnel several times a year, gaining a pattern of training needs from which to improve performance.

The shop begins on the telephone and ends onsite. As we have stated, the first human contact the prospect has is that all important call to the community. How you, the leasing consultant, describe your community and its benefits and motivate the caller to visit is the key. Jackie uses a unique story to demonstrate: "It's kind of like a strip tease. You don't want to reveal too much all at once on the telephone; you want to give the caller just enough excitement by painting those detailed mental pictures. Leave the caller anxious enough that it entices them to visit the property, quickly, and see the whole thing for themselves!"

The shoppers use a general form that includes all aspects of the shop beginning with the telephone conversation. The shopper listens to the inflection in the leasing consultant's voice as they answer the phone and determines the excitement level. Most of the question-based concept is listed on the included sample Telephone Conversation Script.

Throughout the call, other "point valued" moments the shopper evaluates include:

"Did the Leasing Consultant…"

- Ask for the prospect's name and use it throughout the conversation?
- Ask important questions that helped to uncover the caller's wants and needs?
- Ask the caller why they were moving?
- Explain about the apartment home in detail, talk about the benefits of living at the property, and tell the caller about the management company?
- Ask about the marketing source from which the caller got your information?
- Ask for a contact number: cell phone, email address? Pre-close the sale by making an appointment to visit the property?

The shopper will assess if based on the enthusiasm, knowledge, and connection the leasing consultant made with them; (if actually looking for an apartment) are they prompted to visit the property? The shopper provides all this information to your management company for future training purposes.

Unlike shoppers who are sent to monitor and gauge the leasing consultant's sales abilities, a tester from HUD (The Department of Housing and Urban Development) is NOT there to judge your sales ability, but to "test" you for housing discrimination practices. HUD testers can be sent from an anonymous source, a current or former resident, a disgruntled prospect who was denied their application (not qualified by your criteria), or the HUD office may just be monitoring the general area.

Here is how the process typically works:

- It begins with two different groups or individuals of different ethnic backgrounds that are selected to do the test.
- As the telephone call is generally the first part of the process, both groups or individuals call the property, at different times generally the same day, asking for the same basic type of apartment, having the same basic qualifications of a number of people, move in date, price range, needs, wants, etc.
- The whole point of this is to determine if you treat "one group or individual" different from the other group or individual.
- Both groups will visit the property, again within hours of each other to make sure they get the same staff members.
- Finally, the entire report is written up to compare the two calls and visits to determine if there were any possible discrimination issues that occurred.
    - On the Telephone: Not taking enough time to go through the process with one of them, or not being as enthusiastic, or not giving the caller motive to visit.
    - In Person: Differences in the greeting, the tour, overcoming objections, closing the sale, etc.

In Closing...

The first apartment community Kate worked at employed eight Leasing Consultants. They were all very competitive because they had great incentives to lease apartments. The Manager, Glenn, was also very competitive (he went on to become the president of a huge company!) He frequently created leasing contests to keep the leasing office fun and all eight of them engaged in raising their game. One month, as they had their usual leasing meeting, Glenn was giving Kate special recognition for the leases she had closed in the past few weeks. For that month, and the two before that, she was the top Leasing Consultant in the office. The other team members were growing tired of the positive attention she was receiving, and she could feel the animosity increasing. It started to seep out in their words and actions. In this meeting, one of her co-workers seemed to have heard enough. The co-worker spoke up and accused Kate of stealing all the traffic that walked in. Glenn asked Kate if this was true, and she said no and backed up her response by quoting her phone-to-visit conversion ratio, which proved the majority of her traffic originated from a phone call. In other words, she was creating her traffic from her calls. She did not have time to take the walk-in traffic because she was usually busy with her phone appointments.

Don't forget about the phone as a vital leasing tool in your office! Answer your ringing phone with a smile on your face, a great attitude, and the knowledge you need to lease your apartments, and watch as you create your own traffic and increase your leasing power.

Chapter Review

Phone calls seem to be rare these days, so when someone takes action to pick up the phone; you know it is important to them. In the world of leasing apartments, this is a very good thing. You now have an advantage over all your competitors to earn this lease – you have a person on the phone who wants to talk to you!

Preparation is crucial, so do your homework first. Research your community and others, have accurate and thorough information in front of you, and be ready to focus on your caller when the phone rings.

Ask the caller's name. When you do, you are reaffirming that the caller and their needs are where your focus should be – on them. Always remember that the caller can tell when you are not listening, making them feel less important. The resident or future resident should feel like you are interested in what they have to say and their business is important to you. Pull away from distractions and make this important caller the center of your attention.

On the phone you have only a few talents to use to make that great impact - your tone, your word choice, and your attitude. Have a great attitude and expect every call to be a prospect or resident - be nice before you know who is calling.

The customer can sense when you are using a script and that will seem very impersonal. You want to have a conversation that will get you to the lease faster than any script - if you do it right! Lose the script and do not interrogate the caller. We must remember it's not about just filling in a guest card in the order the card is written; we need to ask the questions in a "flow of information" that is comfortable for the prospect to give. Work on your ability to develop a conversation with callers and guests and you will see your closing ratio improve because you are able to know your customer a little better through a productive conversation.

Utilize open-ended questions ("qualifying questions") to allow the prospective resident to really tell you about their needs. Open-ended questions also get the conversation started and will extend the amount of time and interest the caller will give you. It will also allow you to build a natural rapport with the caller, helping you sell without doing a hard sell. It is important to build trust with the caller, and the easiest way to get there is for them to feel like they are talking to a friend on the phone, not a salesperson. You must see your job as helping someone find a home and use that desire to help them drive your presentation on the phone. The customer appreciates sales people who are focused on serving their needs versus trying to sell them something they do not yet know they want.

Use closed-ended questions with pushy callers or those in a rush to get the most pertinent information. A closed-ended question generates an absolute answer and does not require the prospect to elaborate. If the caller is obviously in a serious rush, help them get what they need. To build rapport and trust with this type of caller, immediately acknowledge that their time is valuable. Do this by asking for their contact information and recommend you talk when they have more time.

We recommend that you never give out the price right up front in the conversation as it doesn't add any "value" to the dollar amount. You must show the value through discussing the benefits of living in your community.

It is critical that you understand the law and ensure each and every phone call abides by the law. Be familiar with answering questions correctly about Section 8 Communities, Tax Credit Communities, and difficult questions about your community. Be familiar with the Fair Housing Act and ensure every transaction you have with a caller or visitor is in compliance.

When you are conducting the verbal tour, you want to link items at your property and features in your apartments to the caller's needs and wants. Use this information to focus your verbal tour on their hot buttons. Describe your community and the apartments in detail with adjectives that bring life to the words and allow the prospect to visualize what you are describing. You never want to rattle off a list of amenities. Take time to describe each amenity and use the information you have learned about this specific customer in that description. At this point, you are making a strong connection between their needs and your apartment community. Conduct your phone tour as you would in person – paint a picture of your community and apartments for them and entice them to come out and see it in person. The customer appreciates sales people who are focused on serving their needs versus trying to sell them something they do not yet know they want. Use the information you gathered during your conversation, and serve your future resident with solutions to their own needs.

While leasing in person, your job is ABC, Always Be Closing. On the phone, you want to never hang up without AFA – Asking For Action. Even on a call you want to perform the closing action. This typically occurs at the end of the call and should almost always include asking for an appointment – however, sometimes it is asking for the lease. Every Leasing Consultant should consider generating their own traffic as part of their job. This is your chance. Set an appointment and your next new resident will be walking through the door.

Setting a specific time says to the customer that you are busy, there is a demand for your apartment community, and you are a professional. Adding a personal testimony or even a third party validation coupled with the urgency will also help drive interest.

Follow up with your calls and pay attention to details. Be sure to document your calls, and watch your conversion rate. Compare your stats within your office and company if possible – it will help you understand how you're doing and hopefully encourage you to always be improving your phone technique.

SAMPLE Unit Marketability Check List
by Jackie Ramstedt

Knowledge is power. Design your own form to help your leasing team understand the unique selling features of every available apartment home. By walking each unit and creating this checklist, the leasing consultant can more accurately describe the apartment over the telephone and emphasize during the leasing demonstration. The form is easy to create as a Word.doc and change as new units become available to lease. It's especially helpful during lease up seasons.

Date Walked: The actual day the leasing consultant walked the unit.

Unit Number including Building Number: Both are important, especially in garden style apartment communities with different buildings or addresses.

Size of the Unit: Two bed, one bath…two bedrooms, two baths…two bedroom townhome?

Square Footage of the Unit: Not only the square footage of the unit itself, but what it also includes; balconies, patios, enclosed yards, etc.

Date of Vacancy or Number of Days Vacant: This is crucial to getting those units leased that are losing money! If it has been several days or months, walk this unit often to find out what is needed to get it leased!

Parking Location: Everyone wants a "good parking spot". Know the location of which space goes with which unit. Also remember to let the prospect know about special location parking for guests, boats, motorcycles, RVs, campers, etc.

Front Door Location: Does this unit have a private entrance? Corridor or hallway view? What is the proximity to stairs, trash receptacles, elevators, or interior amenities such as conversation areas?

Floor Plan Advantage: Based on the uniqueness of a floor plan, make sure to have one main concept to discuss: (example) this particular floor plan is the only one with a fireplace, built in book cases, kitchen pantry, wrap around patio or balcony.

Finally, list the features of this particular unit and create the following information to talk about.

Include a chart to assist you in pointing out the amazing features of your vacant apartment homes. Add as many features/benefits as you can!

Features	Benefits	Emotional Appeal
Fireplace	Helps with Heat	Comfy, Cozy
Built-In Desk	Space Saver	Unique

"Conversational Telephone Script for Your Prospects"

Call Date: Appointment Date:
Call Time: Appointment Time:
Leasing Consultant:

Greeting
- "Thank you for calling (property name), this is (Leasing Consultant's Name.) How may I help you today?

Opening
- "I'm so happy that you called...again, my name is (Leasing Consultant's Name), and may I ask with whom I am speaking?"
- Customer's First Name: _____
- Customer's Last Name: _____

Getting to Know Your Customer
Begin asking open-ended, qualifying questions with the following statement:

- "(Customer's Name), May I begin by asking you a few questions?"
- "What specifically are you looking for in your new home?"
    - _____
    - _____
    - _____
- "Do you have any special housing needs?"
    - _____
- "May I ask why you are moving?"
    - _____
- "How soon do you need to move in?"
    - _____
- "How many people will be occupying your new home?"
    - _____
- "Will you be bringing any pets?"
    - #of pets _____
    - Kind of pets _____

Confirming Needs and Quoting The Price

- "Based on what you have told me, (Customer's Name), I think we have the perfect apartment for you! Apartment # _____!"
- Begin describing the specific unit that best matches their needs.
- End description with… "And that particular apartment home rents for only $$$."

Describing the Community & General Market Area

- Briefly describe the community, amenities, location conveniences, services provided, etc.

Setting the Appointment

- I would love for you to see this beautiful apartment and our community. What is a good time for you to visit, perhaps today?
- Try and get the prospect out immediately while they are excited.
- Set a time when YOU are available. Remember YOU are the one that has convinced them to come out.
- NEVER JUST TELL THEM THE OFFICE HOURS!!!
- Give them "choices" of days and times, such as: "I have an opening in my schedule for this Saturday. Would you like to come in when we first open at 9:00 AM or is this afternoon better for your schedule?"
- Record the appointment time on the guest card!

Contact Information

- "In case something changes with the schedule, what is the best way to contact you?"
    - Email address: _____
    - Home phone: _____
    - Office phone: _____
    - Cell phone: _____

Confirmation & Directions

- "(Customer's Name), I have really enjoyed talking with you today and I look forward to seeing you (Appointment Day & Time.) Do you know where we are located? May I help with directions?"

Final Close

- "Please feel free to call if you have any further questions and don't forget to bring a valid photo ID and your checkbook! I know you're going to love our community! Thank you for calling and I will see you (Appointment Day & Time.)"

Administrative Duties & Reminder Contact

- Finish out the guest card completely!
- Prepare yourself by walking the unit you described to the prospect.
- Immediately put traffic information into the computer - don't wait!
- Let other office staff know about your appointment time.
- Make a "reminder contact" the day before the appointment to confirm the prospect's time and once again, get them excited about the visit and prepare them to CLOSE!

Chapter 6
The Psychology of Leasing
By Lisa Trosien

Leasing apartments is more than just being an upbeat, positive person who believes in their community. Smart leasing pros know that people buy from people they like – and there are ways to get people to like you more than they already do. We'll talk about those ways in this chapter, along with a few more ideas to help you increase your leasing success by using some amateur psychology.

Ready? Let's get started!

It's getting harder and harder to sell these days, isn't it? Prospective residents are distracted by 'bright shiny objects' like new construction apartments, rehabbed apartments and even by their cell phones as you try to take them on tour throughout your property. They are also distracted by 'things' they HAVE to HAVE – like the newest iPhone, the newest technological advances or the 'must have' accessory.

Our attention spans have been affected by the addictive nature of internet browsing. Back in the year 2000, we had an attention span of 12 seconds. And while that's not huge, by 2013 our attention had dropped to 8 seconds. That's a fifty percent decrease! And it's really bad when you realize the attention span of a goldfish is 9 seconds. (StatisticBrain.com) Yikes! So, we have our work cut out for us while leasing apartments…we have to do our best to keep the attention of our prospect.

We also need to accept the fact that in today's market, *the prospect has the power*. They can go online and read reviews on any number of websites such as ApartmentRatings.com and Yelp. They can see exactly what apartments are coming available through real time availability software. They can execute their entire leasing experience online without ever coming through your doors if they don't want to. They know your prices, too, and maybe even know if you utilize a software product that manages your pricing.

This recent article in the Minnesota Star Tribune ("Young Savvy Renters Have Taken Charge of the Market", StarTribune.com) discussed how social savvy renters are well prepared when they enter your property:

> "*Social networking is so huge, and there's so much info out here, they know right away if the two-bedroom apartment they're looking at is overpriced or if it's a good deal,*" he said. "*They can quickly see what their friends have been looking at and can share that information.*"
>
> -Brad Tongen, owner, Renters Network

Society today has been described as 'the microwave society.' The definition of a microwave society, according to UrbanDictionary.com is:

> "*The mindset of wanting (and nearly getting) everything RIGHT NOW. Technology has made gathering or sending information extremely fast and we've begun to think that everything in life should be available on demand.*"

Don't fight it. Work with it! Acknowledge the fact that the prospect today is well educated and has done their homework. Just make sure that the prospect doesn't know more about your product – or your competitors – than you do.

Setting the Stage

I'm a firm believer in the 'home court advantage' so here are some tips to create the ideal setting in your leasing office. After all, retailers set up their stores all the time to get you to spend more money, so if you want to make some small changes to your leasing office to help increase your leasing, I say go for it!

Color: If you're a suburban community with lots of drive by traffic, make sure your seasonal plantings include the color yellow. Yellow is the first color processed by the human eye, so it may help your property catch the eye of the person passing by. If your property is in the city with walk by traffic, having the color yellow in your planters can also help get a bit more attention. If you want to learn more about color visit the website colormatters.com.

Scent: Having a pleasant scent in your leasing office can also help. A mixture of lavender and chamomile can help anxious prospects to relax a bit more. The good old standby of freshly baked bread or cookies can help, too. If you're looking to develop a signature scent for your company, there are companies out there who will help you do just that. Scent Air, (scentair.com) is a company that is utilized by many management companies in our industry to help create their own unique, signature scent. If your budget doesn't allow for something like that, consider finding a scent that is created by a company like Bath and Body Works and use it throughout your entire portfolio. This can give you the flexibility to quickly change scents with the seasons if you so desire and take advantage of sales and coupons offered by retailers who carry the fragrance you've selected.

Music: Background music is important in setting the stage at your apartment building. But what to play? Try to select a radio station or music package that matches your demographic. Example: Your property caters to the 18-34 demographic. Would the Sirius XM station "Classic Vinyl" be the best choice? Probably not. Experiment with a few different genres. Ask your residents what type of music they listen to most often. When you've hit the right note with your musical choice, typically your residents or prospects will comment favorably on it.

Begin at the Beginning

A snappy, cheesy greeting on the phone isn't going to cut it. By answering "It's a great day at ABC Apartments, my name is Lisa

Leaser, I can help you!" mostly succeeds in irritating people. Stick with the tried and true "Thank you for calling ABC Apartments, this is Lisa, may I help you?" or something similar. Catchy greetings say, "I AM TRYING TO SELL YOU SOMETHING" and we all know the vast majority of people hate to be sold.

It's the same with visitors to your property. One of my last onsite jobs required me to greet every single visitor to our community (other than residents) with the same greeting: "Welcome to ABC Community! What size apartment are you looking for?" I found that particular greeting was very annoying to most people. It started me off trying immediately to sell, rather than trying to help them fulfill their needs, which are clearly the most important to them. When I stopped asking that question and instead began with a warm greeting that asked how I could help them – "Hi! Welcome to ABC Community! How can I help you today?" – my closing percentage increased. Needless to say, we dropped the pushy version and went with the better, more helpful welcome.

Asking for Anything

When you are talking with your prospective resident on the phone, you have some key things to accomplish. At a minimum, you need to find out:

- What size apartment home the prospect needs
- How many people will occupy the apartment
- What is the prospective resident's budget for housing
- Whether or not they have a pet
- When they need the apartment home
- How the prospect heard about your community
- Why they are moving

Starting off your call with a barrage of questions to the prospective resident is absolutely wrong. After all, the prospect doesn't care about YOUR needs. They only care about THEIRS. So how do you keep them happy and get your questions answered? Easy – answer some of their questions first and then ask one or two of your own. By fulfilling some of their needs, they are more likely to fulfill some of yours.

The Imaginary Sign

Mary Kay Ash, the founder and creator of Mary Kay Cosmetics, had a great technique to help her be successful in her business. It's so easy that anyone can do it. She simply imagined a sign hanging around the neck of every person she met that said, "Make Me Feel Important." So start all of your dealings with everyone imagining this sign, and you'll be extremely successful.

Are You New to Leasing?

If you're a new Leasing Professional, use that to your advantage! We all love to help new people succeed. Think about the last time you were somewhere and the person assisting you was new to the job. You probably had far more patience with them than you would with a seasoned associate. You may have actually talked a bit louder or even a bit more slowly to make sure they had time to process your request accurately. And you probably didn't mind that the transaction took a bit longer. When you admit to your customer that you are new, they will try their best to help you succeed. Being new isn't a disadvantage; it can actually help you secure more leases early in your career! Don't be afraid to tell your prospect that you're new to the job and may have to ask for help to give them a correct answer to their questions. Showing vulnerability helps lay the groundwork for a closer personal connection.

LT Tip *Village Green Management, a highly respected property management company with 40,000 apartment homes across the United States, has their new associates wear a pin that says, "Please Be Patient. I'm a little green. Village Green Companies Trainee." What a brilliant way to let prospects and residents alike know their associate is new to the job!*

Finding the Perfect Apartment

I'm a graduate of the Dale Carnegie Sales Course. I took it when I was a Leasing Professional to help sharpen my skills in sales overall. I love to sell, and this course seemed like a perfect fit for me. One of the most important things I learned from that course was to use this question when trying to lease apartments:

"In order for me to find you the perfect apartment home, I need to ask you a few questions, okay?"

I use that question while completing the guest card for the prospect. It's a great question for a lot of reasons:

- You ask for permission to question the prospect about their needs and wants in an apartment. Not one single prospect has ever said 'no' to me when I asked this question. It lays the groundwork for a great qualifying interview.
- It gives the benefit to the prospect up front. They know that they'll get 'the perfect apartment home' if they let you ask questions. Why would they ever turn you down?
- They focus hard on answering the questions accurately because they know it will benefit them in the end.

It is essential that you make the prospects needs and wants the focus of your time with them.

Are You an Ambivert?

You probably don't know if you're an ambivert because it's quite possibly the first time you've even heard that word. Ambiverts are people who have more or less equal parts extrovert and introvert as their personality type. Why is that important? It's important because ambiverts are the most successful salespeople.

It makes sense. Extroverts can sometimes overwhelm their prospects with their larger than life personality. Their enthusiasm for their product may keep them from being good listeners. Introverts can be too quiet or too reticent to actually engage the prospective resident and ask the proper questions to find the appropriate solution for the customer. The ambivert personality takes the best of both personality types and makes the sale.

How can you use this information to help you lease more apartments? If you're an extrovert, maybe you need to 'dial it down' a bit with your customers. If you're more of an introvert, you probably need to 'crank it up' in your presentations. Whichever personality style you have, remember to always keep the prospects' needs first and foremost in your presentation.

Making Yourself Likable

It's important to make yourself likeable in a sales situation. Warren Buffet, the enormously successful entrepreneur, has even talked about the importance of likability. "I've walked away from some great deals because I didn't like the people I was dealing with" is a quote attributed to Buffet. If you think about it, it makes perfect sense. Why would you want to buy from someone you don't like? Prospects who like you are much more likely to lease from you.

LT Tip *Remember; people can go anywhere and rent an apartment. But they can't go anywhere to rent an apartment and get you. The personal selling dynamic is crucial in our industry.*

Being likable should not be confused with simply being nice. We've all known people who are nice that we didn't particularly like. It takes more than just kindness to be a likable person. People who are really likable have mastered what is called "The Art of Social Jiu-Jitsu." Here are the skills you need to be a Social Jiu-Jitsu Master.

Skill #1: Focus

Social Jiu-Jitsu masters know that they have to 'be present' to succeed. By being present, I mean being in the moment. You can't be thinking about picking the kids up from soccer, or that really cute guy (or girl) you met the night before, or the grocery list you need to write. Masters of Social Jiu-Jitsu focus on the moment and the person (or people) in front of them. That's a big part of being likable.

Skill #2: Ask the Right Questions

If you start off by asking a prospect where they are from, you've done a great job of breaking the ice while beginning your completion of the guest card. This can segue nicely into, "So what brings you here to (insert your city name)?" This can help you avoid that tricky and prying question, "Why are you moving?" that so many prospects don't want to answer and so many Leasing Professionals don't like to ask. You'll get an answer to the question *without* having to ask it in such an uncomfortable manner.

Remember, completing the guest card should be a comfortable and conversational process. You don't need to always go in the exact order of the form. Make it a pleasant experience. And ask questions that may not even appear on the card, such as, "Do you rent now?" If they don't, you've potentially uncovered an obstacle to getting them to lease. They may have a house to sell before they can move in.

Another great question is, "What other apartment communities have you seen?" This helps you learn about where they are in their search. Are they just starting out? Have they already seen five high rises, two garden communities and a mid-rise? If they have viewed some buildings already, ask them what they have seen that they liked or didn't like.

Skill #3: Be Polite and Respectful

Successful salespeople always say "Thank you" and "You're welcome" along with other phrases that let the customer know their needs are number one. If you treat the prospect as you would treat an honored guest in your home, you should be fine. Offer refreshments, make sure your prospective residents are comfortable and always provide a clean, welcoming environment. Remember, there's simply no excuse for dirty, broken or unpainted surfaces in your property.

When they tell you what they do for a living, inquire about their job. Ask them how long they have been working at that particular job or for that company. Let them talk about their favorite subject: themselves!

Skill #4: Make Them Feel Smart

No one likes to feel dumb, ever. Especially when they are making a large ticket purchase, such as leasing an apartment. If your apartments rent for $750 a month, on a one year's lease, you are actually 'selling' a $9,000 item to someone ($750 x 12 = $9,000). That's an expensive purchase! No one wants to think they made a mistake spending $9,000 – so make sure your prospect feels like they are making a great, SMART decision.

Have the answers to their questions ready by being an expert on your property, your company and your neighborhood. If you don't know the answer, the correct answer is, "I don't know the answer to that question, but I'll get it answered before you leave today." And then make sure you DO get that question answered for them in the time frame you indicated.

Skill #5: Be Confident in Yourself and Your Product

People buy from confident salespeople. After all, if you're not confident in your product, why should your prospect be confident enough to buy it from you? Make a list of all the great reasons why people would want to live at your property. Start small – list only 15 reasons. Then after that, list fifteen more, then fifteen more, and so on, until you've reached the magic number of 105.

Start with your amenities – that's easy. Then move onto what's great about the location of your community, your great staff, the apartments themselves. Keep your lists growing a little more every day. This will help you believe in your community even more than you already do, increasing your confidence.

If you're ready for an even more interesting technique to increasing your confidence, study the work of Amy Cuddy, an associate professor at Harvard University. Cuddy discovered that 'the mind shapes the body' when it comes to helping create confidence. Cuddy's TED talk on confidence, available on the TED YouTube channel, has had almost 4 million views. Simply go to ted.com and search Amy Cuddy. It's a great talk and a wonderful use of your time!

Parrot-Phrasing (not paraphrasing)

People who have attended my seminars or have utilized my private training and consulting services know that I am a research geek. One of my favorite authors to study is Dr. Robert Cialdini. His website, InfluenceatWork.com, has a wealth of knowledge to assist you in sales, marketing and management of your communities.

Dr. Cialdini has found that 'parrot-phrasing' - where you repeat the customer's exact words back to them - creates feelings of liking and helps to strengthen relationships. Wait staff that do this with their customers' orders in restaurants see tips 70% higher than their coworkers who don't repeat the order to the customer.

What does this mean for you? Simply parrot-phrase what your prospect wants while either on the phone or in person. Use their exact words back to them and ask them to confirm that you understand what their needs are in their new apartment home.

The Prospect Has the Power

In our "microwave society" where everyone wants everything now, there is a side effect that we need to recognize to be successful in sales: the prospect has the power.

Let's take off our property management hat for a minute and pretend we are a prospect in today's rental market. We'll probably Google what we are looking for and then focus our search on the top results of the first page. (Most people do not bother to go any further than the first or second page of search engine results. A study on SearchEngineWatch.com shows that the number one organic position on Google search engine results gets 33% of the website traffic. Position number two drops to approximately 18% and the corresponding results degrade from that point onward.)

We'll probably look at the apartment that we want through an ILS such as Rent.com or ApartmentGuide.com or we may go to the management company website itself, and narrow down our search to a specific property or two that catches our eye. We may take advantage of viewing a 3D fly-through or a video of a model apartment. We'll definitely look at the floor plans. We'll most certainly take that virtual tour of the amenities and read all about the property itself. We may even click on the 'check availability' button if it's available, so we'll know exactly what apartments are offered in our time frame. We can event rent it online if we want, by submitting an application and allowing the management company to check our credit. But wait a minute…we need to check one more thing before we make any decisions on that apartment.

So what do you think that one thing is?

Just like all of our rental prospects, we want to know what other people think of this community.

So, we're off to a ratings website, such as ApartmentRatings.com, Yelp or maybe some other site where we can see reviews from (what we hope are) real renters who have lived at the community in which we have an interest. We're definitely not alone in our desire to view ratings and reviews, as it's been reported that as many as 60% of consumers head to ratings sites before making a buying decision (ConversationXL.com). And after they read those reviews? A 2014 survey from the firm Dimensional Research shows that approximately 90% of consumers are influenced by online ratings.

Now, let's review what you may have just learned about an apartment community without ever setting foot in the door or speaking to a Leasing Professional:

- We know the rent for the apartment style we want
- We viewed the floor plan
- We watched a video (or took a 3D fly-through or a virtual tour)
- We toured the amenities
- We know the qualifying criteria
- We know exactly what apartment we can get in our time frame
- We can apply online and reserve the exact apartment we want
- We know what current and former residents are saying about the living experience at the apartment community

Clearly, the prospective resident of today has a wealth of knowledge about your property available to them before they ever talk to you. Respect that. Ask them if they've seen your website and what they saw that they liked. You'll save them (and yourself) some time if you can find out just how much they already know.

LT Tip When you feel like you have all the power and the information, you tend to focus too much on your own point of view. The point of view of the prospective resident is what matters here – not yours.

Your Mom Was Right….

Did your Mom ever tell you to sit up straight? Well, Mom was right. How you carry yourself makes a difference. A recent Ohio State University study found that people who sat at their desks with poor posture were less likely to think positive things about themselves. Sitting and standing up straight not only makes you think more positively about yourself, it makes others think more positively about you as well.
The same can be said of your walk. If you walk leisurely to the door when greeting a prospect, you communicate that the prospect is not important to you. If you tend to walk at an average speed, try increasing your speed by about 10-15% when you are walking out to greet a prospect or resident. They will notice and take it as a sign of respect. Now, remember not to walk too fast when you are walking *with* prospects. It's always best to match their speed when accompanying them on your property tour.

LT Tip Whether you're leasing an elevator building or a three story walk up, make sure you take the time to let your prospects know where you are headed on your property tour. A few seconds before you are turning, tell the prospect, "We'll be turning left here." If you're exiting an elevator, make sure you tell the prospect which way to go. People like to feel smart, and it's your job to help them feel smart during the tour by letting them know which direction they need to go.

The Smart Phone

Do you have a cellphone? My guess is that you probably do. According to PewInternet.org, 90% of American adults have one. Over half of those phones are smartphones. And I am guessing that it seems as 100% of your rental prospects seem to have smartphones and they keep them out the entire time you are trying to tour them through your property, right?

A year ago, one of my consulting clients came to me and asked how to work with the prospect that ALWAYS had their phone out. Their leasing teams were understandably frustrated. Prospects were constantly on their phones, either Facebooking, Instagramming, Tweeting, texting or talking. The Leasing Professionals needed a solution. And so what did I suggest? I told them to simply ask the prospect to put their phones away while they were touring so they would be sure to see everything the apartment had to offer.

The results of my brilliant advice?

Complete and utter failure.

Why? The prospects WANTED to use their phones, and no one was going to keep them from using them. So, what did we decide to do? Like the old saying goes, "If you can't beat them, join them." At the start of the tour WE ASKED THEM TO HAVE THEIR CELLPHONES HANDY. Why? To take pictures of our community! To share their pictures on social media with their friends. We told them to text, Tweet, Instagram, Snapchat, Facebook or whatever they wanted to do with their photos. In other words, we let them have the power, and we guided them on how to use it. The result of that brilliant advice? Success!

A Word or Two about Models

One of the biggest mistakes companies make with model apartments is putting them in the very best possible location. With the exception of a lease-up property, models should be placed in the least desirable location on your property. Why? Simple.

The model is a sales tool to sell the floor plan of the apartment. It gives decorating ideas to the prospective resident. It helps them visualize living in the apartment home.

Placing the model in one of the most desirable locations creates a couple of problems:

- The prospect wants THAT exact location, which s/he cannot have. It makes the location they end up with for their apartment seems inferior.
- It takes a highly desirable apartment off the market, one that could probably get top dollar in rent. Never a smart idea, except during a lease-up.

Placing the model in a lesser location typically takes a tough to move apartment (that may sit vacant for a long period of time) and turns it into a useful sales tool. There's an entire chapter in this book devoted to model apartments. Familiarize yourself with it, and you'll find your models are excellent sales tools for yourself and your team.

Don't forget scent and music in your model!

The Contrast Principle

The contrast principle is simple in sales. Just remember to show the smaller space first. Small will feel big; big will feel big. Here's an example:

Your prospect wants a two bedroom apartment. Your two bedrooms have a distinct size difference between the bedrooms. The master bedroom is quite large while the second bedroom is much smaller. Make sure your prospect *tours the smaller bedroom first*. If they tour the larger bedroom first, the smaller, 2nd bedroom will feel even smaller than it actually is.

If your prospect is torn between two different styles of apartment homes, always show the apartment that is smaller first, and then move onto the larger apartment.

Small Commands

Using small commands with your prospects throughout the demonstration of your apartments can also help you to lease more. Ask your prospects to do things like open cabinets, look in the refrigerator, test the water pressure and more. The more they touch the apartment home, the more likely they are to lease it.

Typically, I like to remove the entry doors to rooms in model apartments. It helps the tour flow more smoothly and makes the apartment seem larger. Just make sure you are not removing the doors to walk in closets. Keep those on and always close them after the tour. Why? By keeping them closed, you can ask the prospective resident to open them and walk into the closet to experience the size and layout. Remember, the more they touch the apartment, the more likely they are to lease from you.

LT Tip *Remember to NEVER enter a walk in closet or other small room ahead of your prospect. You should always keep yourself between the prospect and the exit door to the apartment.*

Memory Points

With the average apartment prospect viewing five apartment homes when they are searching for a new place to live, your tour needs to stand out from not only a customer service perspective but from a "Memory Point" perspective. This is a part of leasing that can be really fun for both yourself and the prospect.

To create a memory point in your model, add something different or unexpected to the model. You can tailor it to the demographic you are trying to reach or simply use an item or items that are unusual and memorable. Here is a quick story of how I used memory point marketing to lease a large amount of two bedroom apartments:

The president of a company came to me with a dilemma. They had a property with a large vacancy issue that existed in their two bedroom apartments. Their typical two bedroom renter was a family with children. They needed to move some two bedrooms fast and wanted me to go in and take a look at the model to see if that was an issue.

A tour of the property showed that the model was indeed positioned incorrectly. The smaller of the two bedrooms, typically the bedroom for the children, was decorated as a den. I quickly switched out the furniture to a bunk bed and made the room more child-friendly. I then accessorized the rest of the apartment with Bob the Builder items. The kids' bedroom became a haven for Bob the Builder with bedspreads, curtains, rugs, posters and toys. I even found a Bob the Builder life sized cutout to place in the bathtub. Bob the Builder toys were scattered in the corner of the living room as though children really lived there. I followed the theme with plastic dishes at the dining table and more. We printed royalty free Bob the Builder coloring sheets off the internet for the kids to color. The only thing we didn't do was change all the names of the leasing staff to "Bob" (just kidding).

Within three weeks, we leased every single apartment home.

Now, you don't have to over accessorize like we did to achieve Memory Point Marketing successfully. You can do it with a simple, unusual piece of furniture, a unique lamp or even stocking your model refrigerator like Planned Property Management does in Chicago. Their "Wow Fridge" is a staple of their successful brand and the brainchild of some pretty smart people there. They stock it with snacks, sodas and more and allow visitors to take something from it on their tour. A stocked fridge is a great memory point that matches every demographic.

Reaching Agreement

It's pointless to demonstrate apartments without asking your prospect if they would like to lease the apartment you've mutually selected. Closing the sale is a natural part of the demonstration and should come easily to you. After all, your prospect wouldn't take the time to come and look at your apartments without any interest in potentially leasing one, would they? We've dedicated an entire chapter in this book to closing the sale, but I just want to give you some pointers from a psychological standpoint to help you out.

When you finish touring the apartment home with the prospective resident, ask them a simple question, "So, what do you think?" (or some variation thereof that asks them for an opinion on what they've seen). This seemingly simple question can hold the key to whether or not you lease that apartment home. You'll get one of two answers:

- I like it
- I don't like it.

Either answer lets you know what the prospect is thinking. If they like the apartment, ask them to lease. If they don't like it, ask them what they don't like about it. Perhaps it's an objection that you can solve. If the answer initially is "no" when you attempt to close, don't give up. Eighty percent of sales are made on the fifth attempt or after, so make sure you follow up with them at least five times after the initial visit.

Would You Like Fries with That?

We've all been asked by our friendly McDonald's drive-through person whether or not we'd like fries along with our order. There's solid reasoning behind that question. Once a customer has committed to purchasing an item at a given price, *the add on's are easier to sell.* So, if you're working with a customer who has made a commitment to take an apartment at a given price, upsell them on a garage or reserved parking space for an additional fee. Simply ask, "Would you like a reserved parking space with your apartment as well? It's only $X more." You'll find it's easier to sell it at that time than previously in your demonstration, especially if the prospect has a pre-defined monthly budget in mind.

In Conclusion

While selling to today's apartment prospect is more complicated than it used to be, utilizing the tips outlined in this chapter should help you to successfully close more leases. If you're interested in learning more about the psychology of sales, I've listed several online sources in the "Resources" section below to help you.

Resources

Websites
Influenceatwork.com
Marketingdonut.com
ApartmentExpert.com
Facebook.com/Apartmentexpert
RentandRetain.com
PsychologyToday.com
Forbes.com
Mindtools.com
Socialtriggers.com
Copyblogger.com
BusinessInsider.com

Books
Influence at Work, by Robert Cialdini
Yes! Fifty Scientifically Proven Ways to Get to Be Persuasive, by Robert Cialdini
To Sell is Human, by Daniel Pink
Why We Buy, by Paco Underhill
Influence: Science and Practice, by Robert Cialdini
Thinking Fast and Slow, by Daniel Kahneman
Drive, by Daniel Pink
Predictably Irrational, by Dan Ariely
Brainfluence, by Roger Dooley

Chapter 7
Competitive Selling: The Role "Value" Plays in the Pricing Game

By Jackie Ramstedt, CAM, CAPS, CAS

We live in a very competitive world that is constantly evolving and changing, which means that we will frequently be drawn into situations where we need to sell "against" a competitor, rather than simply selling what our property has to offer. If you want to stand out and set your community apart while staying ahead of your competition, then now is the time to take a look at how you and your teams are conducting business. There are simple approaches you can take that, when implemented, cause your employees to lease more, add more value for your resident's perspective of spending their hard-earned dollars, and ultimately, increasing your property's performance, cash flow and the bottom line. Throughout this chapter, we will discuss the many aspects of the role value plays in the residents' perspective of comparing what they pay with what they actually receive. Learn how to effectively counter objections during lease renewal discussions and, most of all, create a better, more comprehensive approach to selling value against your competition.

We all have budgets. Some of us are carefree and don't think much about watching what we spend as long as we still have "money in the account" and know we will be paid on certain dates. Others have elaborate Excel spreadsheets or apps that keep track of every penny earned, spent and what we spent it on. We can all relate to how budgets fit into our lives, but sometimes we want something so bad, we are willing to sacrifice in other areas to get it - something of value that fulfills that part of us where logic makes no sense, but it just "feels good."

When our prospect starts their journey for a new apartment home, more times than none, price is an important determining factor. Not as the final decision necessarily, but definitely a major component in closing the deal. Their past will govern their future decisions. If they currently live in a community that offers no incentive to stay as a resident, coupled with a lack of caring for them as a resident, no wonder people are willing to "pay to move," sometimes just on principle alone!

To get a better demonstration of this concept, ask yourself this question: If YOU wanted to move into an apartment community today, what would be your top three "must haves" based on your personal lifestyle? Often the answer is directly related to likes and dislikes of where you live now.

- If you are currently struggling with a lack of closet space, then possibly one of your answers might be, "larger and more closet space."
- If you love having a corner unit apartment with a wrap around patio or balcony, again, you might insist that the new apartment home have the same thing, or at least a good view with lots of windows.
- If you absolutely hated living on the first floor with all the noise of people walking up and down stairs, you might want to consider looking for an apartment either in a quieter location or on a higher floor, maybe even preferably a top floor with no one above you.

So how does this help with understanding what our current residents want? As with your residents, it certainly will be of great influence when someone is selecting an apartment that YOU would be interested in living in! If not, these are going to be your "hot buttons" for the leasing consultant to have to overcome in order to close the sale on you. The same applies to your residents.

Same, But Very Different

When communities are relatively the same in product quality, services provided; amenity selections and price, what makes one community "worth the money" over another is subjective in the eyes of the buyer. Some comparisons between your comp properties and your community are basic expectations to the customers. If you have a pool and your competition has a pool or location is a strong factor for selecting this market area that is considered more of an "expectation" for the basic needs of the resident or prospect. Those basic needs and wants are part of the criteria for meeting their particular set of preferences in an apartment home. However, if you have something your competition, in fact, doesn't have, then that is your competitive marketing advantage.

A competitive marketing advantage focuses on those unique exceptions that make the decision to lease at your community more appealing. Even if those advantages are not initially needed, the "value added" approach thinking concept is like icing on the cake. People "want" more than they "need." Some items can be bragging rights to your residents of "My property has something yours does not!"

Here are a few examples of those value added items:

- Dry cleaning or laundry pickup and delivery services: Not necessarily a "necessity" but more of a luxury service if you ever need it.
- Dog walking services: Pets are growing in popularity especially in apartment living. Having the availability of a professional dog walking service helps solve those pet lovers' dilemma of tight work schedules and caring for their beloved animals.
- Eat-Out-In: Partnering with local eateries and grocery stores for food delivery is another "hot" marketing advantage.

- Heath conscious amenities: From having local health food stores hold "lunch and learn" cooking sessions, to establishing a property Mall Crawl group who walk the local mall for exercise, becoming more healthy in hopes of living a longer, more productive lifestyle, is a national focus.
- Core family activities: Nothing is more comforting to people with children than to know your community caters to the "littlest residents" too. After school activities, learning opportunities, exercise programs, and holiday parties, are all part of the added value concept. Properties who believe in having a well balanced event calendar for ALL their residents find real value in these services and activities.
- Love your neighbor: All properties struggle to maintain a harmonious environment for all their residents. Encouraging your residents to refer their family members, friends or people they work with to move into your community actually has two very important motivational advantages:

  - The property gets traffic that comes with an endorsement from one of your own residents who feel it's such a great place to live, they are recommending it to others.
  - It gives the property an opportunity to "thank" the resident for that referral with incentive packages that range from actual discounts off their rent, preferred parking spots, free access to paid amenities, to upgrade amenities for their own apartment home.

Please Note:

By giving the resident an upgrade in their apartment, the resident enjoys the benefits of the upgrade without having to pay for the upgrade. It also positions the apartment for a higher renewal value, so when their renewal time comes rolling around, they already have that "value added."

Dollars and Sense

My mother, Miss Ruby, lived to be 95 years old. She was such a mentor to me and gave me guidance when being a business woman wasn't even popular yet. She worked for a small department store where she was in charge of an entire floor of goods. I worked for her during my high school years and learned so much about value. She taught me the difference between being frugal and cheap when making decisions about what the company would purchase to sell in the store. "The customer has to feel they are getting their money's worth, no matter what the price," she said.

Mom only spent her own money on things she considered valuable, an investment of sorts, saying it had to "make sense" to invest her hard-earned money. I've always tried to look at the world using this very premise, whether speaking about the value in people or things. Many people just don't "see" the value in an item until they really need it, as in insurance. They don't see a reason to take their time to evaluate their choices, based on complaints that "It's just too much hassle," or "It's too confusing," before actually purchasing. This is exactly why we need to do it for them!

In the multifamily industry, we have long been challenged with this same dilemma when trying to convince our residents that we really do care about them, while still increasing their rent, year after year. To them, the longer they stay the more money they have to spend.

Using Mom's principle of "getting your money's worth" with our residents, they expect to be rewarded for their loyalty and, in some cases, even expect to not pay the same amount for rent as those "new residents" who haven't shown their loyalty as the current resident has.

So how can we show our residents that the value in staying at our community instead of considering to move to another apartment community?

It's Not the Money; It's the MONEY!

Price + Value = Profit! Analyzing market trends and pricing can be somewhat confusing when it comes to creating a rent schedule that meets both of the owner's expectations and what the market will actually bear during a certain performance cycle. Many markets still suffer the pains of the "days of the deal" giveaways while others, such as my home town of Austin, Texas, seem to have weathered the storms of lowering rents.

So what is the best way to compare your prices against the competition? To begin with, you must have a very thorough market survey reporting system. Whether you are with a large management group or a small, single investor owner, make sure your rents are comparable to the other properties of your size, age, and amenity makeup, and that you are leading the market in that area.

When you call for updated information from your comps, why do you get the feeling the information is either incomplete, the person giving that information is less than forthcoming with crucial data, or worst of all, flat out lying to you?! Never assume the information is correct. Gaining relevant and meaningful information can be challenging. I suggest you get out of your office, get in your car, and drive over to that property to see for yourself!

I know what you will say, "But they know me there. How can I get the information I need if they know who I am?" Good question! So the answer is to begin building a relationship with your competition based on truth and mutual respect for each other's communities, to honestly give correct information so BOTH of your properties may be successful. This relationship building between competitive properties in a general market area makes for solid business relationships that can build on your reputation and even develop into long lasting friendships. I have managers and leasing professionals whom I knew when I was still managing my properties that I still have as friends today!

Networking is key. We looked out for the market area as a whole, helping each other when times were tight. For example, if I only had traffic looking for one bedrooms, but didn't have any currently available, but the property next door did, I referred them to that property. In kind, that manager and leasing team did the same for my community. Building that "friendly competitive" relationship helped all the properties in the market area to perform better for all our management companies.

Whatever You Can Do I Can Do Better!

Understanding how to handle the competition is an art in itself and could mean the difference between success and failure. Know how your competition stacks up against your product and how your competitor leverages the sale. You should be as knowledgeable about your competitor's property and their apartments as if it were your own. If you can outsell your product with your competitors, then you know what you must work on for your community to come out on top. You have found your own community's weakness.

Be familiar with as much of your competitor's information as you can. Collect their brochures, advertising information, and download any web site or internet promotions. Find out how they will use it and how it benefits them in their approach to selling. What are their sales advantages? Never knock the competition! This is a bad business practice and will make you and your communities look bad. Instead, address each of their advantage points with the benefits and features of your own products and services, diplomatically. It reminds the prospect or resident that you are a professional company and don't resort to negatively talking about our competition. Your reputation will speak for you and your property with long term, happy residents who are satisfied and continue to "vote with their rent dollars" year after year.

Every apartment community feels they have the "best" of everything, including their staff members, comparable size apartment, square footage, recreational and inside-the-unit amenities, resident activities, etc. However, the proof is really in the pudding, so to speak. If that was their bragging rights when their residents leased, but throughout their lease term, they had numerous situations where that was NOT the case, the community lost its value for them.

- "We are always here for you!" – Half the time when the residents came to the office, the "out of office sign" was on the door. And to make things worse, the "clock" on the sign said they would be back at 1:00 and its 3:00!
- "Our service technicians are here 7 days a week to answer any of your calls." – Many residents find that their emergencies are ignored, costing them dollars in damaged property from leaks and more.
- "We have lots of parties and events all year long for our residents!" – The only activities the property had last year was a chili cook off in the fall, and a swim party in the spring both of which have limited appeal. And worse, it was the same 10 people who attended, most of which were the property's staff.

You can see that, as my father used to say, "Your word is your bond, and others judge you by what you say about others!" He also used to tell me, "Jackie, if you don't have enough energy to mow the whole yard, at least mow the front yard! People will notice your efforts!" **And he was right.** People WILL notice your efforts when put in the most effective and noticeable place.

Knowledge is King

To be competitive, know everything about your property and your market area. When you have that confidence of knowing your property well, it is easy to recognize and overcome objections, which saves time and gains your residents' respect.

Knowing your property not only helps your resident with questions and concerns, it actually helps educate them. It is an invaluable advantage. Sometimes people like to confuse the process by asking insincere questions, but using your confidence and knowledge you can easily turn those questions around with telling them about the positive aspects of your community.

Look at areas that include current residents, prospects, competitors, and the economic environment (your neighborhood.) Your residents want to work with sales people who are professionals, experts, great advisors, and valuable resources. If you want to improve your closing ratio, make a more memorable first impression that differentiates you from your competition. A good first meeting will make you your prospect's first choice and create a long lasting relationship for years to come.

Most leasing consultants throw information at the prospect or resident and expect them to make a decision without first finding out some major facts:

- Do they qualify? Who is going to be occupying the apartment?
- What are the resident's future plans? Do they need conditional lease terms based on job relocation, buying a house, etc.?
- What are their needs vs. their wants? What would add value to their lives?

Most customers, today, are looking for the same thing – savings of time, effort, or money. Taking time to make their life easier has become a bigger priority than money. Why? Because everyone is insanely busy.

Start by selecting five strengths and advantages and then five weaknesses and disadvantages of your community. Knowing these will help you identify and develop good selling strategies. Let's make a list of these with counter suggestions for the disadvantages or weaknesses.

List your top five strengths and advantages of your apartment community. Here are some questions to help jump-start your thoughts. They are created to help you think "outside the box" for your answers. In order to be truly unique, with value added aspects, we must dig deeper for more meaningful answers.

Advantages and Strengths:

- Historically, what is our community's reputation in the area?
- What do we have that our competition doesn't?
- What do our current residents think about our staff?
- What additional amenities do we have that are not normally seen on most properties?
- What has our occupancy trend been over the past few years?

Weaknesses or Challenges:

- Why have we lost good residents in the past?
- How do we compare to other communities, price-wise, in our market area?
- Has crime increased in our area, causing the de-valuation of the general market area?
- Is there any new property construction that is causing a strain on our closing averages?
- Do we still have the "value" of interior amenities to command higher prices?

Always be asking yourself, "If I lived here, how would I feel about the quality of the apartment homes, the professionalism of the staff, and the overall feeling of 'home'?" Keeping this foremost in your mind will force you to keep evaluating these processes the prospects and residents go through, reminding ourselves that the happiness of our residents depends on our quick responses to change.

Creating Desire for Action

In order to understand how to create a desire for action, you need to have an understanding of **why** people buy, **what** motivates them, and **how** they make buying decisions. Essentially, people buy to satisfy their physical or psychological wants and/or needs. Keep the focus on the resident and solving their problem, and in the end they will go with - or stay with - the company that best understands them, sympathizes with them and provides solid ways to solve them.

The two main driving forces for why people buy are logic and emotion. Most people buy emotionally and justify their purchases logically. At the beginning of your relationship, making a good impression on your residents will win over their confidence quickly:

- Always Be Professional: Sometimes the simplest steps are the most often forgotten. Dressing professionally. Smiling. Shaking hands. Speaking with compassion. Listen!
- Don't Give Price Right Away: How many times do you greet an apartment prospect coming through the door, only to have them immediately ask about the price of the apartments.
- Understand their Total Lifestyle Needs: Matching the person to a particular apartment location that specifically fits their lifestyle needs can make a huge difference in their satisfaction level.

- Establishing Good Rapport: Let your conversations flow naturally, use the prospects answers to open the doors of opportunity for future questions.
- Don't Just Show the Apartment, SELL the Home: The prospect is a captive audience which gives you the opportunity to continue building rapport and expanding on all the wonderful features that match their interests, actually selling themselves on the idea of living there.

Being Different Is Good

Curiosity is a powerful aspect of sales where you can engage the prospects and residents to see and hear more openly. The number one mistake consultants make in leasing apartments is to not ask for the customer's business. Too many feel uncomfortable with this process, but ultimately, you have to have faith in your own ability. Do you provide great service and a wonderful living experience? Then feel confident about asking for their business!

Prepare a list of ten ways that you're different from your competitors and share this with your prospects during their initial leasing experience and your residents during renewal time to help build curiosity. The differences between your competition and your community must be **relevant** to your prospect's or resident's needs. If they don't care, it's not a valid point of difference. Each valid point:

- Must be **specific**. Use exact figures because, the more precise the number, the more convincing it becomes. If the turnaround time for your service requests average "same day service" compared to the competition's 24 -48 hour turnaround, this is a significant difference.
- Must be **credible** and believable. Don't make up things just to sound better. People aren't stupid; in fact, most people are quite savvy. They already know if what you are telling them is true.

- Must be **provable**. Back up your claim with testimonial letters from current and former residents who can substantiate your claim.
- Must be **demonstrable**. Do this with worksheets, analysis and demonstrations. Sometimes people just need to "see it on paper" to believe it.
- Must be **real differences**. Avoid the "cheaper can be better" claims unless you can bring to bear strong evidence. You're better off claiming "value and reliability" as your property's strong point.

You can add more value if you have more information about your customers, and the greater your competitive edge will be. Understand as much as you can get about their current situation and, just as importantly, about their plans for the future. Learn about their concerns, their issues and their problems, and their lifestyle goals. You cannot know too much; you can, however, say too much.

Many salespeople lose out in a competitive selling situation because they overlook minor differences between themselves and their competition. Do not prejudge the importance of any differences, for what might seem minor to you may be of significant importance to your prospect.

If you help people to see that what you are offering is more relevant to their particular situation, they will hopefully be more "open" to hearing about your information. If the people really feel that you're on their side, you're much more likely to win their business.

Never lose sight of the fundamentals when dealing with a fiercely competitive marketplace. People buy from people that they believe are similar to themselves; they buy from people that they like, and they buy "people," not necessarily the apartment or the community. You have a better opportunity to land a sale if you're in front of a prospect. You'll struggle to do this remotely as most people can't visualize well. They need to actually see it to make the decision. When you are "face-to-face," you can judge the customer's reactions to your proposal, and you have an opportunity to question them more comprehensively. You're there, and the competition isn't.

The Days of the Deals Are Done

In some situations, the only way you can beat the competition is by doing some type of deal. However, it makes sense to avoid as many price-war situations as you can. Especially in today's world, trying to sell value by lowering prices just doesn't make any sense. Either the apartment is worth the money you are charging or not. Period.

I always remind our leasing teams that it's easy to reduce prices or give large discounts or concessions when we are starting our relationship with a new move in. What happens when a year later during the renewal process when we have to raise the rent, sometimes by quite a hefty amount? Within the past few years, some markets are experiencing renewal rate increases that are trending as much as $200.00 more per month. How are we justifying this much of an increase?

Think of this in reverse. Maybe if we qualify our new prospects based on what the renewal amount will be a year from now, they would be able to incorporate the new rental amount better because they are already making more money at the time of move-in. In other words:

- If the amount of rent for an apartment is $1,000.00 per month today and your qualifications to live at your community states, the applicant must make three times the amount of the monthly rent.
- Therefore, 3 times $1,000.00 = $3,000.00 per month, gross income.

- However, if we changed our qualification standards to 3.5 times the monthly rent or $3,500.00 per month, gross income, a new resident would be able to comfortably absorb the renewal increase as they are making more money now, but paying less. Make sense?

Now I'm not suggesting gouging our residents with these huge rent increases, but you have to remember we are a property owner's representative and their goals are to increase the value of the asset (the property) every year. It's our goal to comply with the owner's expectations of our management performance AND keep the residents happy and feeling they are, indeed, getting the value for their rent dollars.

A Good Offense Is the Best Defense

There are eight basic ways to defend against a lower price. If you master them all, you'll spend a lot less time negotiating and a lot more time closing deals. These eight, great differentiators are the keys to defending a high price against lower priced competitors:

#1: Features. Something in your sales pitch is different from the competition.. This can be something major, such as a new rehab, or upgrades, like new carpeting or granite counter tops, or even something small or not expensive to create, like accent colors for special rooms.

#2: Branding. People relate to purchasing from well known business and automatically think of its products and services as superior, or buy it more or less automatically when confronted with a choice. If your management company is well known throughout the city, then branding this advantage can be very beneficial.

#3: Convenience. Location, location, location. If your community has ease of entrance or access to local businesses, transportation, or close to desired shopping area, you have more value.

#4: Quality. Your product, even if exactly identical otherwise, is better made, lasts longer, and/or has better options such as environmental "green initiatives" in the construction of the property itself or the services you provide.

#5: Personality. The resident prefers doing business with you personally, because you've built a long-term relationship with them and their family and friends.

#6: Integration. Your community fits better with other aspects that the customer is going to purchase or is likely to purchase. Examples might be a partnership with a local landscaping company which is creating "planter boxes" or area plots for growing vegetables.

#7: Mutuality. Your business relationship with the residents is important! They want to do business with companies they feel are mutually beneficial.
#8: Strategy. The resident perceives the relationship with you and your company as strategically valuable.

Whenever you find yourself selling against a lower price competitor, you should start positioning and continue repositioning your relationship with your residents to emphasize as many of these differentiators as possible.

Telling, not Selling

It is vitally important to focus on telling, not selling. Picture a scenario where the prospect is sitting across the table from a leasing consultant. The consultant has just introduced themselves and their company and explained a little bit about what they do. So now the prospect turns to that leasing consultant and asks, "What makes you so different than these other properties in this area that I have already visited?"

Here are some very significant things to remember before answering this question.

- You can't sell on what your competition does best and you don't; you have to sell on what you do best and they don't.
- You never want to be known as the lowest price company. Why? Because price is the easiest thing for your competition to duplicate. Let's face it - anyone can drop their prices!
- The hardest thing for your competition to duplicate is extraordinary service, convenience and value. Why? Because extraordinary service takes much effort!
- As a customer, you can buy anything you want off the internet, and you never have to talk to another sales person ever again. However, face-to-face selling is very different.
- The willingness to do the hard work will separate you from your competition because your competition may only be willing to do things the easiest way.

There are two essential characteristics that successful sales people and successful business people have:

- They have the ability to sell more than just their products or services. They utilize all aspects of the community; the services provided, and the general market area to collectively make the sale. Even the staff, particularly the maintenance team, can be a huge sales advantage. After all, service is one of the most fundamental aspects of leasing instead of buying a home. The service, your team, provides can make or break your occupancy. Statistically speaking, residents view the maintenance team as a more valuable asset than the management team. They seem to relate better with them, as they are the ones who come into their homes and take care of their requests.
- They positively love what they do! It's amazing that so many people in our industry don't show this. Even if they do love their job, it seems they are always so stressed,

overworked, complaining, and in general, just miserable. Yet when asked, they always say, "Oh, yes. I love my job." Remember people are observing you and making assumptions of how much you care about being a leasing consultant. (Oh, and by the way - yes, you are leasing consultants, not agents; you don't take tickets like a conductor on a train! You help people with their decisions to move into a new home!) So as the song goes, "If you're happy and you know it," then show it and act like it!

The Ace Up Our Sleeves

As we just discussed, maintenance is one of most valuable assets a community has to offer. Once inside their home, the focus shifts from the excitement and anticipation and of the "new home" to the upkeep and preservation of the working mechanisms within the home. This is where the value of the maintenance team comes in. Typically, the maintenance team is the core of any community. They are there years longer than most management personnel. Their relationship is based on personal trust with the residents which equates to a bond that can last for years. While recently working with a client in the St. Louis area, they had a resident function which I attended. I went from resident to resident asking various questions about how they liked living at the community and what, if any, suggestions they might have to make their home a better place to live. Here were some of their responses…

- "If you ever get rid of the maintenance team, I'm moving!"
- "This is the first apartment where I feel the competency of the maintenance personnel is top notch."
- "Why isn't the office staff as friendly and helpful as the maintenance team?"
- "Well, I'm not happy with the rent increases these days, but it's still worth having the great service the maintenance does in keeping the building beautiful and what they do for the residents."

Really? I was sure they would be asking about why the rents were going up, or be in need of new appliances, or complain about the pet waste or noise. No, it was all about praising the efforts of the long term maintenance team, singling out each one by name and giving me their reasons for, as they said, "just loving" them.
I guess when we think of adding value to the marketing equation; we sometimes miss the aspect of what the residents think is of most value. So let's talk about how to use your maintenance team as that key connection while advertising

- Add up all the years of experience each of your maintenance team has collectively. Then use that number to advertise the professional experiences for your team. "Our property has over 60 years of combined experience and excellence in serving our residents." I can sure see this as a banner ad on your property or company web site.
- Highlight one member of the team each quarter. Interview them and write a "Get to Know Your Service Team" article for your newsletter, website, resident portal communication section, or better yet, contact your local newspaper for a great human interest story. They are always looking for those good content ideas.
- Have a "Celebrate Your Service Team Appreciation Week". Have all of the residents write thank you cards to your team and present them during the party/celebration.
- Have sister communities or neighborhood business join the party and share their stories of your team.
- If you make it a week-long event, have T-shirts made for your maintenance team that says something like: "They love me! They really do love me!" or "Ask me why I'm smiling!" or "Company Rock Stars!"
- Have each member of the maintenance staff take a photo and have them framed in the clubhouse or office with the words: "Our Award Winning Members (or if not award winning; then Super Heroes) of Our Service Team, Serving

You for (put number of years as a team) Years!" Place the framed photos on your "Wall of Fame" which makes for a wonderful feature for those who visit your community. It shows how much you appreciate your team.

Anyway you look at it, celebrating the importance of your maintenance and service teams are a positive and certainly worthwhile focus from the current resident's perspective. So celebrate those who serve our residents best - our awesome maintenance teams!

Reassurance versus Encouragement

Years ago there was a popular book called "Men Are from Mars, Women Are from Venus" by John Gray that talked about the general differences between men and women and how vastly they differ in their ways of communication. Although this might not hold true for all men and women, based on the book's concept, it seems that women need more reassurance that they are making the right decision when choosing a new apartment home. Women struggle with making mistakes and are cautious of being misled by unscrupulous sales people.

Although there are many factors that are taken into account when making major life decisions, women need more information to ensure confidence in their decision. Typically, women are more concerned about the aesthetic aspects and appeal of the new apartment home, the safety of the location and surrounding area, and the resident profile mix. Interior design, color schemes, comfort, and safety are paramount to their decision.

On the other hand, men tend to need more encouragement that the decision they already have made is a good one. It sounds similar to the women's concerns but isn't. Men tend to make a decision first then look for supporting evidence to validate their decisions. Their concerns are more statistically based: "How much will the electric bill average?" or "How often is preventive maintenance completed?"

If you remember that selling to anyone should be about matching the apartment and amenities to the individual's lifestyle, whether man or woman, you will be more successful in not only leasing to them now, but renewing them in the years to come. The key is to keep up on what the resident deems important.

Let's talk for a minute about renewal letters.

Instead of using plain white paper, go to a stationary or office supply store and buy some very nice parchment or professional letter paper. This immediately shows the value of the information and sets this letter apart from other apartment community correspondence.

Rework the wording throughout the letter. Remove the negative phrases like, "Your lease is about to expire," and replace with positive ones such as, "It's time to celebrate the anniversary of your move-in day!"

Begin with an explanation of what has happened over the past few months on the property or the surrounding community area that supports the increasing value in their new rental amount. Share with the resident a "state of the property" evaluation noting the improvements from last year to now. Some examples are listed below:

- "We have so enjoyed having you with us this past year. As you may have noticed, we have done some wonderful improvements showing your rent dollars hard at work."
- "Thank you for your business and confidence in us! We have enjoyed providing you with the best service possible this past year. As you may have noticed, our area is

expanding with new businesses and restaurants. Growth such as this reflects that this is a great location to live!"
- "Wow! What a great year for our community! We have had wonderful activities that have, hopefully, been of great benefit to you! Our desire is for our residents to truly see the value of living here at our community." List some of the recent activities and/or changes and how they were indeed benefits to your residents.

Relationships are delicately balanced situations and timely communication with your residents throughout their lease term keeps them informed and hopefully content enough to not move at the end of their lease term. Gentle reminders of what's going on in the market area coupled with supporting documentation (newspaper articles, etc.) regarding the improvements and or growth in your area shows the residents that the entire community is increasing in value; not just their rent.

Renewing Our Vows of Commitment

We have heard numerous times over the years that the resident decides to renew their lease the day they move in. Their positive or negative experience of that day will either be the foundation for a "smooth sailing" long-term-relationship or a "stormy seas" battle over every single issue throughout their lease term. If residents have a negative experience living at your community, when they leave, they may tell the world what "blood sucking landlords" we are!

Creating a resident retention program that is incomparable to that of the competitors' will add value to the residents' living experience all year long. If residents decide to compare properties, having a top-notch resident retention program will absolutely make a positive influence in evaluating the true value of their current home.

The best way to begin building a positive relationship is to manage the prospect/future resident's expectations. Here are a few suggestions that will allow you to create a positive impact prior to move-in day!

New Resident Orientation

Set a date and time for the new residents to come in and sign paperwork. Try to avoid having the lease signing on move-in day. Move-in day is hectic!

- Prepare all the lease, resident handbook, etc., for the resident. Review the paperwork explaining each paragraph in detail asking the resident if they have any questions. This may be the only time you will have their undivided attention so make it count!
- The day the residents sign their lease, be prepared to give them a move-in gift. Residents will appreciate their move-in gift more this day as move-in day is normally a bit chaotic.

A note about move-in gifts: Using necessity items like paper products are fine as "supplemental" gifts in the apartment itself. Water in the fridge, small soaps in the bath area, and toilet paper in the bathroom (wrapped or at least with a sticker showing it is a new roll) can be appropriate. Find out what matches your property's profile and give something that is memorable and different! For example at a student property, give gift cards for food, backpacks or bicycle locks. Urban/downtown properties have chosen to give pedometers, water bottles, gift cards to local eateries or WiFi locator key chains. Be certain to periodically review your existing residents and their lifestyles to come up

On Move-In Day. (Prior to the resident arriving)

- Go to the apartment and check the temperature. Comfort is very important for that initial first impression.

- Put bottled water in the refrigerator and place paper products and "smell good soaps" in a basket in either the kitchen or bathroom.
- Use a roll of plastic that is "sticky" on one side and place it on the carpet over the traffic areas. The plastic will protect the carpet and will come in handy if there is inclement weather on move-in day.
- Let existing residents know that they have a new neighbor moving in and encourage them to introduce themselves! If you don't have time to personally notify the existing residents, door hangers are available at several great resource companies.
- Place a sign at the parking space closest to the front door of the apartment building reserving a spot for the new resident on move in day. The sign should read, "Welcome to Your New Home! Reserved for a New Move-In Today!" This helps with those awkward moving trucks having to park far away. Remind the new resident that the parking spot will be reserved just for move-in day. Finally, as the new resident begins to un-pack, have your maintenance team walk by a few times a day to pick up empty boxes. Helping the resident by taking away unwanted boxes will assist them in getting settled in their new home more quickly.

When the Resident Arrives On Move-In Day

- Walk with the resident to their new home.
- Hand the keys to the new resident so they may open the door their new home.
- Take a "Move-in Condition Sheet" and assist the resident in making note of any item(s) that may need attention. Please do not hold the mailbox key as hostage for the completed Move-In Condition Sheet! This practice was eliminated in the 1980's.

After The Resident Moves In

Begin contacting the resident on a regular basis. Start within a week of their move-in date. Contact them via phone cal, visit to the apartment, letter, card, on-line survey, email or text. Gather feedback as to the satisfaction level of the resident's move-in experience. So not to overwhelm the resident or be bothersome, spread the contact throughout the first 30, 60 and 90 days of their move-in. Effective examples of contact might be:

- Have the Community Manager contact the new resident and ask about how the move went as a whole. Did the resident feel the staff did a good job? Did the apartment's quality deliver through cleanliness and appearance and meet their expectations and satisfaction levels?
  The Lead Maintenance person should contact the resident to set up a time to visit the resident at their apartment. While there, he/she can discuss with the resident the service request process and procedures. Also beneficial would be for the maintenance person to share some "helpful hints" such as:

    o How to turn off the water supply line behind the toilet. Overflowing toilets are quite a mess to clean.
    o Demonstrate how to use the re-set button on the garbage disposal. Also educate the resident on what is not appropriate to put in the garbage disposal. Some residents will not be aware that putting grease or too many vegetable peelings could cause future problems.
    o How the heating and air conditioning systems work and the proper use of the wall thermostat.
      Show them the proper way to use anything specific to the apartment that would be beneficial for the resident.

- Finally, after 30 days or so, send the resident a "comprehensive survey" of the move-in process, staff performance, apartment living expectations, parking, amenities used, and any other area of concern with which you would like feedback. Surveys can easily be done on-line with a link in an email. Making sure you are respectful of the resident's time. A basic 10 question survey will only take moments to complete. Consider giving the resident a 'reward' of a gift card for taking time to complete the survey. Reward the behavior you want repeated!

In addition, having support from a corporate level can be quite a plus. As a show of "top-down" support, a District or Regional Manager should send a note to the new resident introducing themselves. The correspondence should welcome the resident to reach out to the District or Regional Manager if, at any time, they feel like they are not getting complete satisfaction. Or, welcoming the resident to let the supervisor know of an outstanding customer service issue that was taken care of "over and beyond" the resident's expectations. In addition, the resident should be welcomed to contact the supervisor in the event of "discontentment" over a particular challenge with the onsite team.

Having an open line of communication is vital to keeping good "checks and balances" of all who are involved in the resident's experience.

Please note: This can be of great influence when used correctly. A quick email or printed form letter to the **new resident** welcoming them to the community assures them that you, the supervisor, have complete faith that your team will do a great job. It is in no way meant to "override" or "undermine" the authority of the onsite team. On the contrary, it is meant to provide confidence in both the onsite team and the resident that things will be taken care of professionally, promptly and properly.

During the Lease Term

What we think, what we know, or what we believe is, in the end, of little consequence, compared to what we actually do. In the in-between-time from the move-in day to the beginning of the renewal process, typically 120 to 90 days prior to the end of the current lease agreement, there are so many opportunities to "add that value" back in again. Great "moments of truth" could be at any of the times we come in contact with the resident. Use these opportunities to solidify their confidence in us as the "right place to live for them."

- At First of the Month – During Rent Collection: Ask if there is anything they need in their apartment home.
- While Performing Service Requests: If the resident is home, ask if they need any further assistance.
- Calling Back on Service Requests: Have the maintenance team make a few of the follow-up calls.
- At Resident Functions or Parties: Talk with your Residents about "their" feedback.
- During "Shows" with Prospects: If you see a resident, wave and greet them by name.
- Walking Through the Community: Take a moment to stop and ask how residents are doing.
- On Resident Portals and Web Sites: Remind your residents of just how much you appreciate them!
- After Hours On Call: Thank the resident for making us aware of their problem and the opportunity to fix it.

So What IS a "CSI" Rating Scale?

CSI or a Customer Service Index is what other industries use to see if their products and services meet or exceed the company's expectations of what their "good customer service" programs are. We all think we are doing a good job of providing good customer service, but what constitutes "good?" Who is doing the rating? Are we or are they, the residents?

Actually, it's a combination of both. We have to be aware of our plans and programs and how effective they really are, especially when comparing them to our competition's efforts. So more importantly, how the resident perceives our efforts makes for that higher CSI rating. We may think we are doing a bang up job, when, in fact, according to the resident, none of that matters! So what does?

There are three vital aspects when analyzing your customer service programs.

1. Measuring All Levels and Timeframes of Service: As we have shown you in the information listed earlier in this chapter, there are crucial, memorable points of contact during a resident's tenure that have more weight and can change the resident's opinion of our service efforts. How we respond to the information gathered during that time will let us know if we are doing well or not.
2. How is The Customer Rewarded for Their Loyalty?: If we add up all the rent your residents pay and multiply that times how many years they have been there, the lifetime value of that one resident is enormous. When you put a dollar amount on a piece of paper, most people expect something in return equal or greater than their investment. How are we rewarding our residents for their tenure or lifetime commitments?
3. How The Customer "Felt" During the Experience: Since we often don't hear from the bulk of our residents, sometimes this is hard to answer unless, of course, we are asking them.

Creating a World of Value

The only sustainable competitive advantage is your ability to learn faster than your competition. We all attend seminars and company meetings in person and webinars online, trying to gather enough global information to create a world class experience for our prospects and residents alike.

We have discussed at great length and detail in this chapter some of the moments of truth for our customers where we have a real shot at making things more valuable, offsetting the money they pay. How can we incorporate these ideas into our plans to increase the value of the real estate asset while increasing the value of the dollars our residents spend in rent?

- Give your residents a place to vent! As with a maintenance request for repairing a leak, the sooner we find out about the problem, the faster we can respond and correct it. If your residents know they can "vent" either online via email, a phone call, or in person, our job is to listen and fix the issue best we can. Many leasing people hate dealing with some residents because "some" residents and their issues are "unfixable." That's all right, but they still need to vent. Supply avenues that your residents may do just that, and over time you will begin to see the intensity of the venting will slow down. It's when there is no place to do this that the corked bottle begins to explode.
- Hire people who love serving people! We all say we love working with the residents, but the truth is some people are just the "burr under our saddles." Sorry, that was a Texas thing, but you know what I mean! So to keep things balanced, while interviewing potential new employees make sure to add some, "So, tell me how you would handle this situation…" questions. By doing so, you will find out more about that person's abilities and skills to handle the variety of circumstances that happen daily on our properties. Have

meetings with the staff to remind them of our goal to keep the residents happy and paying rent! So smile! Now, go back to work.

- Be innovative with service! Some of our best ideas for customer service come from our maintenance teams. Ask them how we can be better at taking care of the residents. I have seen several great ideas come from a brainstorming meeting with the entire staff. Among the many great ideas that have been implemented, we were able to implement better timing of how the service requests were completed, even begin competition within portfolios to challenge other properties to be efficient enough to boast "same day service." Reach out to other businesses in your area! We get "tunnel vision" sometimes when trying to come up with new concepts. Why not use other industry concepts in your area? We all have the same customers; we just call ours residents.

- Remember your reputation! Oh, my...reputation management has been on the forefront of hot topic conversations for several years now. Disgruntled current or former residents and even former employees vent about their dissatisfactions online, "airing their dirty laundry." Remember this: one person's opinion, especially if it's a negative one, really doesn't hold much credibility these days. It's when you have a series of issues that people take notice.

There are some great companies in our industry that their sole purpose is to help you manage your property and company's reputation on the internet. Check with your local apartment association, state association chapter, the National Apartment Association web site, www.naahq.org, or other industry organizations to see whom they have as members and whom they recommend. As my Daddy always told me, "Jackie, your reputation is not only about you; it is about whom you associate with, whom you partner with, and ultimately that reflects on your family, your mother, and

ME! So don't get into trouble where people look bad on the family. Our reputation is precious, and we ALL work very hard to maintain our character and credibility." See Daddy, I remember.

A New Level of Thinking

What have we learned from this chapter? What are your "takeaways" that will help you and your team to increase the value of your rents and convince your residents your property and all its services are worth it when considering selling against your completion?

Albert Einstein observed, "The significant problems we face cannot be solved at the same level of thinking we were at when we created them." That's quite an epiphany when you stop to think. When thinking about effectively adding value to goods and services, one must think about these two areas separately. Adding value to physical items or the "goods" will have a completely different thought process than adding intangible services. Both aspects center around the human element, we must create and define those differences with diverse goals in mind.

For example, increasing the interior value of the apartment home might consist of upgrades of appliances, cabinetry, hardware on cabinets, countertops, flooring, window treatments, sinks, tubs, shower rods and shower heads, etc. The decisions of which one to install are primarily based on our financial ability to "afford" those luxuries coupled with wear and tear on the current items in the units. The only effect the resident has on this decision is if they want them, see the value in having them, and are willing to pay for them as an added amenity.

However, when considering adding valuable services for our residents, we have to take into consideration what our residents need and, more importantly, what they would appreciate and/or justify paying for those services. Necessities are expectations, while true benefits will take some real digging and matching with your current resident profile.

Chapter Review

Trying to convince someone of what the real value is in any product or service is difficult at best. When our prospect starts their journey for a new apartment home, more times than not, price is an important determining factor. Not as the final decision necessarily, but a major component in closing the deal. Their past will govern their future decisions.

When communities are relatively the same in product quality, services provided; amenity selections and price, what makes one community literally "worth the money" over another is subjective in the eyes of the buyer. Some comparisons between your comp properties and your community are basic expectations to the customers.

A competitive marketing advantage focuses on those unique exceptions that make the decision to lease at your community more appealing. Even if those advantages are not initially needed, the "value added" approach thinking concept is like icing on the cake.

Nothing is more comforting to people with children than to know your community caters to the "littlest residents" too. Core family based values with after school activities, learning opportunities, exercise programs, and holiday parties, are all part of the added value concepts. Properties who believe in having a well balanced event calendar for ALL their residents find real value in these services and activities.

All properties struggle to maintain a harmonious environment for all their residents. Encouraging your residents to refer their family members, friends or people they work with to move into your community, has two very important motivational advantages. First, the property gets traffic that comes with an endorsement from one of your own residents who feel it's such a great place to live, they are recommending to others. Secondly, it gives the property an opportunity to "thank" the resident for that referral with incentive packages that range from actual discounts off their rent, preferred parking spots, free access to paid amenities, to upgraded amenities for their own apartment home.

Building mutual relationships between competitive properties in the general market area makes for solid business relationships that can build on your reputation and even develop into long lasting friendships. I have managers and leasing professionals whom I knew when I was still managing my properties that I still have as friends today! Networking is key. Building that "friendly competitive" relationship helped all the properties in the market area to perform better for all our management companies.

Every apartment community feels they have the "best" of everything, including their staff members, apartment size, square footage, recreational and inside-the-units amenities, resident activities, etc. However the proof is in the pudding, so to speak. If that was their bragging rights when you leased, but throughout your lease term, you had numerous situations where that was NOT the case, the community lost its value for that resident.

Most customers, today, are looking for the same thing – savings of time, effort or money. Today time to make their life easier has become a bigger priority than money. Why? Because we are all insanely busy.

Start by selecting five strengths and advantages, and then five weaknesses and disadvantages of your community. Knowing these will help you identify and develop good selling strategies and effective counters to overcoming objections.

The two main driving forces for why people buy are: logic and emotion. Most people buy emotionally and justify their purchases logically. You need to have an understanding of why people buy, what motivates them, and how they make buying decisions. Essentially, people buy to satisfy their physical or psychological wants and/or needs. Keep the focus on the resident and solving their problem and in the end they will go with, or stay with, the company that best understands them, sympathizes with them and provides solid ways to solve them.

Relationships are delicately balanced situations and timely communication with your residents throughout their lease term keeps them informed and hopefully content enough to not move at the end of their lease term. Gentle reminders of what's going on in the market area coupled with supporting documentation (newspaper articles, etc.) regarding the improvements and/or growth in your area shows the residents that the entire community is increasing in value; not just their rent.

Curiosity is a powerful aspect of sales where you can engage the prospects and residents to see and hear more openly. The biggest mistake leasing consultants make is not asking for the customer's business. Too many feel uncomfortable with this process, but ultimately, you have to have faith in your own ability. Do you provide great service and a wonderful living experience? Then feel confident about asking for their business!

The differences between your competition and your community should be based on a few solid principles such as, they must be **relevant** to your prospect's or resident's needs. If they don't care, it's not a point of difference. They must be **specific**. Use exact figures because the more precise the number, the more convincing it becomes. If your turn around time for your service requests average "same day service" compared to the competition's 24 -48 hour turnaround, this is a significant difference. So they must be **credible** and believable. Don't make up things just to sound better. People aren't stupid; in fact most people today are quite savvy. They already know if what you are telling them is true.

You can add more value if you have more information about your customers, and the greater your competitive edge will be. Understand as much as you can about their current situation and just as importantly about their plans for the future. Learn about their concerns, their issues and their problems, and lifestyle goals. You cannot know too much; you can, however, say too much.

Never lose sight of the fundamentals when dealing with a fiercely competitive marketplace. People buy from people that they believe are similar to themselves; they buy from people that they like; they buy "people," not necessarily the apartment or the community. You have a better opportunity to land a sale if you're in front of a prospect. You'll struggle to do this remotely as most people can't visualize well. They need to actually see it to make a decision. When you are "face to face," you can judge the customer's reactions to your proposal, and you have an opportunity to question them more comprehensively. You're there, and the competition isn't.

There are several ways to defend against a lower price. #1: Features. Something in your sales pitch is different from the competition. This can be something major such as a new rehab or upgrades, as new carpeting or granite counter tops or even something small or not expensive to create accent colors for special rooms. #2: Branding. People relate to purchasing from well known business and automatically thinks of its products and services as superior, or buys it more or less automatically when confronted with a choice. If your management company is well known throughout the city, then branding this advantage can be very beneficial.

"What makes you so different than these other properties in this area that I have already visited?" Before answering that question, there are significant things to ponder first. You can't sell on what your competition does best, and you don't. You have to sell on what you do best, and they don't. So you never want to be known as the lowest price company. Why? Because price is the easiest thing for your competition to duplicate. Let's face it anyone can drop their prices!

An essential characteristic that successful salespeople and successful business people have is the ability to sell more than just their products or services. They utilize all aspects of the community; the services provided, and the general market area to collectively make the sale. Even the staff and particularly the maintenance team can be a huge sales advantage. After all service is one of the most fundamental aspects of leasing instead of buying a home.
Your maintenance team is one of most valuable assets a community has to offer. Once inside their home, the focus shifts from the excitement and anticipation and of the "new home" to the upkeep and preservation of the working mechanisms within the home. This is where the value of the maintenance team comes in.

When we think of adding value to the marketing equation, we sometimes miss the aspect of what the residents think is of most value. So let's talk about how to use your maintenance team as a key connection while advertising. Add up all the years of experience each of your maintenance team has collectively. Then use that number to advertise the professional experiences for your team. "Our property has over 60 years of combined experience and excellence in serving our residents." I can sure see this as a banner ad on your property or company web sites!

If you remember that selling to anyone should be about matching the apartment and amenities to the individual's lifestyle, whether man or woman, you will be more successful in not only leasing to them now, but renewing them in the years to come. The key is to keep up on what the resident deems important.

People have difficulty in sometimes telling us the truth of how they really feel. I know, I know, you know someone who doesn't have that problem at all! Maybe our resident retention programs "lack luster" and the only contact we have with the resident is the legally required, 30 or 60 day letter of renewal stating the rental amount is going up.

Remember to rework those renewal letters! Instead of impersonal "copied, fill in the blank" type letters, use nice parchment or professional letter paper. This immediately shows the value of the information and sets this letter apart from all other correspondence. Rework the wording throughout the letter. Remove the negative words like "your lease is about to expire" and replace with positive words such as "it's time to celebrate the anniversary of your move in day!"

Begin your renewal initiation with an explanation of what has happened over the past few months on the property or the surrounding community area that supports the increasing value in their new rental amount; a "state of the property" evaluation from last year to now.

Create a resident retention program that shows our residents all year long, that we are the best place to live! Begin with a New Resident Orientation. Set a date to have the new residents come in to go over all the paperwork without the headaches the moving day brings. Prepare all the lease, addenda, resident handbook, etc. for the resident. Go over the paperwork explaining each paragraph in detail asking the resident if they have any misunderstanding or concern of a particular area of the lease agreement. This may be the only time you will have their undivided attention so make it count.

What we think, what we know, or what we believe is, in the end, of little consequence, compared to what we actually do. In the in-between-time from the move in day to the beginning of the renewal process, typically 120 to 90 prior to the end of the current lease agreement, there are so many opportunities to "add that value" back in again. Great "moments of truth" could be at any of these times we come in contact with the resident. Use these opportunities to solidify their confidence in us as the "right place to live for them."

CSI or a Customer Service Index is what other industries use to see if their products and services meet or exceed the company's expectations of what their "good customer service" programs are. There are three vital aspects when analyzing your customer service programs; measuring all levels and timeframes of service provided, how the customer is rewarded for their loyalty and how the customer "felt" during the experience.

We have discussed at great length ways of making the apartments and services we offer more valuable thus offsetting the money the resident pays for rent.

References and Resources

Men Are from Mars, Women Are from Venus by John Gray, Ph.D. – This book gives great insight to the differences in the way men and women think, rationalize, and act. www.MarsVenus.com

www.WalktheTalk.com – This web site has numerous varieties of books, eBooks, videos, free resources, and newsletters. I personally have contributed to one of their books, "Working from a Distance." These are easy to read and immediately adaptable to everyday situations.

Increasing Occupancy: Resident Retention Edition by Mindy Williams, www.RentandRetain.com

Drive by Daniel H. Pink – This is a fascinating book that captures the essence of what makes people do what they do. Web site www.DanPink.com

Reading People by Jo-Ellan Dimitrius, P.D. – Terrific information about how personalities predict behavior and how to understand the process. www.amazon.com/Reading-People

Chapter 8
Demonstrating for the Deposit

By Don Sanders

In this chapter, you will be presented with demonstration and touring strategies for vacant apartment homes, model apartment homes, interior building amenities and exterior building amenities. Knowledge will be gained of not only how to demonstrate the aforementioned, but also how to prepare them for the demonstration prior to the tour.

Creative ideas for marketing overall resident use of the community amenity offerings during tour will be suggested. You will learn tricks-of-the-trade, on how to get prospective residents physically involved in the tour process and how to read their buying signals.

Suggestions will be given on how to more creatively present and narrate otherwise standard features within the apartment home. Emphasis will be put on creating a demonstration style that sets you apart from your competitors.

The goal of this chapter is to promote demonstrations that go beyond presenting the basic information, to strongly focus on presenting a tour that describes the apartment and amenities, but also a lifestyle. For the experienced, this chapter will be a review that will assist in fine tuning their process. For the new, this chapter will provide the step-by-step basics, as well as advanced strategies for apartment home and amenity demonstration success.

Demonstrations That Set You Apart

Welcome to one of the most critical steps in the rental process, where the prospective resident finally gets to see, touch and feel the product. As my father, a former truck driver, would say, "This is where the rubber meets the road." Interestingly enough, many

Leasing Specialists and their supervisors believe the demonstration process only refers to an apartment home and amenities, when, in fact, it refers to far more.

From the second, the prospective resident can see your community from the road; the tour begins. That's right; curb appeal, signage, landscaping, resident balconies and patios, building maintenance, etc., are all critical dynamics within the tour process. Just like all human beings, judgment begins the second any of our senses are stimulated. When a prospective resident arrives at the community, their tour objective, be it conscious or subconscious, is to see and experience as much of the lifestyle that the community can provide as possible. This not only includes the visual aspects of the asset, but also possibly a taste of the professionalism and customer service that they might encounter on a daily basis should they choose to call your community home.

Most experienced multi-family housing professionals have heard or used the term, "Tour Path." The tour path refers to a pre-established path with amenity stop points throughout the community. Most communities suggest that all employees providing tours follow this path. This established tour route is critical for two main reasons; it provides a prioritized path for your maintenance team to focus on each morning insuring a clean well maintained guest experience, and it ensures all customers see the same thing, therefore, reducing any potential fair housing issues.

Unfortunately, many multi-family housing professionals believe that the tour path begins at the Leasing Specialist's desk, moving to the clubhouse, to the amenities, model and/or vacant apartment home and then ends back at the Leasing Specialist's desk. However, as stated earlier, the tour starts the second the prospective resident lays eyes on your community. Therefore, as professionals often commissioned or receiving performance bonuses, we not only owe it to the company but to ourselves to include the drive by, entrance and the inner community lane to the clubhouse as critical pieces to our pre-established tour path. This means each morning as we drive into our community of employment, our eyes need to be wide open to any issues that might cause a prospective resident to have a less-than-positive moment of judgment. So be sure to look for poorly hung banners, overgrown landscaping blocking the monument signage and garbage along the entrance route. Look for fountains not working, leaning inner community signage, trees in need of trimming, poorly marked resident parking, and anything else that might cause a resident to assume that you, your colleagues and owners do not take pride in your community. If your community happens to be a hi-rise or a mid-rise, you'll need to check the sidewalk leading to the building, as well as the parking areas and path from the parking area to the leasing center, including the building lobby and the elevators.

For purposes of this chapter, let's assume that the first impression of the drive-by, entrance and roadway to the leasing center/clubhouse are in outstanding presentation shape. Up to this point, all prospective residents are guaranteed to have a positive first impression. Let's move into the meat of demonstration preparation and techniques.

As stated earlier, visitors to your community are not merely hoping to receive a tour of an apartment home but a tour of a "Potential Lifestyle." That lifestyle demonstration begins with your actions the second they walk in the door.

They say first impressions are established within the first 7 seconds of observing or meeting someone. So let's begin our focus on the concept of customer observation. When a prospective resident enters your leasing offices, what do they observe? Do they observe clean, freshly painted walls? Do they observe the artwork hung evenly? Do they observe well organized business-like desks, free of clutter and multiple personal items? Or do they observe entrance doors cluttered with handwritten notices? Or do they observe dusty silk trees with foam, newspaper stuffing and leftover holiday decorations visible at the base? Or do they observe corners of torn crepe paper on windows and doorways leftover from parties of yesteryears? Whether it is conscious or subconscious, these observations either start your tour out positively or negatively. These observations start your tour out with customers feeling you pay great attention to detail and cleanliness or that you don't care. So let's face it, who wants to live in a place, where management doesn't care?

Quick, the first five seconds are gone with them noticing the leasing office; time to let them notice you. My mother always said, "If you are good at what you do, you can sell an Eskimo ice." So I have learned that no matter what the product or environment, an awesome Leasing Specialist can turn any demonstration experience into a positive memorable one by following three simple rules.

Rule #1 – Personality is Everything
If you were to read a "Help Wanted" ad for an experienced tour guide, you would not expect it to request a quiet, introverted and shy personality type. You would expect quite the opposite. You would expect outgoing, creative and with a great sense of humor. Well, that is exactly what your prospective resident expects, as well. That means when they walk in the door, they expect you to JUMP-SHAKE-&-PERCOLATE! They expect you to JUMP up from your chair, come to them with a level of excitement, SHAKE their hand and put on your PERKY personality. We have all had the opposite happen; where you enter the office, the employee remains behind the desk and merely asks how they might help you. This employee is hard to remember, hard to bond with, and their behavior does not elicit an emotional attachment, all of which are important steps in closing a deal. So remember, the next time someone walks into the office, JUMP-SHAKE-&-PERCOLATE!

Rule #2 – Preparation is Everything
When preparing for a tour, whether it is setting the appointment over the phone or meeting a client for the first time as a walk-in, it is imperative that you get some key information that will allow you to be successful with the next rule to be introduced. This information is directly related to their lifestyle needs, regarding both

the community and their future apartment home. Knowing if they are active people, knowing if they are cooks, knowing if they are entertainers, etc., are all great pieces of information that you can later use during your community and apartment demonstration. Likewise, knowing what types and sizes of furniture they have, knowing the colors of their furniture, knowing what artwork or another display needs they might have, etc., will come in equally as useful. Finally, knowing the names of each person and pet, if applicable, is a winning tool not to be skipped over for future use.

Rule #3 – Customize Everything
Let's face it, the majority of us are not selling anything that unique. Most of us are selling a living space that has a certain number of bedrooms, a certain number of bathrooms, a kitchen, some closets, off white walls, neutral carpet or tile throughout and a patio or balcony. Of course, there may be granite, crown molding, plantation shutters, mini-blinds, etc., that give some apartment homes a slight competitive edge, but typically there is an added price point that clients must deem investment worthily. However the real selling point is YOU! You are unique, and you are part of the lifestyle they are considering purchasing. So the key is to set yourself apart from your competitors. Make your tour unique by customizing the demonstration. Use their names, their children's names, their pet's names and point out amenities that apply to their lifestyle you learned about during the information gathering process or space that applies to their furniture and décor needs. The goal at the end of the demonstration is for them to feel as though the community and apartment home were designed specifically with them in mind, designed to meet their unique individual needs.

Now that you know the three preliminary rules for demonstration success, it is time you face the facts. While you are sitting there gathering all of this information, they are taking advantage of the time you have given them to judge you as a professional. That's right; they came to tour the community and you are part of that tour. So you have to ask, "How do I look?" Did I take time to do my hair this morning, or did I just throw it into a ponytail? Did I iron my clothes today? Did I polish my shoes today? Did the coffee stain come out of my shirt? Are my fingernails clean, groomed and polished? Is my name tag on straight? Is my shirt neatly tucked in? Does my breath smell good?

All of these dynamics play into the final assessment of who will be managing their lifestyle investment and if they are worthy. So you have to ask yourself each day if the people you come in contact with will believe that you visually appear and professionally act worthy of managing the collective investments of both the prospective residents and the residents who live here? Very few employees are given the responsibility to represent a multi-million dollar asset without the direct supervision of the owner. As community employees, we need to take our position extremely seriously. We need to be prepared to constantly be on tour!

So, we look awesome; we have activated our positive, outgoing personality traits; we have gathered all of the information possible about our future residents without sounding like an interrogator, and they absolutely love us. Now it is time to begin the physical tour process.

Typically, the tour begins in the portion of the property where the Leasing Center is located. The clubhouse or clubroom is often home or neighbor to the majority of the community amenities. As you may recall, during the initial interview we found out what our client interests may or may not be. That knowledge should not necessarily eliminate showing an amenity on the tour path, but it may dictate the length of time we spend viewing and describing the amenity. Throughout the next few paragraphs, we will explore pre-tour preparation steps for amenities and dynamic demonstration content that should be presented in regards to some of the industry's most popular interior clubhouse amenities. From there, we will move to the model apartment and vacant apartment demonstration, and then conclude with outdoor amenities.

As we begin to explore how to successfully present and demonstrate interior amenities, you will recognize one action item is consistently repeated, and that is that the amenity should look open and active. We give tours throughout the day during business hours. We cannot guarantee that every amenity will have a resident actively using it during our tour. However, that does not mean that the lights, televisions, music and any other items should not appear on and in use. Turning everything on should be part of the opening for business morning routine.

Billiards Room
Of course, your billiards room will be equipped with pool tables that are in great repair with beautifully maintained felt and the equipment needed in order to shoot a rousing game of pool. The consistent display of these items is critical to making the amenity seem worthy for a tour and to attract the aspiring and established "Pool Sharks" that you are touring. Upon entering the billiards room, you want it to appear active; therefore, lighting should be turned on first thing in the morning and remain on throughout business hours. If the billiards room is equipped with televisions, then these, too, should be on, at a moderate volume level possibly tuned to a sports channel. The pool balls should be racked and set for a new game when not in use and two cues displayed at crossing angles on the table. Additional cues and chalk should be displayed in an organized storage rack. Prior to entering the room, be prepared to suggest scenarios for your prospective resident's usage and enjoyment based upon what you learned regarding their lifestyle and needs.

Let's pretend your clients are a young, vibrant couple who expressed their love for entertaining. This scenario would give you the perfect opening to suggest that, after one of their awesome weekend lunch parties, he could bring the guys over to shoot a game of pool and watch the game, while maybe the ladies enjoyed relaxing on their new apartment balcony with a glass of wine. The goal is to get them to picture utilizing all that is offered.

Another great practice is to have prescheduled events for each amenity. You could highlight your "Billiards Tip Tuesday" program, where a local billiards expert comes in and provides tips the first Tuesday of every month. You could highlight your pool league tournaments that occur the last Thursday of every month. Alternatively you could highlight your billiards drill night (see link to billiards drills at the end of this chapter in the resource section)contest that occurs the second Friday of every month.

Theatre

The theatre can be one of the community's most exciting amenities to demonstrate if active and represented correctly. When demonstrating the theatre, it is important that you know some basic statistical information, allowing you to impress any audio visual nerd joining your tour. For instance, you may highlight the fact your theatre is home to an 84-inch flat screen television, to a projection system with 3200 lumens, or to a cutting edge Bose surround-sound system. These tidbits of electronic statistical information can set you apart from your competitors, sound impressive to even those who don't understand, and possibly put you one step closer to getting the application and deposit. Just like other amenities, it is imperative that the theatre look and feel active, even when not in use by residents. Therefore, having the lights dimmed, a movie playing and possibly the smell of freshly popped popcorn are great marketing tour strategies. No popcorn machine? No problem! There are companies that produce buttered popcorn flavored room air freshener. (see air freshener link in the resource section) Another option is to have a video or PowerPoint presentation that loops, showing the highlights of what your community has to offer. As with other amenities be proactively prepared to present scenarios that apply to your prospective resident's potential use of the amenity.

Let's pretend you have a single resident who just received a job transfer and will be new to the area. You can invite them to your highly attended Sunday night football party or your Thursday night

Reality TV viewing, thereby giving them the opportunity to meet other residents and make new friends quickly.

Game Room
Game rooms are quickly becoming a huge draw for renters. While typically appealing to families with teenage children, or young bachelors, this amenity is proving to appeal to a wide range of residents. Of course, while Wii, Xbox, PlayStation and Nintendo are the video forerunners for popularity, the retro standby of old school air hockey or Pac Man is still appreciated. I have been on multiple tours of communities with game rooms. To this day upon entering a game room, I always wish the tour could pause for a few minutes so I could play one of the games. One time while touring a community in Raleigh, NC, the Leasing Specialist quickly recognized my affection for air hockey and leaped at the opportunity to bond with me. We played a five point game, of which she intelligently let me win and then we moved on to the next amenity. Hands down, this was the best community tour I have ever taken.

As previously directed, be sure the lights are on, music is on and the game room appears to be active during business hours. While demonstrating the game room, be sure to point out the variety of gaming systems and game discs available for the residents to check out. If your prospective resident has age appropriate children with them, invite the children to explore the room, possibly even give him or her five minutes to play a game while you speak to the adults, or challenge them all to a game.

As a side note, this is also a great place to let the kid(s) entertain themselves while applications and deposits are being executed with the adults.

Cyber Cafe
Many communities confuse business centers with cyber cafes. Cyber café implies an area where one can work on their personal laptop via WiFi, get something to drink, all while sitting in a

comfortable chair. If your cyber café doesn't have these three items, then it is probably a business center. I love the cyber café in my building, and it is widely used in the morning. I think many residents are tired of paying an outrageous price for a cup of designer coffee at the corner boutique java joint. I believe they appreciate the opportunity to start the morning out close to home. I know I love going to the community cyber cafe, getting a cup of coffee, firing up the laptop, cleaning up emails from the night before, and putting together my attack plan for the day, all in the comfort of my building prior to driving to work.

Key selling points to introduce your prospective residents to while touring would include making them aware of the WiFi connectivity and what amenity areas it covers, such as; the pool area, the game room, etc. It may sound basic, but pointing out ample availability and convenient locations of electrical outlets for laptops will definitely set you apart from any prior competitor tours. Obviously the word café implies availability of something to eat and/or drink so they will need to be introduced to their options. While some communities offer complimentary beverages, many communities have added both drink and snack vending machines. Be sure to let them view what's available; if complimentary, offer them something to take along on the rest of the tour, making access to cups with lids a necessity. Don't forget, be proactively prepared to present viable scenarios based upon what you have learned about your customer.

Let's pretend your prospective resident is a busy single mom of school aged children who works from home. You could suggest that after she sees the children onto the school bus each morning, she could swing through the Cyber Café to start the day off right, grab a cup of java, sit by the fireplace and answer emails she received after close of business from the prior day.

Business Center
A great staple to community amenity packages continues to be a professional business center equipped with desktop computers, printers, copy/fax machines and other office resources, sometimes

inclusive of a conference room. Many communities find these most utilized after school by students who do not have access to computers. While I believe that to be true, I also believe they are an underrated social amenity as well, where a great deal of peer tutoring occurs. Additionally, many families only have one computer, with multiple people wanting to use it, so this amenity often solves a supply and demand challenge.

While touring this amenity, be sure to point out the number of computers available to the residents, the software programs loaded and available on the computers, and the capabilities of the printers.

Additionally, don't forget to highlight any programs you may have in place, such as after school mentoring from 3:00 pm to 5:00 pm Monday through Thursday, or the ability to reserve the conference room for small meetings or introductory software training seminars you may offer to your residents.

Like all other amenities, keep lights on, computers on, and printers loaded with paper so upon touring the amenity looks active.

Fitness Center
The fitness center is consistently the most requested amenity in the multifamily housing industry. Oddly enough, experience would suggest that probably less than 25% of the renters originally intending to utilize the facility actually use it upon becoming a resident.

Demonstrating this amenity can be a little tricky if not well maintained. Fitness centers often have rubber flooring and mats that, unfortunately, fill the room with an unappealing odor. Add the sweat from daily workouts, and you can have an aroma disaster on your hands. Therefore, in preparation for the tour, be sure that automatic time released deodorizers are in place, filled and in working order. Citrus based deodorizers tend to be most effective in neutralizing these odors.

Again, this amenity must appear active even if not presently in use, so be sure the lights, music and televisions are turned on and left on throughout business hours.

Knowledge of the fitness equipment is beneficial. Do a little research regarding the brand of fitness equipment your center contains, where it is manufactured and what makes it special. Sharing this trivia could put you far ahead of your competitors if touring a fitness savvy prospective. Fitness equipment is typically divided into three simple categories; strength (i.e. free weights), endurance (i.e. treadmill) and fitness (i.e. ab machine.) Because treadmills, ellipticals and free weights are the most used, be sure to point out if you have multiples of any or all. Of course, if your community offers other gym amenities, such as towels, disinfectant cloths or filtered water, be sure to include those items in your features to point out, as well.

With today's focus on healthy eating and regimented exercise, many communities utilize their fitness centers to offer classes regarding nutrition and health. Often nutritionists or trainers can be found in your resident base, or with a little outreach, can be identified in your neighborhood. By arranging these quarterly information seminars, you have one more thing to promote while touring.

I once was on a tour where the consultant hopped on the treadmill in her high heel shoes and demonstrated the equipment incline while telling me about the quality of the equipment. I am not for sure I would recommend this, but, I will never forget that tour. She certainly set her community and herself apart from all of the other tours I did that day. She later joked that if I could do 500 chin ups, she would give me my first month free. Luckily, she never gave me the opportunity to desperately fail at that challenge. Instead, she quickly moved us along.

Locker Room
Much like the fitness center, the locker room, too, needs constant aroma management. The automatic time released citrus deodorizers here are critical.

Often it is left up to the prospective resident of the opposite sex to do a self-guided tour of the locker room. Therefore, it is important that you draw their attention in advance to key features you want them to notice in your absence. So before you turn them loose, be sure to let them know what they are looking for such as; private shower stalls, dry sauna, toiletry shelves and outlets by every mirror, shower soap and shampoo dispensers, etc.

Party Room
This amenity if promoted correctly can be a great selling point for potential renters as well as an awesome source of ancillary income. A party room is typically a somewhat generic room with tables, chairs, televisions and possibly a kitchenette that the residents can rent for special occasions (such as birthday parties, bridal showers, graduation parties, etc.)

Since the room is typically generic, offering the host the opportunity to hang themed decorations, it is not always the most exciting room to tour. One of the ways to spice up the tour is to have a PowerPoint slide show of past party pictures looping on the television. If there is no television, then an iPad presentation or old school photo album of pictures will suffice. This gives the prospective resident some insight as to how the room can be set up, how great it can look, as well as introduce them to the entertaining opportunities the facility could provide.

An interesting way to introduce this room might be to ask the question, "Does anyone have an upcoming birthday or anniversary?" Hopefully, they will answer "Yes" and then you can show them the perfect place to have the perfect celebration!

Now that we have covered the industry's most popular amenities typically found in the clubhouse, let's move to the apartment home itself.

There are two types of apartment home setups that we provide tours of, the first being a fully furnished model apartment home, and the second being a vacant made ready apartment home. The model provides an opportunity for the customer to see how standard sized furniture fits within the space while the vacant allows them to imagine how their furniture will fit in the space. As you may remember, at the beginning of this chapter we discussed the importance of finding out information regarding the furnishings the customer owns. This knowledge will ultimately allow you to assist them in imaging an arrangement in the vacant apartment home. But for now, let's start with some key demonstration points that you should apply while showing either.

Just like the amenities, each morning your model and targeted vacant made ready apartments should be inspected for presentation readiness. Everything in the model should be turned on. Motion-activated sensors that turn everything on upon opening the door is a fabulous time and energy saver.. Great attention to detail truly pays off when presenting these apartments, especially in the vacant made ready apartment homes. Below are five quick steps to implement each morning to insure demonstration worthiness.

Step 1
Check all lighting to insure that no light bulbs have burned out, inclusive of closet lighting and appliance lighting.

Step 2
Turn on all faucets for a few seconds to remove any air that has built up in the water lines and to remove any initial rust that may be expelled from the faucets.

Step 3
Flush all toilets and put all toilet seats and lids down.

Step 4
Check to make sure all blinds are consistently opened and angled evenly throughout the entire apartment home, allowing maximum light to filter into the rooms.

Step 5
Do a quick inspection of each room and closet as well as outdoor living space and storage areas to make sure everywhere is free from any debris that may have blown or been tracked in, inclusive of expired insects. This step should also include a quick check of overall cleanliness, such as finger printed windows or mirrors, water spotted sinks or faucets, etc.

Now that we have inspected the apartment home or model for demonstration worthiness and are comfortable that it passed the test, let's discuss how to transition from the clubhouse to the apartment home with the prospective residents.

If walking to the apartment home, attempt to walk beside the future residents, not in front of them. This allows for a more comfortable conversation that puts them at ease. If the width of sidewalk or hallway does not accommodate, be sure to pause and face them intermittently, or perfect the skill of carefully and slowly walking backwards for very brief moments. If in a golf cart, be sure to take your time, allowing for the ability to have eye contact with each person on the tour. That may mean that you have to briefly stop the cart in order to ask or discuss something with anyone riding on the back. This brief stop makes them feel important and included.

While we have not discussed demonstrating exterior amenities yet, your tour path may offer the perfect opportunity to highlight some of these amenities. Definitely take advantage of that logical path to prevent having to circle back.

Upon arrival to the building, take time to point out exterior architectural features. Those features may include items such as;

terra cotta barrel tile roofs, decorative window mulleins, accent shutters, ornate lighting fixtures, unique balcony railing, etc. After introducing those features, ask the question, "So what do you think so far?" You want to take their "buying temperature" throughout the tour. While you do want to get honest answers from them, you also ultimately want to promote positive responses as often as possible. Therefore should you get a negative response, you need to be prepared to handle the objection in order to turn it into a positive outcome. One of the most important parts of conducting a demonstration is to get the client to say that they like things as many times as possible. The more times they say it, the better your chances are that they will fill out an application, put down a deposit, and call your community home.

Next, we verbally move them in, acting as though they have already become residents, by asking the question, "Are you ready to see YOUR new apartment home?" It is critical during the demonstration process that they consistently hear us refer to the community, apartment and amenities as being theirs. It promotes them to actively consider the community as their future place of residence. Comments like; check out your resort style swimming pool, step onto your balcony and take in your view, look at the size of your new walk-in closet, etc., is an important demonstration tool that will increase your closing ratio success.

Guessing that 99.9% of the prospective residents we tour are respectable trust-worthy human beings, it is always important to keep your personal safety in mind. Prior to stepping into the apartment home, you need to perfect a physical demonstration technique that puts you between the client and the door at all times, with you being closest to the door. Some communities install door stops at the base of the doors that can be flipped down with your foot, so the door remains open during the tour. Others suggest carrying compact rubber door stops. If this is the case, prior to placing the door stop under the door, invite the client to move forward and explore the kitchen without you. This gives you the opportunity to monitor their position, comfortably bend down to place the stop in position, and then join them in the kitchen to point out key features and benefits.

Prior to moving onto specific tips for showing vacant make readies or models, let's discuss the overall objective that you want to achieve while doing the physical apartment tour. SET YOURSELF APART FROM YOUR COMPETITORS. The goal is clear and simple: if you have the same tour style, if you highlight the same apartment features, and if you use the same vocabulary as your competitors, then you become oatmeal - plain, boring and beige. Therefore, to conduct a "Rock Star" tour that is sure to close the deal, you need to know and experience your competitors personally.

Over the years, competitive market surveys have become automated and easily accessed without having to visit a competitor's community. I believe this to be a sales tragedy! There is no way you can compete as effectively with your sales approach by looking at a report, versus having experienced the product personally. If you are a closeted spy, then shop the competitor as a potential renter. By doing this, you get to truly experience the full demonstration and sales experience that you are competing against. However, if you don't have the secret squirrel personality trait, then be upfront and honest with them. Let them know who you are and what you want, and reciprocate by inviting them to view your community. Whichever the approach, you need to make a commitment to gain first-hand knowledge of what you are competing against, both the product and personalities. A written inventory of amenities and pricing will never allow you to become a stellar demonstrator of your community.

I was a Leasing Director for a huge community that was 34 years old. The community had historically been quite successful, until a brand new community was built nearby that was offering rent equal to ours. I shopped the community on the weekend and was lucky enough to get the "Leasing Consultant from Hell." The reason I say lucky was because there was no way I could compete with the new product, but my staff could definitely compete with the customer service experience the competitor was providing. The next week we redirected and started focusing on giving the greatest customer focused tours known to mankind.

Additionally during our meetings we would inquire if the prospect was visiting any other communities. If they stated our new competitor, we would offer to set up an appointment – of course with you know who! It was amazing to see how quickly we turned our challenge around and fully succeeded at holding our own. This experience truly made me realize that while the product is important, the customer service and personality of the demonstrator is pivotal in regard to the decision of the prospective resident.

Take the time to view a competitor's product and get to know their sales team! By doing so, you will be able to more effectively provide your prospective resident with a more unique and memorable demonstration approach, inclusive of pointing out nuances and differences of your community versus communities they have toured or are planning on touring.

So we are now at the front door of your potential bonus or commission, and it is time to show them what you've got! Of course, you are confident that the key easily works in the lock since you used it this morning when pre-checking the apartment for tour worthiness. So you put the key in the lock, ask them one more time if they are ready, therefore, building anticipation, open the door and say, "Welcome to your new apartment home!"

Having invited them to step inside, you are most likely standing in the foyer that leads to a main living space, or the main living space itself. There is a huge mistake that both novice and experienced Leasing Specialists continue to make, and that is announcing the rooms upon entry. I would suggest that 75% of the tours I have taken, upon entering the living room, the Leasing Specialist has said, "This is your living room." Really? Do you think that I am that stupid? Are you worried I might put my bed or dining room table in here? Announcing the rooms is merely stating the obvious, an unmemorable waste of breath lacking commission or bonus driven creativity.

If you did your job well initially, having gathered pertinent information about their furniture, you could introduce the living room in a far more creative and memorable way, a way that motivates them to think about their personal items in this specific room. Realtors often say, "If you get them to decorate, you can get them to move in!" Same applies to rentals. Instead of announcing the rooms, start by asking them to picture a piece of their furniture in a specific location within the room. "Picture your sage green sofa placed upon this beautiful mocha ceramic flooring, with the chaise near the glass sliding doors, so while stretched out relaxing you have a beautiful view of the lake. Also notice, the adjacent cable-ready wall provides more than ample space for an entertainment center to accommodate your 72 inch flat screen television. Where would you picture putting your club chair?"

This conversational give-and-take during the tour makes the demonstration process more interactive and productive. Additionally, it sets you apart from your competitors; you are most likely the only one who invested the time to understand their space requirements.

Throughout the next few pages, we are going to discuss how to tour standard rooms within an apartment home while sharing what tools to come prepared with, what features to point out, what specific information to introduce and measurement facts you should know in order to provide a stellar tour. Much focus will be placed upon pointing out important features, especially convenience features, which prospects do not notice during tours. Additionally, I will share creative marketing ideas I have seen that have insured memorable tours to prospective residents and proven to have increased Leasing Specialist closing ratios.

Living Room

Let's start with the measurement facts one needs to be equipped with. A standard sofa is 8'w x 3'd, a standard club chair is 3'w x 3'd, a standard end table is 2'w x 2'd, a standard entertainment center is 5'w x 2'd and a standard cocktail table is 4'w x 2'd. Therefore, a living room would need a wall approximately 12' long in order to accommodate a sofa and two cocktail tables. Hopefully your living room walls meet those requirements. If so, point it out. Typically, people place lamps on each end table. If you have electrical sockets on both ends of the wall near where the end tables would be placed, be sure to point out that convenience. Additionally, highlight the unobstructed wall above the sofa, free of sprinklers or smoke detectors if applicable, great for hanging oversized artwork. Next, draw their attention to the other wall that will easily accommodate a standard sized entertainment center plus a club chair. Point out the cable connection and outlet location that provides for easy electronics set up. Point out the additional outlet that would be perfect for a floor lamp by the club chair. Move on to important features like ceramic/porcelain/marble flooring, crown molding, vaulted ceilings, decorative lighting and all other upgraded features. End by pointing out standard features that you and your competitors share, such as climate control ceiling fans and window blinds. While in the living room, be sure to discuss space usage. For instance, if the living room is open to the dining and kitchen area, be sure to discuss how it is nice for entertaining, since all of the guests can easily communicate with the host while he or she is busy in the kitchen.

My favorite creative demonstration marketing idea that I have seen in a living room model was a "Did You Know" looping PowerPoint on the television. Each slide had the heading "Did You Know?" and a picture of what the slide referred to and the competitor comparison. For instance, the slide might have had a picture of their floor plan and said, "Did You Know…our living rooms are 18 square feet larger than the average of our competitors?" "Did you know…we are one of the few communities that accept dogs over 35 pounds? "Did you know…we are one of the only two communities in the area that provide assigned parking?" This slide show offered the prospective resident an opportunity to receive important information, without causing the Leasing Specialist to sound like a pushy salesperson. The PowerPoint presentation also had other interesting facts, such as the combined years of experience of the community management team, the number of employees who chose to live onsite and some recent apartment association awards they had won.

Dining Room

The average rectangle dining table is 6'w x 4'd; standard round tables are 48" in diameter and dining chairs are 2'w x 2'd. Therefore, a dining area needs to be approximately 10' wide in order to comfortably accommodate standard tables and chairs, though slightly smaller will work. Typically there is not a great deal to point out in dining areas unless they are oversized and can accommodate a sideboard or china cabinet. When demonstrating the dining area, stick to outlet location, unobstructed walls for artwork, crown molding, vaulted ceilings, flooring and lighting. If open to the kitchen and living room, point out the entertaining benefit, as well as easy access between the kitchen and dining area.

One of my favorite creative demonstration marketing ideas I have seen in the dining area was a housewarming party set up. Each of the place settings had name cards at them, such as; "My Mom," "My Dad," "My Best Friend," and "Me." On top of the plate was a menu with the name "My Welcome Home Café." Like a real menu, it was divided into Appetizers, Entrees and Desserts, all relating to the rental process. Under appetizers, Tangy Tour Kabob's were complimentary while Ahi Application Rolls were $85. Under entrees, Mac & Move-In Fees were $1, Month and Pet Rent Panini was $25 a Month. Under dessert, the Customer Service Custard was complimentary as was the Package Acceptance Parfait. The drink list was never ending ranging from the 24 Hour Maintenance Magic Martini to the Courtesy Patrol Colada. I thought this was a very cool and non-threatening way to present pricing. It was hard to let the pricing impact you negatively because you were so caught up in the creativity.

Kitchen

The kitchen happens to be one of my favorite rooms to demonstrate. There are so many effective ways to creatively point out features in the kitchen that will help you to seal the deal. Let's first start with cabinets; all kitchens have them, they just all look a little different. Your challenge is to make your kitchen seem better, even if it is equal to your competitors. The first step is to know the facts about your kitchen. Know how many kitchen cabinet doors you have. Know how many total shelves those cabinets collectively contain. Know how many kitchen cabinet utility drawers you have. Know how many kitchen pantry shelves you have. Also, know the linear feet of counter top space.

Most Leasing Consultants enter the kitchen and say something on the order of, "This is your kitchen, and it comes equipped with all of the appliances you see here." Imagine being able to say, "I am sure you have already noticed that your kitchen boasts having 16 cabinets, giving you 44 shelves of storage. Not to mention, 3 utility drawers, a pantry with 6 shelves and over 12 linear feet of counter top space." Those statistics are impressive, and something the average client will not take notice of without your prompting. Statistics like that sprinkled among the statements drawing attention to the energy efficient appliances, granite counter tops, brushed nickel hardware and the garbage disposal will set you apart from your competitor. Many of you reading this will not consider implementing this strategy. The difference between you and those who do will be recognized by the dollars in your pocket versus the dollars that could have been in your pocket. Being successful at sales requires dedication and uniqueness. Let everyone teach you what they can, and then build on it making it uniquely yours. Do not let your goal be to only emulate others.

I have seen many kitchen demonstration ideas used during apartment tours, most standard such as having refreshments in the refrigerator or gifts in the cabinets. I do not want to discount those ideas; I think they are very important, and you should continue using them. If you are not using them, then you should institute them. The creative ideas I am suggesting should be used in addition to those previously identified.

I love kitchens that smell like kitchens without making the rest of the rooms smell like kitchens. A great way to accomplish this is by having coffee mugs filled with whole French Vanilla coffee beans, ground cinnamon and vanilla extract. Merely put the beans in a zip lock bag, add the cinnamon and vanilla shake them up, and pour the mixture into the mugs and display. As prospective residents enter the kitchen and walk past the display mugs, they will notice the aroma. This is better than a commercial plug-in or automated dispenser that is designed to allow the aroma to travel throughout the apartment home.

One of my other favorites may seem old school or too crafty, especially for a Class A community. But believe me, it works everywhere, and prospective residents love it. Obtain an egg carton in good display shape, preferably a cardboard one. Go to your local craft store and buy a dozen white plastic eggs, and miniature items such as eyes, hair, jewelry, etc., which you can use to turn your eggs into egg people, somewhat like Mr. Potato Head. You will display the carton opened, and in the lid you will have the title, "A Dozen Reasons To Live At _____ Apartment Homes." Each egg person will then have a speech bubble glued to them, expressing one of the top 12 reasons to live at your community. You can include items such as the fact you provide emergency maintenance 24/7 - or that you had a 92% renewal rate in 2013. You could announce a specific apartment association award your community won.

Alternatively, you could present that you have the largest floor plans among all of your competitors. My experience has been whether, in a Class "A" metropolitan loft development or a rural "C" level community; prospective residents love the commentary surprise. When invited to get a beverage from the refrigerator, they run across the egg people and cannot help but read 12 more reasons why they should call your community home. Who knew a refrigerator could be so entertaining and informative?

During an apartment community takeover in San Francisco, we began using magnetic refrigerator picture frame. I could have never anticipated how popular they would become, to the point of my employees asking to have them customized for children and pets. The frame was produced with the community name; logo and telephone number printed on it with the tagline, "Our First Picture at Our New Apartment Community."

While on tour, our Leasing Specialists would pay special attention to identify the moment when their clients got excited about something. They would whip out their cell phone, tell them to pose in front of the amenity, and would take their picture. When they returned to the office, they would print out the picture, put it in a magnetic frame and hand it to the prospective resident. Soon after the program was instituted, maintenance technicians began to report back that they had seen the pictures and frames posted on refrigerators. The program began to snowball; we had frames made for cats, for dogs and kids. Soon our resident refrigerators were covered with community branded magnet frames.

Bedrooms

Measurement facts we need to be equipped with to effectively demonstrate a bedroom are; a queen size bed is 5'w x 7'd, a king size bed is 7'w x 7'd, nightstands are 2'w x 2'd and a standard dresser is 6'w x 2'd. Therefore, to accommodate a queen size bed and two nightstands you would need a wall approximately 10' long and for a king, 12' long. Much like the living room and dining room, you will want to point out important features that may go unnoticed. For instance, if the logical bed wall has outlets on both ends, you would want to point out how convenient that is for nightstand lamps. If the opposite wall has cable connection, you will want to point out how perfect that is for the bedroom television. Of course, you would also want to point out key features like crown molding, vaulted ceilings, climate control ceiling fans, decorative six panel doors, brushed nickel hardware and any other outstanding features that might go unnoticed.

One of the most effective marketing features, I've seen for a master bedroom was a television that had a relaxation DVD playing. The scenes changed from crashing ocean waves to a crackling fire, a rushing mountain river to woods full of chirping birds. Upon entering the room, you immediately felt relaxed. One side of the bed was carefully turned down with a flower and chocolate on the pillow. It truly invited you to crawl in, relax and enjoy your new home.

My favorite demonstration marketing feature for a kid's room was a giant 12 piece 3' x 4' floor puzzle of the Tot Lot (see puzzle link in the resource section.) The Leasing Specialists would let the children know that if they put the puzzle together; the Tot Lot would be the next stop on the tour. This gave the kids a chance to have fun and the adults a chance to talk.

<u>Bathrooms</u>
Much like the kitchen, it is important for you to know statistics about your bathroom. Most bathrooms come with cabinetry beneath the sink. Some of the cabinetry is designed with drawers and some not. If your cabinetry has drawers, be sure to point out that feature, especially if it sets you apart from most of your competition. The next most important item in the bathroom is the medicine cabinet. Know how many shelves are in your cabinet, if they are adjustable, and if they can accommodate family size or taller items such as mouth wash or shaving cream. Next on the list be sure to draw attention to towel bars in the shower or on the wall, as well as towel hooks on backs of doors. Finally, point out upgraded features such as rainfall shower heads, curved shower rods, exhaust fans, ceramic tub surrounds, heat lamps or other notable features.

My absolute favorite demonstration marketing feature for any room ever was one created for the bathroom by a maintenance technician. This young man decided that it would be fun for prospective residents to see real bubbles in the bathroom. Initially, he purchased a battery operated bubble gun from the children's toy department. He attached the bubble gun to the wall. Then he ran a string along the wall and attached it to the door. When the door opened, it constricted the trigger and from behind the shower curtain came real bubbles. Let's just say it was a HUGE HIT with the prospective residents. In fact, it was so popular; they later invested in a bubble machine that they connected to a motion sensor.

Closets
Storage is always a huge consideration for prospective residents when choosing an apartment home. Not only do they need storage for clothes, but also for boxed items such as holiday decorations or life's memorabilia. Therefore, demonstrating and explaining the closet is more than just opening the door. Perhaps your closets have double racks so shirts can be hung on the top, and pants on the bottom or possibly your closets have cubby organizers or additional shelving. Whatever the features, be sure to point them out. If possible, calculate the number of hangers the closet can comfortably accommodate and share that statistic. Another impressive statistic is cubic square footage of closet or storage space. For instance, if a closet is 5'w x 3'd x 8'h the calculation would be (5 x 3) x 8 = 120 cubic square feet. Imagine if you added all of the closets together, you very easily could suggest there is over 500 cubic square feet of closet space. That is an impressive number that will definitely set you apart from your competitor.

I've seen some really creative marketing demonstration items for master bedroom walk-in closets! Among the most memorable were designed to show how big the walk-in closets were. One had a life size decal of the front of a Ford Mustang; that's right; the closet was wider than a car. A second one had a Twister game mat on the floor. The closet was big enough to play a game of Twister. The final one had hangers in every slot, each hanger with a number, and the last one with an oversized number showing 237!

Once, I was on a tour with an experienced new hire. I was shadowing her to observe her tour style to see if I could offer any tips. We were touring a family with two children, approximate ages 7 and 12. She asked the young one to help her demonstrate the walk-in closet by standing in the middle, having her stretch out her arms, spin around and see if she could touch adjacent walls at the same time. Then she challenged the older one to do the same. She ended by asking one of the parents to try and quickly proved that the closets were so big; not even an adult could touch both walls at the same time. When the closet demonstration ended, everyone was laughing; who knew closet demonstrations could be such a positive tone setter.

Patio/Balcony
Outdoor living space is quickly growing to be a requirement for many renters. They want to have that semi-private outdoor space to enjoy a morning cup of coffee or that evening nightcap. Many buildings, today, are being designed with multiple outdoor living spaces for both living room and master bedroom. Know the overall size of the outdoor living space and what furniture it can accommodate. Can it hold the standard round patio table with 4 chairs? Can it accommodate the patio love seat with 2 club chairs? These are questions you need to be able to answer.

When demonstrating the patio/outside area, do not do it from inside the glass doors. Weather permitting; be sure to invite the prospective residents out onto the space to have the full experience. Point out key features such as electrical outlets in case they would like to have a water fountain or plug in holiday decorations. Point out porch lighting, upgraded railing, privacy walls, landscaped views or access to private storage.

My favorite marketing demonstration technique for outdoor spaces are motion activated chirping birds (see bird link in the resource section.) By placing the birds in a potted tree at the door, clients stepping onto the patio or balcony are immediately presented with the sounds of nature. If electricity is available on the patio or balcony, the sound of running water from a fountain is another great source to add to nature's sounds.

Storage

Apartment living offers an awesome carefree lifestyle for many. They don't have to worry about maintenance, lawn care, property taxes and other demands of home ownership. However, with apartment living sometimes come minor sacrifices such as storage space. While a homeowner typically has basement, garage or attic storage, often renters have to become experts at compact living. Additional storage opportunities, even if they come at an additional cost, are important amenities to point out. Leasing Specialists often skip presenting storage opportunities because they are not visually attractive to demonstrate. Be sure not to make this mistake! The prospective resident does not expect them to be beautiful; they are definitely focused on function over form. Take the time to tour the storage space and provide basic facts such as cubic square footage and additional charges.

To demonstrate the size of a storage space, place empty standard sized Rubbermaid storage tubs sitting in the unit creatively labeled; "Your Holiday Decorations," "Your Childhood Memories," "Your Keepsakes," etc.

Some communities also offer designated areas for bike storage. With today's focus on health and wellness, many of your residents will come with bikes in tow. So, be sure to point out community storage features if applicable.

Now that we have covered most of what an apartment home can offer, let's move into exterior amenities that the community may have to offer. When presenting exterior amenities, be sure to attach a benefit to the feature. For instance, does the amenity benefit them by saving them money or time? Does it offer them entertainment options or a chance to make new friends? Most Leasing Professionals merely introduce their clients to the feature or amenity without ever discussing how they could benefit them. Over the next few pages, we will discuss how to tour exterior amenities and provide ideas of how to introduce their benefits.

Swimming Pool
As a fitness center is the most requested indoor amenity, the swimming pool is the most requested outdoor amenity. In most cases, this amenity is typically a show piece, easily seen from the clubhouse interior. In preparation for a tour, it is imperative that all of the furnishings be fully organized. Weather permitting, the first thing in the morning and throughout the day, all the chairs should be placed at the same angle, backs at the same height, and umbrellas up adding a pop of color to the pool deck.

When touring the pool, discuss the benefits that the pool can bring to your client. If they are health conscious, suggest it as a great supplement to an exercise program. If they are workaholics, suggest it as a relaxing escape. If they are a parent, suggest it as a child entertainment venue. If they are new to the area, suggest it as a mix and mingle opportunity.

While near the pool, be sure to present past community activities that have taken place poolside, such as resident parties, scuba lessons, wine tasting events, etc. Present the pool as one of the top utilized amenities that consistently offers a social avenue for residents.

Try to avoid the overused old school description of a "Sparkling Pool." Refer to it as a resort style pool. Be sure to point out features that the pool and deck may offer, such as; a wading feature, a pool cabana, an interesting shape, decorative tile or possibly vending machines.

As a side note, be very careful while touring the pool area. I've heard many horror stories of Leasing Specialists and prospective residents falling into the pool while demonstrating the area. So be alert, monitor both you and your clients positioning in relation to the pool's edge.

Sand Volleyball Court
Sand volleyball courts may be both regional and seasonal in many cases, but a multitude of them exists in communities throughout the United States. For these to remain a viable amenity to point out, they must be well maintained. They need to be well framed, contain a healthy amount of sand, and have a net in good repair.

This amenity is not that exciting to view, so you must be equipped to discuss active programs such as volleyball leagues. A popular sand volleyball activity is glow-in-the-dark volleyball. Black lights are set up at the two ends of the nets and the four corners of the court. Glow in the dark face paint is provided to competitors and those accompanying them to cheer them on to victory. I lived at a community years ago that did this every Friday evening during the summer months. It was a packed house every Friday.

Outdoor Theater
Growing in popularity is the outdoor theater craze. This consists of a blow-up screen, typically poolside since seating already exists, and a projector, (see theatre link in the resource section.)This can be a hard amenity to demonstrate since it is set up only at the time of the event. However, letting clients know of its existence, possibly showing them pictures of the event in action and sharing what type of movies are shown can get the prospect excited about yet another resident activity. Be prepared to present the Monday Mysteries, Tuesday Tangos, Wednesday Weddings, Thursday Thrillers and Friday Fright Nights outdoor theater schedule, a schedule your competitor most likely does not have.

Let them know how this event can save them the hassle of going to the theater, save them the money of the tickets, allow them to meet new friends, and do it all in the comfort of their own community.

Playground
The playground is by far one of the most fun amenities to tour, especially if your clients have children with them. Many communities have an elaborate all-in-one playground, home to multiple slides, swings, bridges, rock climbing walls, spinners and much more. If children are on the tour, be sure to plan an extra five or ten minutes to allow them to explore and play. Often parents or guardians are worried about uprooting their children. If they see the children are excited about the pool, the playground, their new room and other amenities, it helps the adults to make a decision. Therefore, never underestimate the persuasive power of the playground!

At the initial consultation, you asked how many occupants would be living in the apartment. It may be obvious that you have two adults and no children. Don't let this be an excuse not to show the playground. Ask the prospect if they have nieces, nephews or friend's children that might visit? If they say, "Yes," be sure to include the playground in the tour as a convenient amenity to entertain the children while the adults talk.

I know one Leasing Specialist that very successfully demonstrates the playground, oddly enough in advance of the tour. This young lady is very diligent in getting the children's names during the phone consultation along with the caller's email address. She then uses her iPhone and goes to the playground, shoots a short video at the playground of her going down the slide, spinning on the spinner and hanging upside down on the monkey bars – all while personally using their names and inviting them to come visit. The day of the appointment the kids cannot wait to meet the most fun Leasing Consultant ever and have the opportunity to visit the playground.

Pet Park
Many prospective residents are searching for pet friendly communities, and many of those residents are dog owners. Having an area designated and fenced off as a pet park is a huge amenity

for those owners. They want to have the opportunity to let their dogs off the leash to run and get exercise.

No matter how simple or elaborate this area is if you have a dog owner on tour, be sure to include a glimpse of the pet park, sometimes referred to as the "Bark Park." If your park consists of more than just a fenced in area, be sure to take them in and point out the cool features, such as; the wading pool, dog wash station, the rope tugs, the park benches and whatever else may exist.

While I do not recommend offering pet sitting services because of liability issues, if you do have holiday kennels nearby or residents at the community who offer those services, be sure to let them know of those conveniences.

Picnic Grill Areas
Everyone loves outdoor living space. Yet sometimes an apartment balcony or patio is not quite large enough to accommodate a larger group of people nor do most communities want residents grilling on those areas. Community cabanas or pavilions equipped with grill stations near the pool or on the community grounds have become sought after amenities that are highly used by residents.

Much like the interior amenity of a party room; be sure to be prepared to creatively describe these areas during use for a birthday party, sporting event or family reunion. Point out any features the picnic area has, such as; running water, electricity, multiple grills, multiple tables, etc. Again, this is a great amenity to have pictures of, while decorated and in use.

Services
Communities throughout the nation have begun to cater to their resident's busy and active lifestyles by offering convenience services. These services may include; scanning, faxing, copying, package acceptance, plant care, etc. Be sure to mention the convenience services that your community may offer at some point during the tour.

Guest Suite

Having a guest suite to offer your renters is a huge and somewhat rare amenity that can truly help you close the deal. Having guests stay at your home either as a renter or a homeowner can be somewhat stressful. Therefore, being able to offer guests their own separate space or apartment home during their stay is phenomenal. If you have a furnished guest suite, be sure to inform them of this rare amenity. If it is not being used at time of the tour, include it in your tour route. Otherwise, let them know of the size, furnishings inventory, and cost of use.

Because this is an expensive amenity to offer, it must be highly utilized in order to produce enough ancillary income to exceed the vacant rent loss. Promoting it to your prospective resident, and existing residents is important. I know many communities that promote one night use of the guest suite to local vineyards for wine tasting parties, restaurants for tasting events and home product sellers for product parties such as candles. They are allowed to place invitations under doors inviting your residents to attend their events, thereby generating new business while providing your community with ancillary income.

Let's begin to summarize some of the important items that hopefully you have learned while reading this chapter.

First and most important, is that you set yourself apart from your competitor. You must know how your competitors conduct tours, but it is equally important that you not emulate their style and most likely limited content. You want to create your own memorable style and your own memorable content. When the tour is complete, you want your client to be amazed at how unique, professional and informative your tour was in comparison to other tours they may have taken.

Second, don't announce the rooms. Your customer is bright enough to know which rooms are used for what. Take these room-by-room tour moments to point out features they might miss, such as; electrical outlets, television cable hookups, ceiling lighting, decorative window mulleins, cubic square footage, etc.

Third, be sure to stage amenities to be active, even when not in use. Have part of your morning business opening routine to include turning on televisions, playing movies, turning on music, turning on lights, etc.

Fourth, provide the tour participants the opportunity to experience the amenity. Sit at the pool cabana for a few minutes to discuss pet policy. Stop at the playground and let the children play while reviewing the deposit structure with the adults. Step onto the balcony and stand at the railing enjoying the view while discussing scheduled resident activities. It is imperative that they not only see the community but that they experience and feel the lifestyle you are offering.

Finally, have fun! A tour should not be a monotonous experience driven by a checklist of items to review and present. Build humor into the tour, not only by sharing your own personal, humorous style, but also by the use of marketing items placed in closets, refrigerators, cabinets and other key locations.

The demonstration is the final step to closing the deal. This is your moment to shine or to fizzle. Be prepared, know your client, and make them feel special by customizing the tour. Use their name, their children's names, their pet's name and any other personal information you gathered during your prior phone or in person communications.

Most importantly, assume the deal! You are awesome, and your product is awesome! Who in their right mind wouldn't want to live at your community? When the tour is over, it should be carefully staged to end at the point where applications can be comfortably completed. That may be in the quiet comfort of the model, at the Leasing Specialist's desk, the Internet Café or elsewhere. They need to move; you have an apartment they have expressed a liking, it is time to move them in to your community!

So WELCOME THEM HOME!

Resources

http://www.4americanrecreation.com/images/kingsley.jpg

www.89billiardz.com

http://tinseltown-candles.highwire.com/

www.PortraitPuzzles.com

http://shop.nationalgeographic.com/ngs/product/home-d%C3%A9cor/home-accents/motion-activated-singing-birds

http://www.target.com/p/inflatable-home-theater-system-16-x9/-/A-13079826#prodSlot=medium_1_11

Chapter 9
Overcoming Objections: Master This And Close More Sales!

By Mindy Williams

Leasing any apartment means you're going to have to overcome the objections of your potential new resident. This can become a powerful sales ally if you know how to do it the right way. One of the most important things to remember is objections are buying signals, showing you the prospect IS interested enough and is thinking of things that won't work. That means they've imagined themselves living in the apartment, and there is a good chance it will work for them if not for the objection(s).

Moving past the objections of your prospect starts by having confidence in yourself and your product, and having the skills to ask the right questions. What you're looking for is the root of their objection. If they say the bedroom is too small, try to figure out what is it too small for? And, is there a way to make it work?

Overcoming objections is quite simply the biggest challenge for any leasing consultant. Even the newest luxury community can pose uncertainty to the average prospect. Each customer has specific needs and wants they have defined during their apartment search. While there may not be a perfect community, the presentation by the leasing consultant can seal the deal with the right sales presentation.

You probably know that the average leasing consultant is taught to close a minimum of three times during each tour. Did you know a person needs to hear a marketing message at least seven times before being ready to buy? So, work more closing statements and thoughts into your presentation (there are 25 tried and true closing techniques at the end of this chapter.) Closing more than three times (the average), in a conversational manner, gives you a competitive edge. In this instance I mean that a "close" can be an agreeing thought, "Yes, I like the sunlight in this kitchen too."

In "Never Eat Alone" by Keith Ferrazzi, I learned that 95% of sales are made on the 5th attempt or later. Read on for ideas on how to hone your sales skills and how to incorporate more "attempts" into your presentation. The key to a higher sales ratio is persistence, product knowledge, and confidence in overcoming common objections. The strategies here will help you do just that. Remember that the most important part of overcoming objections is preparation in knowing your competitors, knowing your product, and knowing your customers. Understanding common objections and knowing how to respond prior to the objection happening is highly important. Waiting to figure out a way to overcome an objection until the tour itself, may result in a lost sale. By the end of the chapter, you'll be prepared for pretty much anything you'll encounter so you will not have to do much overcoming on the fly.

I wrote this chapter in "bites" so you can absorb and master each section before moving on to the next one. While answering the questions, make sure your answers are in alignment with what you truly believe. A big part of selling is being true to yourself if you can wholeheartedly stand behind what you are saying about your product to your potential customer you'll close more sales.

Seven Tips on How to Overcome the Competition

Here are some steps to help you blow past the competition:

1. Evaluate the marketplace. Know your strengths and weaknesses, as well as your competition.

2. How can you differentiate yourself and your product? How are YOU better? List two here:
3. If you aren't better, become better. Develop a merchant program where local businesses give your residents discounts. Invite a nail

technician to your fitness center, clubhouse, office or vacant apartment. Make sure your internet is the fastest possible speed and is accessible over as much of the community as possible. Expand your service hours. Do whatever it takes.

4. Ask residents and prospects what they want. Our office at Rent and Retain gets many calls asking us what to give to prospects and residents as leasing and renewal incentives. The truth is; we don't know! Residents in Arizona may want water misters on their patios while in Minnesota that's a ridiculous giveaway. Ask, ask, ask your prospects and residents what they want as move-in incentives, move-in gifts and renewal gifts.

5. Continue to thank them! If your residents think you're taking their business for granted, and they can get a better deal elsewhere, they will be history.

6. Get better at your job. Learn more. Do more. Research more. Read more. This only helps you become more valuable. There are many free ideas out there for property management professionals. The All Stars Facebook page (Facebook.com/ApartmentAllStars) is a perfect example. Rent & Retain's website (www.RentandRetain.com) and Facebook page (Facebook.com/RentandRetain) also have free posts weekly on how to increase your occupancy and make your life better.

7. The best advice: Nothing changes if nothing changes. Get out there and find out what needs to be done. This will help you in job security, higher occupancy and hopefully an easier workday.

Five Skills of A Great Salesperson

1. Learn to uncover the real objection. When a prospect says, "I'm going to keep looking," figure out if that's really what he/she is doing. The same principle applies to other objections too. Look at his/her body language (more on that at the end of this chapter), listen to what the prospect is saying, and think of another avenue of

attack. When a prospect says, NO, s/he isn't rejecting you. There is a roadblock there that you need to get around. Listen to what the prospect is saying, drill it down to specific things, then go full speed ahead to find out how they can be minimized.

2. Determine if it is the presentation or something with the apartment. After hearing an objection, if it doesn't sound quite right, try asking, "Was it something I said?" Or, "Did I miss something?" If it was the presentation vs. the apartment, regroup and reconnect.
Once you know what the objection is, or if you could have done something differently, you can do something about it!

3. A great salesperson also needs to know this: What makes you happy? After a frustrating day of doing your best, with sometimes less than stellar results, you need to make yourself feel better. How can you help erase some of the day's frustration? I like to listen to motivational CDs in my car on the way home. What works for others is to take a bubble bath, take a five-minute vacation and imagine yourself on a tropical island, listen to calming music! Taking a slow, deep breath five times in a row can lower your stress level in under a minute. Find pleasant, inexpensive things to make you happy. If you have quick ways to pick yourself up, you'll be stronger mentally. This will help get you back in the game faster.

4. Address obvious objections head-on. Lisa Trosien had terrific success during her leasing career. Lisa mastered getting glaring objections out in the open immediately. The community, where Lisa worked, had a super small hall closet. She showed prospects how to maximize the space BEFORE it became an objection for the prospect. Saying something like, "At first glance this closet seems small. However, if you do X and Y and Z, you'll find you can maximize what is here."

If you have something that is really obvious and you frequently hear it as an objection, try bringing it out in the open early on. That could skip over the objection more quickly.

5. You're in good company. Sometimes you just won't make the sale, no matter how well you presented your material. That happens. Know that, across the country, there are thousands of sales people getting rejected at exactly the same time you are. Reevaluate and see what you could have done differently! Your next chance to do a great job is coming! Any minute now the phone will ring or a new prospect will come through the door. You can do it! Remember what you learned in training, apply some of the sales and service ideas you've learned and tell yourself that YOU ARE A WINNER!

Four Sales Tips To Help With Objections

1. Get permission to follow up. If the prospect does not give you permission to follow up, there is a reason. And, that reason could be their main objection to leasing.

It's okay to ask a prospect why they do not want you to follow-up. Be cautious and try not to use the word "why" as that tends to put people on the defensive.

Instead, if your prospect has an objection, ask for clarification. The more you know, the more you can help find something to suit their needs. Soften the "why" with a "hmmm" or "Just to make sure I understand, why..."

2. If you aren't sold (on the product/location, etc.), the feeling could be contagious.

To be successful, you must feel confident about what you are selling. If you don't, it's time to find out why -- then find a way TO feel confident about it.

When a prospect states an objection, be quiet for a few seconds. A pause will show the prospect that you heard and are processing his/her comment. Give an agreement statement like "I understand." Or, "I hear what you are saying." Or, "I see." Then, address the objection. "I understand what you mean. But what if we did _____ it would _____."

3. Be sincere! Remember people know when they are being "sold" something. The best salespeople develop a rapport with their future customers prior to trying to close the sale.

4. Make your prospect feel comfortable. People remember how you made them feel, but they will not necessarily remember what you said.

Leave them on a high note with a small item such as candy, a cake pop, a cookie, a mint, a promise of a goldfish (one community in Houston gave goldfish as move in gifts), a guarantee you'll hold the perfect apartment for them, whatever works for you (and them).

Close the Sale Right Now After Hearing, "I need to think about it."

"You don't close a sale; you open a relationship if you want to build a long-term, successful enterprise." -Patricia Fripp

Experts agree that if a salesperson lets the prospect "think about it" there is a 95% chance of losing that sale. So, if a prospect says they need time to think about it that means it is time to help them think about it NOW.

Ask:
- "What exactly do you need to think about?"
- "Is there something I could have shown you that I didn't?"
- "Are you unsure about the price?"
- "Is there something that makes you think this isn't the home for you?"

Remember, no one likes to be on the receiving end of an aggressive sales pitch. If the prospect still resists, ask for permission to follow up. Also, ask what the best method for following up is: email, phone call, Facebook, texting, etc.

Overcoming The Top Three Objections

In a poll on Rent & Retain's Facebook page (Facebook.com/RentandRetain), the three most common objections across the country are: price, storage, and "I need to think about it." Let's take a look at ideas to help overcome these top three objections!

1. Price

Whether you run daily specials or are utilizing a revenue management system, price is always a huge concern. So, how do you come back after your prospect says that the apartment is not within their budget?

- Estimate what your prospect pays in utilities. Whether you offer energy efficient appliances or if your community includes utilities like water, cable, or trash removal, there are savings to be noted.
- Determine what luxuries your prospect pays for outside of their housing expenses. For example, a gym membership could be cancelled in lieu of your community's fitness facility and pool. Or, your clubhouse may offer free wi-fi and a coffee bar to cut down on trips to Starbucks. If utilities or wireless internet are included, that's a big savings!. A prospect can save approximately $120 a month by not having to pay for cable TV and internet. If cable and internet are included in the rent, that will be a big plus for the prospect to live at your community.
- Create value. While many want to pay less for rent, they are generally willing to pay more if they feel they are getting a good deal. Talk about all the perks offered by your property such as the resident events, maintenance-free living,

upgraded anything (carpet, flooring, window treatments, microwave, drinks/towels at the pool, etc.) Phone charging stations are very popular. Do you need to offer a "charge" as a perk? Add extra outlets if you can, have a "charge" center in your leasing office for prospects and residents. Remember that charging stations and additional outlets are new services that people didn't need a few years ago. There was a recent poll on Facebook that asked where people charge their phones. The top two places people charge their phones are the kitchen and bedroom. If you can add a power strip under the kitchen counter or somewhere accessible, do it and use it as a selling tool!

2. Closet Size/Storage Space

How many times do we hear a prospect say that they have too many clothes or shoes? Or have a prospect ask about additional storage space? Below are some ideas that will help with maximizing storage space!

- In the model apartment, include space-saving devices in the bedrooms and closet areas. Adding built-ins to offer additional storage space in the closet is a selling feature. I just bought a built-in for our family room, and it looks so much neater and I have way more storage space. Not to mention, as a resident perk, the prospect will not need to purchase a bookcase or TV cabinet.
- Sell the space that is offered in the apartment home. If there is more cabinet space, showcase it. If there is outside storage, mention it. If there are open areas in the floor plan, suggest an armoire, enclosed bookcase, or other larger storage furniture. More times than not, there are other storage options in the apartment that the prospect did not consider.
- Negotiate a deal with a local storage facility to offer residents of your community exclusive savings on storage

rental with flexible leasing options. In return, you will offer free advertising for the storage facility via community newsletter and social media platforms.

3. <u>"You are first place I've looked." "I'll think about it." Or, "I need to speak with my spouse/roommate."</u>

All of the above are common responses heard when asking a prospect to commit to filling out an application and leaving a deposit.

- Explain carefully about supply and demand as it relates to your current pricing or specials. Offer to hold the apartment for 24 hours as a courtesy because you are confident s/he will be back.
- Ask the prospect where else they have looked or plan to visit. Know your market and competitors so you can have a good, solid conversation about your community as it compares to others. Make sure to highlight the benefits of your community instead of focusing on what others have that you do not. One of my favorite expressions is, "Blowing out someone else's candle doesn't make yours burn any brighter." Stay classy when pointing out what you have that others do not. Definitely mention the differences.
- People become connected to others as well as places. Make this a comfortable experience that will become a reality for their future. Give them the physical address of their new home and tell them about the lighting, landscaping and other features of that specific apartment. Don't forget to introduce them to all team members at the community including your maintenance team. Resident testimonials work well here, both on flyers and on your Facebook page. This creates a sense of community and belonging that is so important.

Overcoming Objections Cheat Sheet

People think about what you tell them to think about. For instance, think about a chocolate milkshake. So, what are you thinking about right now? Most likely it's a chocolate milk shake!
During your sales presentations, be careful of how you present ideas, especially as you overcome objections. If you say to a prospect, "We don't have enough parking for guests, but there is plenty on the street." Many prospects will not hear anything after the "but." So when you try to overcome the objection, phrase it something like this, "There is plenty of parking for your guests on the street."

In an effort to easily overcome objections, make a 'cheat sheet' of common objections listing ways to overcome each.

Write down the most common complaints and objections that are encountered at your community. Work as a team to brainstorm several ways to overcome each obstacle. Prepare questions for each objection that will help you seek out and search for the root of the issue and address the real needs of your customer. Be prepared to meet each objection head on, and remember to first validate the concern of your customer by communicating your understanding of their concern.

The best method for dispelling a person's objection is seeking out the exact root of their concern. What does that mean if they say the bedroom is too small? What is it too small for? Is there a way to make it work?

Your "cheat sheet" will come in handy day after day. The more you practice overcoming objections, the easier it will be for you.

Evaluate objections on a regular basis to ensure that you are up-to-date with the climate of the market. Objections can change with a changing market Here are some tips on making your cheat sheet:

- Listen to objections from current customers and make a list.
- Are the reasons behind the objection valid?
- Hone your listening skills for any and all new information you may gather.
- Respond to each objection clearly and sincerely. Be certain you overcome the prospects specific objection, even if that means asking more questions!
- Establish yourself as a valuable resource and apartment expert – not as a cheesy salesperson.

After you offer a resolution or solution to the objection, make sure the prospect feels good about it. Get a feel for if your suggestion works by saying, "What do you think, does that work?" "Does that sound okay?" Or, "Other residents have found X to be okay, do you agree?"

Make a list of the three most common complaints or concerns about your community:

1.

2.

3.

Write down as many reasons you can to overcome these three concerns! Narrow down your very best responses so you have an answer on hand ready to neutralize the three most common objections.

For example:

- "Is the closet really too small if you hang your winter coats in the hall closet?"
- "Your gym is 10 miles away? If you use our facility you'll save time and gas not to mention the cost of a gym membership!"

Objection #1 is
_____

Two questions to ask to see if it really is a valid objection:
a.
b.

Objection #2 is
_____

Two questions to ask to see if it really is a valid objection:
a.
b.

Objection #3 is
_____

Two questions to ask to see if it really is a valid objection:
a.
b.

When A Prospect Graces You With a Valid Objection

Objections are usually just scratching the surface of the real problem. You must ask questions to get to the root of the objection before you can come close to closing the sale.

Focus on the problem, not the symptoms. Simply asking, "Could you please explain that a bit more for me?" or "What exactly do you mean by X?" after hearing the objection could help you both uncover the root of the problem.

The basics never go out of style! That counts for dieting, choosing a spouse, deciding what to wear to your holiday party (stick with a classic outfit, no cleavage, please!) and the basics always work for selling! Follow what you've been taught, and you'll do fine.

Remember as a leasing consultant your goal is to help people find a great home. However, like anything, if you don't use it, you lose it. So practice good sales techniques every day.
It is also important to ask the right question after an objection or need is stated.

If your prospect says, "I need an apartment with lots of closet space," hopefully you can honestly say, "We have tons of closet space (or ways to maximize your closet space) here at Rent & Retain Apartments."

What if you don't have tons of closet space? Ask more questions to find out why the prospect needs lots of closet space: Ask a few fact-finding questions like:

- "Please tell me more about what you need the space for."
- "What types of things do you need the space for."
- "If I may ask, is it for storage or for everyday items?"

See how the questions really help dig a bit deeper so you can determine if it is a deal-breaker or something that can be tweaked to make it acceptable?

Get To The Root of the Objection

- Ask one question at a time to uncover more information.
- After you ask a question, be quiet. The story of what this apartment will become is theirs to tell, not yours. This helps uncover any uneasy feelings.

- After they have finished, remain quiet for 1-2 more seconds. Use this time to process what they've really said, and make sure that you're responding to their actual concern, not just what you're expecting them to say. Maintain eye contact so they know you are still engaged and present.
- Follow-up their answer with a related question.
- Remember that it takes about 7 seconds for someone to formulate and ask a question, so if there's silence, don't scare it away by talking through it. Let them think.
- If the room is too small to be both a spare bedroom and a home office, décor and design solutions might be just what the future resident needs so they can see the room in a different light. Pinterest can be a great source for ideas here, as can an IKEA catalogue. Pictures can speak volumes in these instances.
- Respond to each objection clearly and sincerely. And make sure you overcome their specific objection -- even if that means asking more questions.
- Establish yourself as a valuable resource -- not as a cheesy salesperson.

Great Follow-up Questions to Ask With Objections

- "What are you paying for rent now?"
- "Which communities are you comparing us to?"
- "I hear you saying you don't like X. What would you prefer in terms of X?"
- "If it weren't for _____, would you like the apartment?"
- "Could you please explain what you mean?"
- "Could you be more specific?"
- "How did you come to that conclusion?"
- "Hmmmm. What are you basing that on?"
- "I understand your concerns about _____. Have you considered _____?"

- "What would having a _____ do for you?"
- "I understand. What else?"
- "Could you give me an example?"
- "Why are you considering that?"
- "How would that work?"
- "I hear that you don't like X color. What colors do you prefer?"

<u>Crash Course In Body Language</u>

As a refresher, here are quick tips on how body language can help improve spotting when someone has an objection.

<u>Eye Contact</u>
In general, people will keep looking at something they like. So watch for which floor plan their eyes might linger on.

Most Americans are comfortable with eye contact that lasts about three seconds. When we are intent on listening, and we want to know more about what the person is saying, we tend to keep eye contact for longer than three seconds. So, if someone is really listening to you, they'll look you in the eye for longer. Longer eye contact means you are maintaining their interest. If they aren't giving you eye contact or signals they are listening, ask a question or do something to shake things up to get them involved in the conversation, this works for kids and husbands too!

<u>Body Position</u>
When people agree with you, they'll smile and nod and lean toward you. If folks disagree with you, or may not like what they see, they'll avoid eye contact, cross their arms or lean away from you.

Forbes.com reports how a person crosses their legs can give you an idea of how they are feeling. If the foot on the leg that is crossed on top points towards you, the person is most likely interested in what's going on. If their leg is crossed, so the top foot is points away, the person is <u>not</u> interested.

Five Keys to Closing the Sale

1. Listen for what his/her exact needs are.

2. Write down exactly what he/she says so you can repeat it back when you offer your recommendation. This shows you were listening.

3. The best sales people LISTEN for at least 60% of the call/visit before making a recommendation. Good questions are:

- "Is there anything else you need to store/put in the closet?"
- "I have skis and I store them in the storage area on the first floor. Do you have big items in your current closet that could be put in the first floor storage unit? The storage area opens up more room in your apartment's closet for you."

The more details you get, the more information you have, the more options you have for solutions, the more sales you'll close.

You can't overcome objections without finding out what the REAL objection is.

4. What is the BIGGEST thing the prospect will profit from (or benefit from) by choosing this apartment (product)?

5. Why does my prospect need to make this decision RIGHT now? What are two obstacles he is telling me and how can I fix them?

Sales Tips:

When prospects hear a question, their minds are immediately conditioned to begin searching for answers. Keep questions short so they do not miss what you say in the last half of your question.

Remember, their minds are already formulating an answer to the first part of your question.

Become a better salesperson by listening to your customer's FULL question before thinking about how you are going to answer. You might miss the most important question if it's at the end of what the customer is saying. That question could be the biggest objection, you need to hear it.

Closing Lines That Work

Feeling comfortable with closing is another key to sales success. There are a number of closing lines you can use to create urgency or sway a prospect. These work well if you've successfully overcome an objection with a prospect. Right then is the time to go for the close.

Test several out to see which closing lines "fit" your personality and apartment community. Different occasions call for different closing lines.

Here are 25 closing lines from my book "Closing Lines That Work" so you'll always be ready to find the right words to help your customers find the right home. Remember that 95% of sales are made on the fifth attempt or later. These will help you make five or more attempts to close the sale.

1. I have just one left of that model.
2. Do you like the (garden, townhouse, third floor) one best?
3. I find this to be the most _____ apartment
4. You've made a good choice – that's an excellent (location, style, etc.)
5 We have a special that includes _____.
6. We can guarantee the service you will receive will be the best.
7. Would you like me to reserve the style you like best?
8. Would a (ground floor, garden, etc.) home be best for you?
9. Would you like to be able to sign up for the free (internet, maid

service, parking) available with this apartment?
10. This apartment is more expensive, but it's been proven that….
11. Don't you agree that (this apartment has a lot of features; this is a very large apartment, etc.)?
12. It may not be exactly what you had in mind, but since it's our only one, why not take a look at it?
13. I believe I can offer the deluxe model for you at the same price. Let me check.
14. This is the last day before the price goes up.
15. Is this what you wanted?
16. If you want to save (time, money, gas commuting, etc.), this is the home that will help you do it.
17. Why wait when you can move in now? Moving is a pain, let's get it over with as soon as possible. I can hold the apartment home until tomorrow morning if you like – this style is going fast and I don't want you to miss out.
18. Do you prefer the apartment home with or without (two-toned paint, the pool view, etc.?)
19. Why wait when you can move in now? Moving is a pain, let's get it over with as soon as possible.
20. We can guarantee a lower price for (_____ time) if you sign the application today.
21. If you ever have a problem with your apartment home, call me, and I'll take care of it.
22. Have you decided which apartment home you like best?
23. This is the same apartment home that I (or someone else) live in.
24. Yes; this style of apartment home is popular. I've rented ___ of these already this (week or month.)
25. You're making the right decision. This is a great home for the price.

Score Better On Your Next Shop – 5 Tips

How you overcome objections is critical when you are being shopped. Here are five tips to help you.

1. Know your product so you can anticipate objections in advance.

2. Approach the objections in a matter-of-fact manner.

3. Ask smart questions to determine the real reason behind the objections.

4. Help the prospect determine if their objection is a big enough reason not to live at your apartment community.

5. When you open them up to your point of view, and how others have resolved the objection, there's a better chance you'll make the sale. Remember the tried and true sales technique <u>Feel. Felt. Found.</u> When presented with an objection you can say, "I understand how you <u>feel</u>. Others have <u>felt</u> the same way. But then they have <u>found</u> (list reasons here how other residents have seen that objection isn't the road block it currently appears to be to the prospect.)"

Conclusion – Listen To Your Buyers

"You can close more business in two months by becoming interested in other people than you can in two years by trying to get people interested in you." Dale Carnegie

In the classic book "How to Win Friends and Influence People by Dale Carnegie, the most important recommendation is to listen and then repeat and rephrase what you just heard back to the other person. By doing this you are showing the other person you listened and processed what you heard.

Since most people only listen and hear about 25% of what the other person says if you listen and process what you hear from your prospect, and then repeat and rephrase it back, you'll be way ahead of the competition.

Arm yourself with the answers from your checklist, listen to your buyer and help them determine if their objections are really problematic or not, and chalk all non-sales up to experience.

Chapter 10
The Art of Closing

By Kate Good

Many people will flip to this chapter looking for the magic words they can use to guarantee the potential renter will say yes, fill out an application and leave their check. The truth is that if you just want to learn "closing lines" you are on a mission that will NEVER work. The reason is because closing is not a magic line. It is not an event. It is simply a step in the sales process and the process must build on each step. Closing does not work unless you understand your customers' needs through information gathering and rapport building. Attempting a close is impossible and should never be done until you have demonstrated features and benefits of the apartments and your community and discussed and concerns or objections your customer has about the apartment community.

In today's fast paced world, we are all looking for a shortcut. We need things done faster. People don't always want to put the work into something if there is simply "an app for that." Unfortunately, this is one thing in your life that will simply not work unless you put the time in with your customer. Allow me to explain why with a short little story from the first year I was a Leasing Consultant:

The first apartment community I worked at was called The Hamptons. We had 832 apartments over three phases of development and one of the phases was brand new and had 156 apartments to rent. The other two phases already built seemed to have extremely high turnover. I would soon come to find out that because we were located in Ft. Lauderdale this turnover rate was par with South Florida rental communities. All totaled; we had over 200 apartments on our availability sheet, and we needed to get them leased. Fast. As in, do anything for the lease...fast.

We gathered with our Property Manager, Glenn, to put our heads together and create a plan. After a few hours of idea sharing we decided we needed to do a huge open house weekend with search lights, display ads in the newspaper (yes, we still did newspaper ads; this was the late '80's!) On Thursday night, we stayed late to blow up balloons, hang banners, spiff up the models, create mini models, and set up a refreshment station. We cleared a space for a DJ and got the grill ready for a huge open house cook out. We ordered in food for the whole team to feast during our preparations and had a great time as we anticipated a huge leasing event. There were 10 of us working in the leasing office, and all were scheduled to work the entire weekend. We were armed and ready for a big crowd as our goal was to close 40 leases by Monday morning at 10am.

I arrived to work on time on Friday and was surprised to see no one was there. I turned on the lights, took the phone off service and waited. No other team members showed up. It was just me! Soon the calls started rolling in. It seems that everyone got food poisoning except me. I dodged that bullet by avoiding the pizza my whole team devoured because I am allergic to cheese. I enjoyed a sub sandwich instead and was healthy and ready to lease. How was I going to get through our supersized leasing event as the only Leasing Consultant? I quickly did some math in my head and realized that my bonus check would be impressive enough to excite a Vice President!

By 10:45 am I had already shown two apartments and closed the leases. Only 38 leases to go! At noon, there were close to 15 people standing in the leasing office. I started to panic. I stood on a chair and said "Hi, I'm Kate, your Leasing Consultant, everyone with your checkbooks follow me." I lead the crowd through the exercise and laundry room, pool area, passed the tennis courts and on to the model apartment. I tried to talk to everyone but can assure you there was no time for completing a guest card. We came back to the office, and I asked the crowd who wanted to take an apartment off the market. Imagine my disappointment when I went from thinking I would get 10 leases in one hour to closing absolutely not one person in the group! Yep, not one apartment rented. To make matters worse, they never came back, and I did not have a guest card with their contact information needed for follow up.

Why did I strike out with this group of interested renters? I did not earn the close. I mistakenly positioned myself as a tour guide and did not connect with anyone. I did not solve objections or point out features that would hit the customers' hot buttons. I did not sell anything. My close was my opening line asking if they brought their checkbooks!

On that day, I learned you have to **earn** your close by doing all the other steps that lead to it. I learned the importance of relationship building and how it relates to closing techniques. One does not work without the other. So, if you have flipped to this chapter first thinking this is all you need, roll back to the beginning and forget the shortcut. It simply will not work to only learn a few closing lines.

Was Harold Hill the World's Greatest Salesman?

If you've ever seen the old Broadway Musical, The Music Man, you know the story of "Professor" Harold Hill, who goes from town to town selling musical instruments and uniforms for boy's bands. The play starts off on a train full of traveling salesmen discussing the current state of affairs, technology and even a list of products that became useless because of new technology. It reminds me of what happens when you get a group of leasing professionals together.

As the train travels the tracks, the salesmen discuss Harold Hill's reputation and how "he doesn't know the territory." So how does he do it, they wonder. "What's his line?" they ask. "Never worries about his line, he's just a bang beat, bell ringing, big haul, great go, neck or nothin, rip roarin, every time a bull's eye salesman." That's quite a reputation. Spoiler alert: Harold Hill is on the train the entire time. As the train starts to leave River City, Iowa, a town they claimed Hill could not sell, he hops off the train to prove them wrong, and the audience gets to witness one of the greatest sales of all time.

In the big opening number, Hill spends some time getting to know the people of Iowa. He learns their hot buttons and what is important to them. He learns they are very literal and not too much fun. He learns people mind their own business with a chip on their shoulder and are quite stubborn and contrary. He also learns they'll give you their shirt "and a back to go with it" if times get tough. He then plans his "pitch" with a former co-worker. You see, River City, Iowa doesn't have a boy's band, so Hill has to "create a desperate need" for one. He soon discovers it, and the excitement begins.

As Hill goes through his first sales pitch, he hits all of the hot buttons he learned by getting to know his prospects and stirs the town into a frenzy and leaves them convinced they need a boy's band. Now that he has created the need for the band, he can sell them the instruments and uniforms. In our industry, the need for apartments already exists, so the need you must create is the need to live at your community, as opposed to your competitor.

Hill goes door to door selling instruments and uniforms methodically, using various closing techniques along the way. Hill is a master at the art of closing. Remember his reputation? He was infamous. Legendary. But, why?

Leasing must be learned through trial and error, practicing and rehearsing and gaining confidence in your own techniques. The simple truth is most of this book is about how to get a lease, and that is not possible if you simply attempt to deliver one magical closing line. Closing is the very last step but must be part of the entire sales process. The reason why Harold Hill was so successful is he was confident. He mastered more than one closing technique and tailored it to each customer. He created not only a need, but built relationships, trust and made his prospects feel good about their decision. He didn't even know how to play an instrument, but he sure knew the right song to play for each prospect.

Harold Hill began his sales effort with the end in mind. He knew he wanted the town to buy from him, but he had to determine what their needs were. He used these needs to position his product. He then showed the town that buying his product was a solution even while not knowing they needed it. This is what must be done to earn the right to ask the customer to buy. Success happens when we open our close with these relationship building techniques.

Always Be Closing

You've heard the expression "always be closing" before and while there is truth to that statement, it shouldn't be taken too literally. This is what I like to call the "Glengarry Glen Ross" which is a hard-nosed close. Another one of my favorite fictional sales stories, Glengarry Glen Ross, is a movie about real estate. Alec Baldwin plays Blake, the company's top salesman, who is called in to give a "pep talk" to some of the salesmen at an office that is underperforming. Blake teaches them to always be closing. It's very different from Harold Hill's techniques but deserves acknowledgement as some of the philosophy may be valuable in certain situations. However, the foundation is the same, know your customer. Always be closing was broken down into four steps. AIDA.

(A) Attention - Do I have your attention?

(I) Interest - Are you interested?

(D) Decision - Have you made your decision?

(A) Action or close.

"Get out there!" Blake says. "You got the prospects coming in. You think they came in to get out of the rain? A guy don't walk on the lot lest he wants to buy. They're sitting out there waiting to give you their money. Are you going to take it?"

The delivery of this message during the movie is lost on those receiving it due to the aggressive nature of Blake's delivery. They are more concerned about keeping their jobs than the teachings of the top salesman from another branch. However, there is a lot of wisdom in these words. Think about it. Your community has spent a lot of money creating prospects through branding, marketing and advertising. These people are not setting appointments to tour your community. You've already met many of their needs before they even show up for an appointment because today's customer can find out a lot about your apartment community through their online search for their new apartment home. If they are a "drive-by," you've already met their location need at the very least. So, at a very basic level you've met the most important need by having apartments available to rent. You must, at some point, make an attempt to close.

On the other hand, if you are always closing the prospect from the moment they walk in the door, they may feel pressured and uncomfortable. If your end goal is to close a prospect and you have all the necessary tools, then you will always be closing or working toward your end goal.

Most of the time; you will be able to close a prospect without the hard close, but the general technique is useful and can be converted to a more tactful closing technique or combined with another technique to be an effective closer. After all, there is nothing wrong with asking direct questions with certain prospects. The true art of closing comes when you begin to master several techniques, put your own spin on them and customize your close for every unique prospect.

Even Good Car Salesman Know This

What are some things that will help you to close without the high pressure close? Product knowledge, meeting an emotional need, being helpful in their overall decision process, or finding the right apartment for them at the right price can make it a lot easier to transition to the close. It used to be that the car salesmen were successful because of high pressure sales tactics. That is no longer the case. I first noticed a shift in their approach when I looked at buying a Honda Accord. The salesperson took the time to show me all the features of the car. The test drive was fun, and I learned more about the car's unique performance. These are things I would not have discovered simply by kicking the tires.

I was intrigued by this new era of a car salesman and felt that their skills would work in the apartment industry. The Honda dealership two exits up the highway was hiring, so I interviewed and got the job. I was not interested in selling cars; I simply wanted to learn how their new method of sales worked without the high pressure tactics we used to experience from a car salesman. I attended four days of sales training with Honda Motorcar Company. In all, I had 24 hours of training classes with them and not once was I ever given a closing line to use on the car buying public. Instead, we spent much of the time learning why our cars were superior to other in the product class.

The training classes at Honda taught me that people who stop by a car dealership have car buying on their mind. Sure, there will be a few who come by to kick the tires but there was a good chance that they will buy too. People don't waste their precious time doing things that don't serve a desired outcome. If the Honda sales method were to be successful, we had to treat everyone like they were going to buy a car today. This, in itself, was a close, but it was masked in a closing subtle approach but a strong informational approach. By the time that a person was ready to leave the dealer, they would feel that the Honda Accord was a huge value for the money and that buying a new car was a smart thing to do. I started to see the customer asking questions that would satisfy what they needed to know about the car in order to buy it. If I listened carefully and treated these questions as buying signals, the close was smoothly transitioned by answering the question with language that sounded as if the car was already theirs. I was closing the whole time and did not use one single closing line. I was surprised to see that most of the people I practiced this sales technique on asked me if they could buy a car and rarely did I have to ask the customer to make the purchase.

While we only learn one closing technique from Blake in Glengary Glen Ross, and it clearly worked for him, there is so much more to learn from our Music Man example Harold Hill and his techniques. The next part of this chapter will outline some other traditional closing techniques that can provide a foundation for you to build your own personal style. I am confident that I do the work necessary to find my customer the best apartment for their needs. I spend the bulk of my time in the leasing process practicing thorough information gathering and need searching by asking open ended questions and building on the customers' responses. When I pick out apartments to show, they are selected based on these needs. I know I cannot ask them to rent until I successfully overcome objections and show the customer that their furniture fits in the apartments. I discuss their other options in the market and see what I need to know about the customer to be at the top of their list. It is then and only then, that I attempt my favorite closing line. Did you think I was going to tell you now? You will just have to read on to hear what works for me. Remember, the point is not "the line," it is all the work I have done prior to the line that makes it work. I worked hard to develop strong communication and sales skills. You are reading this book, so that proves you are dedicated to your craft. Notice I used the words "your craft?" That is because there is not a script; you have to develop and practice your techniques.

At various times throughout the tour, the leasing consultant has an opportunity to use different closing techniques. Read through these techniques and determine how they can work with your leasing formula for the foundation.

The Bandwagon Effect

A bandwagon was a float or wagon, typically used in political parades or rallies. There would be a band playing music and others singing or dancing and enjoying themselves. The purpose was to show that everyone on the bandwagon was "on board," having a good time together and to encourage others to join in and support that particular political party or campaign. If you weren't on board, you were missing out.

In order to get prospective buyers to adapt to a new idea or product, it is important to show how others are "on board" and enjoying the new product. A strategic tour path can be a very subtle way to use the bandwagon effect. Taking the prospect by busy fitness center, swimming pool or common areas would be a great way to build their excitement and show them how many other people are living it up at your community.

A lease-up community is also a great example of a situation when you might use the Bandwagon close. This technique shows how other people are all lining up to buy the product. In this case, a waiting list is a good thing, especially when construction isn't complete, and there aren't apartments or a model ready to tour. Indicate that the other people are known to or are like the person you are talking to. Hint at how they may be left behind by others or even seen as slow and backward by not buying the product sooner. Combine it with hints of scarcity, showing how the product is so popular you may run out soon. This close works well when there are other prospects filling out applications as the Leasing Consultant is touring the community. Ironically, seeing others jumping on board makes people feel safer in making a decision to do the same.

The Bandwagon closing technique is best used in a situation where the prospect is hesitant to make a decision. They want to be absolutely sure before they sign a lease. The only thing holding them back has nothing to do with the features and benefits of the apartment and the community, but fear of making the wrong decision. This is your opportunity to point out like-minded people who have already made the decision they are afraid to make.

Examples:

"I had three of these apartments yesterday, but two were rented this morning."

"I have another appointment at 4 p.m. for this apartment; you may want to put a deposit down now, so you are sure to have this apartment."

"We have rented 8 one bedrooms this week, it seems like everyone wants this style of apartment."

I also use this flavor of closing when overcoming objections by saying, "I understand how you feel, other people I have rented to have felt that way before, but they found…." and then I say what I think might help close the customer by relieving the concern over the objection. Note there are keywords in this statement that I have highlighted for you again: "I understand how you **feel**, other people I have rented to have **felt** that way before, but they **found."** The words feel, felt and found create the Bandwagon effect to overcome objections and attempt to close the customer.

Assumptive Closing

I grew up in Lancaster, Ohio. When I lived there, it was rather small and certainly did not have apartment communities as you would see today. There were a few places to rent scattered around town, but they did not have pools and workout rooms! When I got to the age where I could make my own decisions, I moved to sunny South Florida and eventually became a Leasing Consultant. I thought it was the best job I could earn for myself because I could not think of a single reason people would not want to rent the apartments at that community I was assigned for work. We had trees, three pools, two tennis courts, racquetball, 21 laundry rooms, workout room and two resident clubhouses. I honestly had never seen anything so grand and with so much to offer.

When I showed apartments, I simply assumed everyone would lease them. I could not imagine that anyone would say no after seeing all that I had to show them. My words and actions were all assumptive in nature. After taking them on the grand tour, I would sit down with my availability sheet and express to the customer that I really hoped I could find an apartment available for their needs. When I did, I circled it on the site plan and wrote the apartment number at the top of the application. As a courtesy, I filled out as much as I knew about this customer based on what I had gathered on the

Guest Card. Then I turned the application, and my pen, over to the customer and began writing a receipt for their security deposit and application fee.

I was surprised to learn a few weeks later at my first leasing class that I was bringing to life one of the most popular closing techniques in our business, the Assumptive Close. To me, it was just my natural approach to leasing, and I have to say, it worked out really well for me. I had a consistent closing ratio of between 65% and 80%.

Over the next year, I started to understand why this sales technique worked. If you start your interaction with a prospect assuming that they will lease an apartment from you, you are using the assumptive closing technique. This positive approach to closing is highly dependent on one particular factor: confidence. Confidence will create more energy and enthusiasm during your presentation. These traits are contagious and will have a positive impact on your prospect.

Simply assume the prospect will rent an apartment as the presentation is given and choose the words you use accordingly. Instead of using the word "if" use "when." Ask questions you know they will agree with and ask them in a way that they can only answer by saying, "yes" or something positive. At no time during the assumptive close do you ask for the prospect to rent, instead you assume they will be renting.

People love to buy things, but most people do not like to be sold. The Assumptive close is low pressure and the prospect is left feeling that they were guided through the leasing transaction by someone who understands their needs and is on their side as opposed to someone who is trying to sell them so they can get a commission.

The assumptive close requires that the leasing professional be knowledgeable about both the apartment community and the leasing process including all paperwork and requirements of the prospect. You may start the Assumptive close over the phone by politely reminding them to bring their checkbook in order to place a deposit or pay their application fees.

Examples:

"By your comments I can tell that you love this apartment. I will go get the application for you to complete."

"I know that having a furnished apartment was the most important feature you were looking for. You can pay by check, credit card or cash for the deposit in order to hold this apartment that includes the furnishings."

Trial Close

Thankfully, this close does not involve the opinion of a jury of your prospect's peers. In fact, it's just as easy as asking the opinion of the prospect along the way and gauging their satisfaction with simple and direct questions, typically during the leasing presentation. A Trial Close is not a normal 'closing technique' but a test to determine whether the prospect is ready to rent. Use it throughout the presentation to take their temperature or "test" the prospect's readiness to rent. If the prospect makes a decision on a minor point such as what floor they'd prefer to live on, it's a pretty good indicator that they will be able to make their final decision much easier. The Trial Close will most likely require the use of other closing techniques but it will help you determine where you are at in the sales process and when to ask for the sale.

The Trial close is effective because it gets the prospect engaged, and if timed properly by a seasoned leasing professional, it gets the prospect used to saying something positive or a direct "yes." Once they say, "yes" once, the next "yes" is much easier. One of the best times to use this technique is after you have successfully overcome an objection.

Examples:

"How does that sound so far?"

"Do you feel there is anything I may have missed?"

"Can you see yourself living here?"

Alternative Close or Which Close

People love to have choices but not too many. Two options are usually not enough, and four options can be overwhelming. The alternative close technique typically gives the prospect three alternatives with a wide price range from which to choose, and you should always sell from the top down. First, offer them something sumptuous and expensive that is beyond their budget, but not so far beyond that they would never consider it. It must be realistic. Ideally, it is something they wish they could afford, but cannot justify the expense at the time (if they do, it is your lucky day!) Secondly, offer them a solid, good deal within their price bracket. It may not have all they wanted, but it is clearly a good value for them. Finally, offer a severely cut-down deal in which very little of what they want is included. They should, of course, go for the middle option.

Example:

"I do have a two bedroom, two bath with full-size washer and dryer and private entrance, but it is a little more than you were looking to pay. You could take the two bedroom two bath within a common hallway, which is right in your price range. I also have the two bedroom, one bath, apartment that is the least expensive. Although it's a basic apartment, it's also a great deal."

Have you ever experienced the potential renter who could not make a decision? They will say to you something like, "Well, if it is meant to be, it will be, so I am going to think about it." This wishy washy person needs you to help them narrow their choices and see why one apartment is best for them. After all that work to find the apartment their logic will lead them to taking the apartment off the market.

Team Close

When you are getting near to closure or if you are having problems, hand over the actual closing to another person. You can frame this as a different process, for example, where your job was to help the customer choose, and the next person is there to negotiate the final details, verify the price or just take down notes.

Examples:

"Now that we've got the perfect apartment for you, my Manager is going to help sort out the paperwork."

"You have said that the price is important to you and Stephanie our Leasing Manager is going to work out the details with you now."

It is also fun to help your fellow Leasing Consultants out by using the team close throughout the day. If my co-worker is walking back from a tour with a customer I will say to that customer, "So what did you think?" or, "When are you moving in?" or, "Which one are you going to take off the market because I have a guest coming in shortly who is also looking for the same apartment." The customer often gets swept up in the energy and excitement, and this certainly helps sway their wills.

Tie Down Close

Whenever you ask a question and then follow it with another question (usually a contraction) you have used a "Tie Down" close. The tie down encourages the prospect to answer the question, getting one more "yes" toward a sale. Also, if they disagree and give you a negative response then you've isolated an objection to overcome so you can handle the problem before moving on. Examples of tie down words include couldn't, wouldn't, isn't, etc.

Example:

"This apartment has very large closets, doesn't it?"

"It would be great to have a fitness center within walking distance, wouldn't it?"

"Your clothing will fit nicely in the large closet, wouldn't it?"

The Ben Franklin

Also known as the T-Bar or the Balance Sheet Close.

Ever run into an indecisive customer that has to analyze every little aspect about your community, the apartment and everything in between? Well, grab a pencil and a sheet of paper and help them make up their mind already! Using the Ben Franklin technique, you start by listing both the benefits of renting the apartment, "the pros" and also the "cons." Of course, the pros (the reasons to rent) will win. You can even write it down like a balance sheet. Make sure the 'pros' column is longer and more impressive, of course. Cons include things they wanted, but are not getting. Start with the cons and keep them short.

But do make it sound credible, as if you are giving them fair consideration. Then cover the pros. Perhaps sound pleasantly surprised as you describe them. Sound reasonable, as if you are on their side. Sound almost as if you are talking to yourself.

Examples:

"Well, although the price is a little higher than what you wanted to pay, you will have extra space in the closets and a fitness center within walking distance and you will no longer have to pay for a gym membership."

"Let's weigh things up. You're going to have an extra roommate in the apartment, but you are well within your budget and will have a full size washer and dryer, and access to a 24-hour fitness center. Doesn't that sound good?"

Pros	Cons
Huge closets	$20 over current budget
Brand new carpet	Only 2nd floor apartments available
Fitness Center	
Bark Park	

Needs and Knowledge

I tuned into one of my favorite late night comedians one evening and heard a great sales lesson. David Letterman invited the top salesman at Saturn Car Company to be a guest on his show. This was in the early years of Saturn, and the country was noticing that this was a "different car company." We loved their commercials, the new shape of their car and the different attitude that was driven in "unsalesman-like" conduct. After a bit of small talk, David invited the salesman to sell him something.

The salesman says, "How about your pen?" With Dave's agreement, they continue.

The salesman asks, "How often do you use your pen?" Dave answers, "Every day."

Next he asks, "Why do you use this pen?" "Because it is my favorite!" replies Dave.

The salesman says, "Would you pay $2.50 for it?" "Yes" confirms Dave.

The salesman ends the conversation with "done."

Why did this sales presentation work? Because the salesman did not talk about the product. David Letterman was not informed of the color, ink life, brand name. No mention of the pen's features and benefits were reviewed. Instead, the salesman relied on needs and knowledge of the customer. Asking, "How often do you use your pen?" identified need. The next question that asked why he uses the pen reveals knowledge. In this scenario, the customer proved they needed and wanted the pen for their own clarity. So when the salesman jumped in with a price the customer says, "Yes!"

So is it that easy to close a lease? Yes and no. Some leasing consultants are so talented at asking the types of questions that discover needs and get the customer talking that they learn exactly how to connect this customer to the available apartment. Digging a little deeper and learning about this customer and their lifestyle is also a necessary ingredient. The savvy leasing consultant can now form their presentation around the needs, and knowledge discovered. When discussing the kitchen, say something about the customer's needs. This creates a connection between the product and the customer. They will see that this apartment meets their needs when they take comfort in the connection to the product. Now closing becomes so much easier because the customer feels like this apartment is made for them.

Before you ever show an apartment, make certain you ask questions to find out what is important to this customer. Using this key information on the leasing tour will help your customer see that this apartment meets their needs.

Product knowledge doesn't begin and end at your own community. You must also know what your competition has to offer.

Emotions Make It Tough To Walk Away

Most men carry their money in their pocket. Women carry their money in their purse which usually hangs near the pocket. Purse and pockets have exactly what we need to take an apartment off the market, currency. So what is the quickest path to that money? You have two choices; appealing to the customers brain or their heart. The brain wants to know facts and figures such as price and square footage. The heart takes a completely different approach. It wants to hear about things that will make it pound a little bit. In other words, people need to feel their heart in their future home.

There are just a few things that get priority space in someone's heart: family and home. So, where does the family live? In the home! They are so closely connected, and a customer needs to see themselves living in the apartment before they will choose it as their home. There is not a closing technique that will replace the need to mentally place their furniture and see their life taking shape at your apartment community.

Keep in mind that today, more than 70% of renters have pets. These furry creatures are now more than man's best friend; they are full time family members. We make decisions that benefit out pets. Some of us buy them souvenirs while on vacation. I will even admit to talking to my sweet puppy, Mrs. Harry Winston, on the phone. **When helping the customer vision living in the apartment make sure you include the WHOLE family in that picture including the ones with four legs.**

If family and home tug at the heart then they are certainly filled with emotions. So the decisions we make for our family and home are very emotional. This is a good thing for sales people to know because you can use this in a very positive way. Don't confuse what I am saying here that this makes people emotional in a freaked out way. Emotions simply mean you care; this is personal, and a person is devoting their energy to it. This is exactly what we need to lease an apartment.

Here are a few questions that spur emotions when considering a place to call home:

- Will it make me feel better?
- Will it make me stay longer?
- Will it save me money?
- Will it change my life?
- Will it meet my future needs?

Are You Helping or Hurting Your Customer?

People feel better when they observe the environment and they find it suits them. They will see that they can find comfort and thrive in all that the community offers. Because the idea of moving can create emotional trauma, it is important that people feel better about the moving process when they visit your community. This can be accomplished by offering help with relocation tasks. This is the part of the move that can be overwhelming and since you work with people who are moving every day your experience can create shortcuts to solutions. The next thing you can offer to keep the customer in a productive state is a leasing office that serves them. I literally mean to serve them treats and drinks (I'm not talking about cocktails here!) Give customers refreshment and a little pop of sugar to give them instant energy. We need them in this state to so that they can think clearly and make a decision.

During this process, you can actually hurt the decision making process by adding stress to an already stressful time. I was sitting with a group of ladies discussing the wedding plans for the woman sitting at the middle of the table. The bride was full of excitement and joy, and this quickly turned when others at the table started to swap the stress. We heard about misspellings on the invitations, the napkins being the wrong color, a tear in a wedding gown, weather ruining the reception and so on. There is no reason to believe that any of this will happen to this bride, but everyone wanted to caution her. This negative energy does not need to be a part of a positive conversation. Watch your comments. You can swap a moving story with a customer that will throw them into a tailspin and the decision making process will stop.

Help the customer by setting their decision making process up for success. Allow the customer time to think. Not everyone is a quick decision maker, and they will need to step away to make their decision. Don't panic, this is why we want you to learn to be masters at follow up. In addition, you want to also leave the right seeds of thought with the customers so that they bloom in their mind when you are not there personally to close the lease. Here are a few seeds to plant:

- Finding a home that meets your needs is a real challenge. Thank you for taking the time today to look at what we have available for you. It looks like we found a home that is perfect for you.
- I am happy to hear that you are giving this apartment serious consideration. That means you really like it!
- We took a lot of time today to pinpoint your needs and find an apartment that meets them. We should hold this apartment for you while you make a decision. I can take it off the market until tomorrow morning.

While there may not be a trick, secret handshake or magic wand that will work on every prospect, there is definitely a trick to **not** closing a prospect and **not** getting a lease. It's simple. Don't ask.

After all, "You miss 100% of the shots you don't take." - Wayne Gretzky

Another important element to closing is knowing what stop you are on their tour schedule. How many other apartment communities are they touring? How many and which ones have they already seen? What did they like about the other communities they have seen and what attracted them to the other communities they are going to tour? I wouldn't recommend asking all of these questions verbatim, rather come up with your own way to work them into the conversation organically. Don't be afraid to compliment the great features your competitors have to offer and don't be afraid to politely point out the features your community offers that are newer or give you a competitive advantage. You don't want to ever speak negatively about your competitors as it may be a turn off to your prospect. After all, your community is on the same short-list as them.

Flat Rate Pricing is a Dead End Street

Many communities tried flat rate pricing during the recession in an effort to fill up fast. While this may have resulted in a nice bump in occupancy, the leasing team was left with all the "less desirable" apartments to lease making their challenges even tougher. The long term problem is that now they have a community where people think that most pay the same amount in rent. The price was typically based on the lowest rent we could offer even though more than half the apartments had higher value. Price the apartment based on the attributes which make the apartment unique.

Why should a person rent the subject apartment over another? The answer to that question will help you see the individual opportunity for this apartment price. Once you move to this type of price structure it is easier to sell a new price on an apartment. The reason is pretty simple; it limits the number of apartments that will meet the customer's needs. If you have 10 one bedroom apartments available and they are all $899 then the customer has 10 to choose from making the decision harder not to mention, you will lose your sense of urgency.

It makes more sense to qualify the customer based on price they can afford and then limit their choice based on this need. Ideally, you want the customer to consider two apartments vs. 10 apartments. The price differential will help to narrow the choices.

Options and Control

Give residents options, and you give them control. Everyone loves control and when you give people options they feel like they have properly researched and uncovered all their choices for an apartment. This should limit the customer from feeling like they need to see more before they can make a decision. The customer now has a decision to make rather than just accept what you are asking of them. Psychologically this will help you get to yes. The options could also be the length of lease or apartment upgrade. Now the customer has control of the decision through choice.

Monthly Market Surveys are Worthless

Information that was gathered about your competition two weeks ago will not help you lease apartments. In today's world, many apartment communities have sophisticated pricing engines which will study market pricing in order to find out the optimal price whereby the apartment should lease without leaving money on the table. If you study your market on a daily basis, you will have the advantage of timely information. When you do so, you will notice incremental changes in the market by companies who are truly committed to managing for a high yield. Tracking these changes will help you understand what is available in the market and how the market is accepting the inventory. You now have data you need to price accordingly.

You may be thinking, how could I possibly call my competition on a daily basis to get this information? My answer is, you don't have to. There are other ways to collect the information, but you still need to study the data. Your property may subscribe to online market survey services that provide this data. Ask your manager to see these reports so that you can learn about your competition. Nothing works as well as simply asking a customer where else they have looked for an apartment and what was offered to them. If I lose a lease to another apartment community, I will call the prospect and find out where they leased and why. This is a market survey that will not only teach me about the renting world around me, but will also give me tips on what I need to do to be a better Leasing Consultant.

Make it Easy

Moving is the worst day of your life. At least I think so! While you are usually happy to move into a new place to call home, the idea of packing all of your things into boxes is stressful. You don't want your things to get broken, lost or damaged! It is also stressful to learn about a new neighborhood, find your grocery store and all the services that make your life easy. It's just not fun, and there are a million better things to do on a Saturday.

A smart Leasing Consultant will do a lot of the legwork for their customers. Show them all the knowledge you have prepared for them. Maps that have local services, websites to get their utilities connected, I even like to point out my favorite shortcuts for getting around town. Take the hassle out of moving. Make it super easy and really smooth by sharing your expertise with the customer. I think it is also helpful to show the customer places where they can get discounts on boxes and moving supplies. Wear the hat of a "relocation specialist" and people will want to do business with you.

Be Observant

Quite frequently, prospects may give you signals that they are ready to lease. They may be verbal or non-verbal. Once you observe a verbal or non-verbal buying signal, you need to stop selling and ask for the lease. You can, in fact, oversell a prospect and in the process potentially lose them.

I hear buying signals all throughout the sales presentation. It is important to capitalize on them each time. A few months ago I was showing an apartment to an older couple. As we passed the mailboxes, the husband asked if those were the mailboxes. I did not point them out as part of my presentation, and I thought that was pretty self-explanatory….they looked like mailboxes! However, then I remembered that people will not say things like this unless they are starting to see themselves living at a certain apartment community.

For our older residents, there are two things that become especially important in their lives: M & M's, but not the chocolate candy that melts in your mouth, not in your hands. Instead M & M's stands for meals and mail. I responded to this customer that yes those are their new mailboxes, and they will be happy to know that their mail will generally arrive between 10 and 11 am. (Notice I used assumptive language when I observed a buying signal?)

Steve Jobs and Closing

Show the customer everything. One thing we heard over and over again when Apple Founder, Steve Jobs, passed away was that he had a gift for imagining what we did not know we needed. Many times you may offer something that the customer did not consider for their list of apartment needs and wants. However, by demonstrating all features and amenities, you may just strike a chord and the customer's interest will peak.

Slow Down

Slow down. Don't be in a hurry to rush through your model. This is your number one sales tool. Invite the customer to take a seat on the couch and continue your conversation with them. Making themselves at home could be what they need to see this as their new home. Here is a tip from the awesome leasing teams at Pacific Living Properties in Sacramento, CA. If you open the refrigerator in their model apartment, you will see festive streamers, drinks and delicious snacks. The PLP team has a long tradition of offering the customer a delicious and refreshing snack. Since there is plenty of yummy treats, the customer does not feel; it is an imposition to help themselves. Then the PLP team member invites the customer to sit down on a bar stool at the breakfast counter, or take a seat on the couch to enjoy their leasing treat. Now, the customer can feel themselves living in this apartment.

You have heard the term; seeing is believing. The customer must see themselves living there to believe this is their new home. Slow down the tour so that the customer can take this moment in. Invite the customer to pull out their trusty smart phone and shoot a video of the apartment, so they remember it.

Broken will NOT Sell

Take what you have and make it a little better. Customers notice when things are broken so fix them. Fix everything. The goal of your apartment community is to have zero defects. The customer may be able to live without a tennis court, but they are not interested in living where the gates don'twork. Just ask anyone who works for Avalon Bay Communities, and they will tell you their motto is "neat, clean and working."

You cannot ask someone to buy something that is broken. Maintenance plays a huge part in your ability to attract people and rent to them. This week have a team meeting and talk about how you all have one goal; to lease and retain customers. Discuss how maintenance is a big part of that closing process.

Don't Even Attempt a Close Until You Find Out What They Need

Sometimes words come out of my mouth, and I think, "That is the perfect way to say that." At other times, I know that I need to put a little more explanation behind what I am saying. The title of this section is not self explanatory, at least not when it comes to leasing more apartments. So many times I hear a Leasing Professional jumping right in at the start of a leasing presentation and "data dumping" on a future resident instead of taking the time to find out what the customer needs in a new apartment home. Then they say, "So what do you think, are you ready to lease?" We are so eager to tell the customer about the apartment but at this point the consultant might as well be saying, "Blah, blah, blah."

The customer is not going to remember much of what the consultant is saying because it does not mean anything to them. To make the things Leasing Professionals say more meaningful we should start by asking what the customer is looking for. Questions such as, "What is important to you in your new home?" and "Are there any special features you are looking for in your new home?" Asking questions to engage the prospect will draw out information about your customer that will make it so much easier to make what you are saying about the apartment much more memorable. Now, when you discuss the apartment, and it's attributes, you can say something like, "Our living rooms have a 14 foot wall which should be big enough for your oversized couch and end tables." Wait to tell them what you know until you can link it to what they need.

This is a critical part of the leasing process which must happen in order for any closing attempt to work. Asking questions and linking their answers to your community as part of your demonstration is like having a custom built apartment for this person. Now when you are reviewing the reasons why this customer should rent the apartment, the things you mention will hit home because they are about the customer and not just the apartment.

Emotions and the Art of Negotiation

The very best professionals are always looking for opportunities to learn. You must be one of them because you are reading the Apartment All Stars Complete Guide to Leasing looking to sharpen your skills. Well, to you I say, "Dig in." It is important that you have the mindset to Always Be Learning. I live by this concept and always challenge myself to find new information.

There is one topic that I have been studying recently to make myself better at what I do and that is the art of negotiation. No matter what my position is in this industry, I find negotiating to be a necessary skill to master. In the sales process, it is an essential for anyone who wants to have an exceptional closing ratio.

We must start by learning the power of emotions on the negotiation process. This means that we make decisions based on our emotions. Yes, there is still the logical side of our brain that is weighing in on this decision, but it is an emotional rush you feel that drives you to say yes.

When are the emotions of your customer most effective to the sales process? In the model or rent ready apartment; it is at this moment that the customer has been taking in all the features and benefits of your amenities on the way to the model. They are really excited and now you show them a beautiful model apartment that is the best home in the community. Whamo! They are really feeling their emotions at this moment. Now is the time to ask for the lease and close it!

Set yourself up for success by placing a stack of applications and pens in the model. Have your availability with you at all times. If you wait to do this when you get back to the leasing office, you are missing the power of the emotional high.

The Three Things Rule

I was once asked by my very first property manager, Glenn Rand, to make a list of "100 great reasons to live at The Hamptons." I will admit it now, when I got to around #54 I started to repeat myself. Honestly, was anyone even going to read all 100 reasons? I had better things to do with my time like eating some frozen Otis Spunkmyer cookie dough! There are many great things about your apartment community. We have all been trained to successfully demonstrate all the features and benefits. But the truth is the customer only remembers what is important to their own personal needs. A wise leasing consultant knows that when people's needs are met, the buying decision is made. Isn't that what we want? Yes, people to make their buying decision while standing in our model or vacant apartment. Then we slide in the application conveniently located in the kitchen drawer or our leasing kit.

Getting to the buying decision is not so hard when you take the time to discover what the potential resident's needs and wants are. To do this, we have to ask open-ended questions that get the customer talking about themselves. In their answers, listen for what might be a deal breaker and what will be a deal maker. I have found that most people have three things they need and want. If you meet these three things, you are a sale maker.

Once you have heard what the customer is looking for, successfully demonstrate the apartment by using their needs and wants and link them to the features and benefits of your apartment community. By doing this, you are personalizing your tour to custom deliver the information this individual customer needs to make a decision.

So what happens if they don't lease right away? Use those three things that were most important to the customer and talk about them in your follow up notes, phone messages and emails. If you become really good at drawing out their three things and linking them to your apartments, you show the customer that apartments are not one size fits all and this apartment was made for your customer.

Doctors Understand the Sales Process

I'm always on the lookout for great sales and marketing ideas and tools. I never thought I would find it while sitting in a doctor's office last week. The visit went like this: determine my name and why I am there, wait in the waiting room to be called into an exam room. Ok, that is not the part we need to learn from, it took 27 minutes to see a doctor! What happened next is what we need to learn. The doctor entered the exam room, shook my hand, asked me questions, asked other questions that were built on my responses, diagnosed my problem and prescribed me a remedy.

Let's review: examine, diagnose, prescribe. It seems like leasing should work this way too. Examine what your customer's particular needs and wants are, diagnose which of your apartment options will meet their needs and then prescribe an available apartment.

The sad reality is that many leasing consultants don't follow this method. When a customer walks in the door they are asked if they want a one, two or three bedroom and based on the response shove a floor plan in their face and start to describe it. This was done without examining the customers' needs. If a doctor prescribed a drug without an exam then he/she would be accused of committing malpractice! I believe shoving a floor plan into someone's face without following the process of examining, and diagnosis is committing leasing malpractice.

Leasing apartments works so much better (and easier for that matter) when we take the time to ask questions of our perspective renter and determine their needs and wants. Then we take them to a model home and use their needs and wants to demonstrate why the apartment is perfect for them. Based on their response we have diagnosed what will and won't work for them. Now it is time to look at our available homes for their time frame and make a selection for the guest to approve. Even if you only have a few options for your customer, take time to discover needs as they turn into your closing tool.

Closing Multiple Decision Makers

Selling to one person is tough enough. Frequently, more than one person is involved in making a decision where to live, and this can complicate things. Different sets of hot buttons and different personalities can create an interesting challenge. Finding common ground and honing in on those features can help you navigate a smoother close. In The Music Man, Professor Hill closes four people at once by literally getting them to harmonize. As Hill helps them find the common bond of singing, they soon forget all of their differences that have kept them arguing for 15 years and overcomes all of their individual objections, making the close easy. Building rapport is even more important when dealing with multiple decision makers than it is with single decision makers. You'll need to earn enough trust so that all decision makers are comfortable telling you what they're most interested in, so that you don't waste time presenting the wrong benefits to the wrong decision makers. This is a great technique for roommate situations, couples and families where everyone has different needs.

For truly complex selling situations such as two friends with different budgets and hot buttons, your best bet is to treat each decision maker as a separate sale. Let's say renter A is strictly concerned about price and renter B is mostly concerned about rules and guidelines for her 80 lb golden retriever. Once you've determined which decision maker is responsible for which facet of the sale, you can stress the appropriate benefits with each decision maker in turn. When speaking with the price sensitive decision maker, you'd talk about the value and the features and benefits of the apartment. You'd present the pet owner with information about your pet policy and the bark park and grooming station Onsite.

And Now, My Favorite Closing Technique!

I promised you that if you read this entire chapter I would tell you my favorite closing line. It's really very simple and easy:

"Would you like Tea or Lemonade while you fill out the application?"

By now you know that using assumptive language, building rapport, discussing needs, pointing out features and benefits and overcoming objections are all part of my closing style. One does not work without the other, and my tea or lemonade line would fail miserably if it came before, or in place of, all the other things I do to lease an apartment. This line is my transition to the next step to lease the apartment. It is not magical because alone it holds no special powers. It works for me because, at this point in my presentation, I did all the work I could to find the perfect apartment for this customer and lead them to see why this apartment should be their future home.

I believe that you now have studied your craft with this complete guide to leasing. The Apartment All Stars are a team of seasoned sales machines, and we have come together to write all of our techniques down for you. Each chapter in this book is necessary for any of the chapters to work.

Chapter Summary Review

Closing is simply a step in the sales process, and the process must build on each step. Closing does not work unless you understand your customers' needs through information gathering and rapport building. The need for living in an apartment already exists, so the need you must create is the need to live at your community as opposed to at your competitor's.

Most of the time you will be able to close a prospect without a hard close, but the general technique is useful and can be converted to a more tactful closing technique or combined with another technique to be an effective closer. After all, there is nothing wrong with asking direct questions with certain prospects. The true art of closing comes when you begin to master several techniques, put your own spin on them, and customize your close for every unique prospect.

The Bandwagon closing technique is best used in a situation where the prospect is hesitant to make a decision. They want to be absolutely sure before they sign a lease. The only thing really holding them back has nothing to do with the features and benefits of the apartment and the community, but fear of making the wrong decision. This is your opportunity to point out like-minded people who have already made the decision they are afraid to make.

If you start your interaction with a prospect assuming that they will lease an apartment from you, you are using the assumptive closing technique. This positive approach to closing is highly dependent on one particular factor: confidence. Your confidence will create more energy and enthusiasm during your presentation. These traits are contagious and will have a positive impact on your prospect.
The Trial Close is effective because it gets the prospect engaged, and, if timed properly by a seasoned leasing professional; it gets the prospect used to saying something positive or a direct "yes." Once they say, "yes" once, the next "yes" is much easier. One of the best times to use this technique is after you have successfully overcome an objection.

The Alternative Close technique typically gives the prospect three alternatives with a wide price range from which to choose and you should always sell from the top down. First offer them something sumptuous and expensive that is beyond their budget, but not so far beyond that they would never consider it. It must be realistic. Ideally, it is something they wish they could afford, but cannot justify the expense at the time (if they do, it is your lucky day!). Secondly, offer them a solid, good deal within their price bracket. It may not have all they wanted, but it is clearly a good value for them.

Finally, offer a severely cut-down deal in which very little of what they want is included. They should, of course, go for the middle option.

When you are getting near to closure or if you are having problems, hand over the actual closing to another person. You can frame this as a different process, for example, where your job was to help the customer choose, and the next person is there to negotiate the final details, verify price, or just take down notes.

Before you ever show an apartment, make certain you ask questions to find out what is important to this customer. Using this key information on the leasing tour will help your customer see that this apartment meets their needs. Closing becomes so much easier when the customer feels like this apartment is made for them.

The customer needs to see themselves living in the apartment before they will choose it as their home. There is not a closing technique that will replace the need to mentally place their furniture and see their life taking shape at your apartment community. When helping the customer envision living in the apartment, make sure you include the WHOLE family in that picture - including the ones with four legs.

Because the idea of moving can create emotional trauma, it is important that people feel better about the moving process when they visit your community. This can be accomplished by offering help with relocation tasks. This is the part of the move that can be overwhelming and since you work with people who are moving every day your experience can create shortcuts to solutions.

Do a lot of the leg work for their customers. Show them all the knowledge you have prepared for them. Maps that have local services, websites to get their utilities connected - I even like to point out my favorite shortcuts for getting around town. Take the hassle out of moving. Make it super easy and smooth by sharing your expertise with the customer.

Information that was gathered about your competition two weeks ago will not help you lease apartments. In today's world, many apartment communities have sophisticated pricing engines which will study market pricing in order to find out the optimal price whereby the apartment should lease without leaving money on the table. If you study your market on a daily basis, you will have the advantage of timely information.

But the truth is the customer only remembers what is important to their own personal needs. A wise leasing consultant knows that when people's needs are met, the buying decision is made. Listen for what might be a deal breaker and what will be a deal maker. I have found that most people have three things they need and want. If you meet these three things, you are a sale maker.

Exam, diagnosis, and prescription: Examine what your customer's particular needs and wants are, diagnose which of your apartment options will meet their needs, and then prescribe an available apartment.

While there may not be a trick, secret handshake, or magic wand that will work on every prospect, there is definitely a trick to not closing a prospect and not getting a lease. It's simple. Don't ask. After all, "You miss 100% of the shots you don't take." *(Wayne Gretzky)*

Chapter 11
You've Got Mail

By Kate Good

The novelty of email used to delight us; now the sheer volume of it aggravates us. To stand out in a prospective resident's flooded inbox, you need to be able to craft quality emails that don't get lost in the crowd or get deleted as spam. Email contact is a vital tool to use in leasing apartments, and you want to ensure you are using it effectively, keeping in mind the quick turn-around time needed in responding to emails. In this chapter, we share tips and tricks to help you capture your recipient's attention, professionally respond to their needs and increase your web conversions and sales.

In the early years of the internet, AOL was king. One of the greatest sounds in the world was the service telling you, "You've Got Mail." People LOVED to get email. I still keep my AOL address for nostalgia's sake, and I miss my personal connection with the AOL man! In today's cluttered and complicated online world, email does not have the glow it once had. In fact, there is no glow at all anymore, and for many, email is a nuisance. People focus on ways to filter and remove the noise that fills their inboxes. Prior to leaving for vacation recently, I spent two hours blocking, reporting, and opting out of email so that I would not have pesky email use up my data limits while traveling abroad. I came to realize how much email I get that I have come to ignore. We don't want our emails to be ignored! So, how do we get people's attention in this busy world? You have turned to the chapter that has this single goal in mind. Your ability to succeed may be the factor that earns you the next lease.

Do you feel like you have more responsibilities today than you did a year ago? I bet if I ask you that same question a year from now your answer will be the same as it is today…YES! How to we cope?

How do we keep up? Each day we are given just 86,400 seconds. Not a second more, and thankfully, not a second less. Yet year after year we seem to have more on our plate, more things vying for our time. It used to take 6 days to get a letter to a customer - now it takes 6 seconds when we send one through email. Yes, things are speeding up, but that has some pitfalls. Now we seem to have more to do and read.

It is Monday, and I am working on writing this chapter. It is now 4 in the afternoon, and I am wondering where my day went. When I look at my productivity, I see that I spent the first three hours of my day reading and answering email. Were any of those emails a standout in my overcrowded inbox? Yes – one. It had a fun picture and a personal message. I felt like it alone connected with me in a sea of 47 emails. Does your email standout?

Luckily in our business, people frequently email us first, usually to express a need, so they are expecting and wanting our reply. Often, our customers are searching for us on an Internet Listing Service (ILS) such as ApartmentGuide.com or Rent.com, and will inquire about several properties via the contact option on the web page. Studies show that the timeliness of your response could be a determining factor if the customer decides to set an appointment for a visit to see your apartments. That does not mean that you can be lazy and ignore the rules of good writing or proper etiquette. Likewise, you must remember your email is often another step in the leasing process, and your e-letter must be well crafted to keep prospective residents flowing into the sales funnel.

Messages from your customers are the most important emails coming into the leasing office. Your customers take on a couple different forms - internal and external customers - and email communication is probably commonplace with both.

External customers include your prospective residents, current residents, and anyone in the community not already doing business with you. While all customers should be treated with professionalism and respect, your external customers are the most vital. In the external customer relationship, they are the only customers. In the internal customer relationship, both sides are typically considered customers.

Internal customers are the folks you work with – especially in other locations and departments, people you do business with like carpet vendors, exterminators, and any other contractors. You may not think of your community's accountant or the HR director as your customer, but they are! They don't rent apartments from you, but you do provide a service to them in the information you exchange towards a common goal. You are also their customer with the services they provide to you!

Nature of Email

Before we delve into email responses and how to craft an effective email, we need to talk about the nature of email. Email, as you know, is a form of mail. But what defines email is the speed in which the message can get from one person to another. We jokingly call regular mail "snail mail" these days because compared to email; it moves as slow as a slug.

So why does this matter? As someone responsible for responding to email, you need to understand that emails cannot wait, at all. If you aren't responding to email within hours, you're not doing your job. We'll talk about some ways to help you with this, like using auto-responders, but for now, you simply need to know that you must respond to email as quickly as possible.

Legal Issues with Email

One more thing we really need to cover before we go over fabulous ideas for writing tush-kicking emails: the law. Whether you know it or not, that little unsubscribe link you see at the bottom of most emails from businesses is there for a reason, and that reason is the CAN-SPAM Act of 2003. A law passed by Congress that regulates commercial email is called the "Controlling the Assault of Non-Solicited Pornography And Marketing Act of 2003," or CAN-SPAM for short. Using the word "assault" to describe email practices scares me! However, we needed drastic action in our country to address the new era of email.

The best way to fully understand the law is to read the examples and materials provided by The Bureau of Consumer Protection (BCP) here: http://www.business.ftc.gov/documents/bus61-can-spam-act-compliance-guide-business

Here are the highlights of CAN-SPAM. The law covers unsolicited email, which means if a prospective resident emails you and requests information, you're clear and free from the stringent requirements of CAN-SPAM. However, for emails you send out to anyone whose email address you collected but did not have them opt-in to messages or is not already a customer, here are the must do's according to the BCP, retrieved from:
http://www.business.ftc.gov/documents/bus61-can-spam-act-compliance-guide-business

Don't use false or misleading header information. Your "From," "To," "Reply-To," and routing information – including the originating domain name and email address – must be accurate and identify the person or business who initiated the message.

Don't use deceptive subject lines. The subject line must accurately reflect the content of the message.

Identify the message as an ad. The law gives you much leeway in how to do this, but you must disclose clearly and conspicuously that your message is an advertisement.

Tell recipients where you're located. Your message must include your valid physical postal address. This can be your current street address, post office box you've registered with the U.S. Postal

Service, or a private mailbox you've registered with a commercial mail receiving agency established under Postal Service regulations.

Tell recipients how to opt out of receiving future email from you. Your message must include a clear and conspicuous explanation of how the recipient can opt out of getting email from you in the future. Craft the notice in a way that's easy for an ordinary person to recognize, read, and understand. Creative use of type size, color, and location can improve clarity. Give a return email address or another easy internet-based way to allow people to communicate their choice to you. You may create a menu to allow the recipient to opt out of certain types of messages, but you must include the option to stop all commercial messages from you. Make sure your spam filter doesn't block these opt-out requests.

Honor opt-out requests promptly. Any opt-out mechanism you offer must be able to process opt-out requests for at least 30 days after you send your message. You must honor a recipient's opt-out request within 10 business days. You can't charge a fee, require the recipient to give you any personally identifying information beyond an email address, or make the recipient take any step other than sending a reply email or visiting a single page on an internet website as a condition for honoring an opt-out request. Once people have told you they don't want to receive more messages from you, you can't sell or transfer their email addresses, even in the form of a mailing list. The only exception is that you may transfer the addresses to a company you've hired to help you comply with the CAN-SPAM Act.

Monitor what others are doing on your behalf. The law makes clear that even if you hire another company to handle your email marketing, you can't contract away your legal responsibility to comply with the law. Both the company whose product is promoted in the message and the company that actually sends the message may be held legally responsible.

If you use an email marketing software program, your messages will most likely automatically include an unsubscribe link, as well as provide your physical address in compliance with CAN-SPAM. The rest, however, will be up to you. So if you're a serious marketer and reaching out to people who haven't requested information or opted-in to receive emails, do your homework and follow the rules.

Email Basics

Emails received by a leasing office come in for many reasons: residents needing help, vendors looking for a check, competitors wanting to know specials, and people within your own company reaching out. We will not cover specific techniques for responding to all of the various types of emails, as this chapter will primarily focus on prospective resident emails, but we should go over some email basics important for all messages.

Let me remind you one more time of the nature of email. It is speedy! If you aren't connected to your computer by the hip, make sure you are checking email regularly and often. Here are some tips to help you remember to check email throughout the day.

Set a recurring alarm on your phone. Use the alarm function on your mobile phone to alert you three or four times a day to check email. Checking email once a day just won't work. Your competitors will beat you to the punch and move ahead of you on the customer's list of places they want to visit. Why? Because your ability to respond in a timely manner is a demonstration of the care and attention you give to residents. This is also true for residents you would like to renew each year. There are many things about customer satisfaction that are in our control, and timely response to their needs is at the top of the list.

Have an assigned time for email responses and follow-up. This is a good way to guarantee focus and ensure thorough responses. You can do this two or three times a day if your office has solid coverage for the leasing floor.

Organize your inbox including using folders and colors where applicable. You can create a folder that says "Needs Follow-Up" and move emails you have not had a chance to respond to yet into the folder and come back to them in a short while, when you have time. Nonetheless, remember timeliness is key – so if you filter emails in this manner, DO NOT forget about them.

It is also imperative if more than one person is checking email that a system is in place to safeguard against two people responding to the same email. Pay attention to the top of the email, where in many programs it shows if you've already responded, and check the sent box if you are unsure.

Writing Skills and Grammar

The first major promotion I received in this fine business was to move from Assistant Manager to Training Coordinator. Back in the day, our main visual in the training room was the flip chart. Because I have never been a contender to win the national spelling bee, I conducted an on-going contest in my training room. If you were the first to point out a misspelled word, you got to take a dig into the prize bucket. While I made my weakness a fun contest for my audience, I was secretly embarrassed. Thankfully, today we use PowerPoint, which has spelling and grammar checks built in. There is still the occasional misspelled word making it to the big screen, but I now have confidence that these errors rarely happen.

All emails should adhere to the rules of good grammar. We live in advanced times, and you can utilize the tools at your disposal to check for spelling and grammar mistakes. If your email program does not have autocorrect or does not alert you to errors, copy and paste your email into a word processing program, like Microsoft Word, to verify your email's body is without spelling mistakes and common grammatical errors. Even today, when I handwrite a thank you note, I often type it into Word first and do a quick check of my spelling and grammar.

While a program's autocorrect can verify and find many errors, it is not foolproof. If you struggle with grammar, spelling, and sentence composition, find a book on the subject or an online course you can take to build your skills. One of my favorite hacks to find mistakes in your writing is to ask someone else to read your work out loud to you. You will quickly identify problems in structure and grammar when you hear your email read aloud.

Years ago, my All Star Partner and co-author of this book, Lisa Trosien, set me up with two email services which taught me a word each day and a grammar lesson. It was like going back to the fourth grade! One of the reasons why the lessons made a memorable impact on me as an adult was I now had practical knowledge of their usage and could put my new lesson into practice that day. There is no shame in my game. I am good at a number of things and know that I need to step up and try harder with the things that do not come naturally. Lisa Trosien is the All Star Partner who organized the writing of this book, and I was very proud that she picked me to write this chapter. It means I have come a long way, baby!

If you're interested in avoiding the most common grammar mistakes, take a look at these articles for the biggest offenders:

http://litreactor.com/columns/20-common-grammar-mistakes-that-almost-everyone-gets-wrong

http://www.businessinsider.com/11-common-grammatical-mistakes-and-how-to-avoid-them-2013-9

http://www.copyblogger.com/grammar-goofs/

Multifamily Lingo

I could write all day in multifamily lingo and anyone reading this book would probably understand me. However, your prospective resident would most likely be confused or, at the very least, have a hard time getting through a sentence littered with our industry's lingo.

Here are some examples using multifamily lingo and the improved version suitable for your prospects:

> Dear Mary,
>
> I've got a make ready I can show on Friday if you wanted to stop by. I'll tell the supervisor to put it on master so anyone can show you.
>
> Thanks,
> Lisa

> **Dear Mary,**
> **I am excited you want to tour the community and walk through the available apartment home. The apartment I was thinking of for you will actually be available for you to see on Friday.**
>
> **I may not be working on Friday but can make arrangements so any member of our team who is here can give you the full tour. Does Friday work for you?**
>
> **Sincerely,**
> **Lisa**

> Dear Bob,
> My LRO requires your lease rent to be at market and, therefore, I cannot come down on that price. I'm sorry if this doesn't work for you, but it is out of my hands.
>
> Sorry,
> Pam

Dear Bob,

    I understand your concerns regarding the monthly rent for the apartment you want. We have systems in place that ensure we treat all people equally and abide by the Federal Fair Housing Act. It is because of these systems that our monthly rent is non-negotiable; we strive to always be fair. If you'd like to come in, I can sit down with you and go over the average utility bills for that apartment and discuss other ways living here may save you on your budget. With our fully equipped fitness center, you might consider dropping your gym membership to save a little. Please let me know how I can assist you.

Sincerely,
Pam

You can see how the verbiage with multifamily jargon could confuse a prospective resident. You can avoid this mistake by taking the time to reread everything you type and imagine how the recipient would interpret it.

The Subject Line

We'll start at the top – the subject line. When crafting a subject line, regardless of the recipient, keep it on point and avoid using exclamatory words, slang, sales phrases, all caps, and punctuation. All of these are red flags to junk or spam filters, not to mention annoying. Let's look at a few different types of subject lines fails:

THE SCREAMER – LISTEN TO ME, I'M IN ALL CAPS! CAN'T YOU SEE I AM SO IMPORTANT?! Never ever use all caps unless you're typing out an acronym or abbreviation like FHA.

The One Word Wonder - "HI!" is probably the worst subject line ever and is also a major red flag for spam filters. No "Hello,"

"Here," "Yay" or "Yes!" either. Just avoid doing a one word subject with all your might - you can do it, I know you can.

<u>The Desperate Plea</u> - PLEASE open me! I really want you to read this. Puhlease, pretty, pretty please! No! Just stop that right now. It is very unbecoming and once again will alert spam filters that you're up to no good.

<u>The Faker</u> – "URGENT!" "Confidential," "Must Read!" and any other subject like that, which tries to deceive your reader into opening the email due to false pretenses is no good. Do NOT do it!

<u>The "I'm So Excited!!!!!!!!!!!!"</u> – We already mentioned to lay off punctuation in the subject line, but if you use it, you certainly never need to use more than one punctuation mark. Do not feel the need to fill out the subject line with fifteen exclamation points to show excitement – one works, and even that you shouldn't be using in the subject line.

<u>The Lying Reply</u> – My absolute biggest pet peeve and a very deceptive practice. Never try to fake your recipient into believing they are getting a reply by starting the subject line with "re:." This practice is not only deceptive; it is downright unethical.

Once you have your subject line, there are several free online testers you can run it through to see if it is likely to be caught in a spam filter. You can do a quick Google search to come up with some or use this site:

http://www.localnews.biz/subjectLine/ValidateSubjectLine.asp

The Body

Now you're ready to get to work on the body of your email. You want your prospective resident to open and read all the way through your email. I did a blog post on this very subject not long ago, and

I'm going to borrow from that to give you some real tips on getting people to read your emails.

I found myself reading my email today, and the whole point was to delete things that did not need my attention. I think many of us do this no matter what day of the week it is, but for this Monday, I was rapidly tapping the delete button. I started thinking about what it takes to get people to read email and found myself doing a search for some expert help.

Here are some tips from Jill Konrath who wants to make sure all of your emails elicit a response.

1. Eliminate Delete-Inducing Words – Get rid of all verbiage that activates the delete response. Here are some serious offenders: exciting, state-of-the-art, solution, partner, leading edge, passion, unique and one-stop shopping.

2. Keep Your Message Simple – Your email needs to be less than 90 words. Use two-sentence paragraphs so it can be scanned. Stick with common black fonts (no colors) and never include more than one link or attachment.

3. Align With Their Objectives – Research your prospect's specific needs, likes and other hot buttons which will help you connect. Relevance is essential.

4. Focus on Immediate Priorities – Identify key events that may be impacting your prospect's priorities and tie your message into that. An example might be if they are relocating from out of state, there are a lot of things that will need attention vs. a move across town.

5. Be an Invaluable Resource – In your e-mails, focus on the ideas, insights and information you can share that will be of value to your prospect in reaching their goals.

6. Craft Enticing Subject Lines – Your subject line determines if your message gets read. Avoid sales hype and focus on business

issues such as: "Quick question re: are you ready to move" or "Welcome home to Green Oaks Villas."

7. Launch a Campaign – Do eight to 12 touches (via e-mail and phone) over a four-to-six week period, with each contact building off the previous one. Provide links to resources. Spotlight the value of visiting today and making a decision.

Using the tips above, let's discuss sending emails to prospective residents. You very likely get the same requests over and over from prospects. I strongly recommend having pre-crafted messages saved for common requests. This will allow you to quickly respond to requests and do so with a message you know is right. Take a look at your requests for apartment information; create standard emails for all of these, and save them in a location where everyone can find them.

There are more varied requests than you may realize. I don't mean just to create messages for people wanting a one bedroom, or a two bedroom etc… You probably get requests from people interested in more than one floor plan, from people interested in short term or furnished apartments, people wanting to know your pet policy, etc. Create well written emails in advance for each of these, and you'll be sure your response is hitting the mark. **However, and this is a necessity, take the time to customize each of the pre-written responses so at the very least you are addressing the recipient by name.** If you can add any additional customization based on their original request, go for it, as it will make it even better. The more your email feels like you wrote it with only the prospect in mind, the better it will be in gaining trust and interest.

Let's look at creating some of these pre-written emails right now. First, what is our goal with an email? You may be thinking that every email has a different goal. No, not really - your primary goal with any email should be to get a response. You may want to lease the apartment over email and may end up doing so, but first and foremost, getting a response is all that matters.

Unlike the subject line, which we already covered, your email will have an opening line, middle and an ending.

Here are my tried and true tips for the opening line, body and signature of your email.

- <u>Never begin with, "Hi, my name is   ."</u> Instead, start off by saying something about them instead of you. Try, "I see that you are interested in two bedroom apartment homes."
- <u>Avoid generic messaging.</u> Just because you're using a pre-crafted message doesn't mean it needs to be generic. Your pre-created messages can be dynamic and inviting, and by customizing the message a bit for each recipient you'll avoid being just another email that says, "We have great two bedroom apartments that start at $950 per month."
- <u>Do not include attachments.</u> This one is hard for some people to follow, but it is a good rule of thumb. Attachments on emails are sometimes filtered off by an email program, and people are often hesitant to open them anyway. Unless a person specifically asks for an attachment, avoid sending one. If you can link to floor plans, photographs or video tours, that is a much better solution than using attachments.
- <u>Ask a great question.</u> When wrapping up an email, end with a fabulous question that will get them to respond. You don't have to ask, "Does that meet your needs?" You can ask, "Does our Hamburg two bedroom with that view of the lake sound like someplace you could call home?"
- <u>Signatures should not be distracting.</u> I believe signatures with links to your online presence are important. Nevertheless, you don't want a signature that is eight lines long and shows up in their email as an attachment (we'll discuss this more in a bit).

Since you're going to have to put your email messages together on your own, I've created a template using all we've discussed so far to help you get it right.

> To: JJones@gmail.com *[Always double check your "To" line on emails. Most programs have an auto fill for the "To" line that will automatically input an email address from your contacts or one that has been used in the past when you begin typing. Check it twice to make sure it is right.]*
>
> Subject: re: two bedroom availability *[Keep it simple and something relevant to what the prospect wants, many times this will be a reply so your subject will be what they had in their original request.]*
>
> Dear Ms. Jones, *[Mr. | Ms. prospect's last name]*
>
> I understand you are interested in a two bedroom apartment home that can be available for move-in next week. *[Keep the focus on the recipient and their needs.]*
>
> Residents in our two bedrooms love the layout of our Hamburg due to the oversized living room and open floor plan. We have one of these favorites coming available for when you need it, and it happens to be in an ideal location, overlooking our fully stocked fishing lake. You would get the benefit of afternoon sunlight on your screened-in patio, as well as be close to your garage, as it is directly across from the entrance. *[Something that relates to their wants and leads to the potential benefit.]*
>
> Does this apartment home sound like someplace you could call home? I can do 11:30 or 2:30 tomorrow for a tour; does that work for you?

If not, you can let me know what time works for you tomorrow or Friday, and I can arrange for a complete tour of the community. *[Ask your questions to encourage a response.]*

Sincere thanks,

Kate Good
<u>Hunington Residential</u>
480-888-5028

Notice how we got to the point quickly; people always appreciate that. We also kept in mind what's in it for them. Everyone likes to know what's in it for them, so tell them! And finally, we didn't add a lot of superfluous information. We've linked our website in our signature line in our example because you don't need to type out, "Here is how you find us online." The prospect emailed you and is smart enough to figure out how to access your website, and they can call you if they have a problem.

Get input from supervisors, marketing personnel, and your team members on creating the emails for your prospect requests for information. We aren't going to go into responding to resident requests, but if you keep the same rules in mind we've discussed in this book, you'll get it right.

<u>Signatures</u>

We briefly brushed on signature lines, but it is time to take a closer look at this component of email messages. Signatures are an important part of an email if they provide relevant information in an expected location. If you fill your signature with information the recipient doesn't need nor want; it is just an annoyance. Let's go over the rules for creating a great signature.

- <u>Save your signature.</u> This may seem like a no-brainer, but a lot of people actually don't know how to create and save a signature in their email provider. If you're using Outlook, create a new email and look along the top ribbon. Click on signatures and create new. If you have a hard time, Google "email signature and [your email provider]."

- Limit your lines. We discussed this earlier, but now I'm going to give you some tips to limit the lines. Use the vertical bar | or the colon to combine information such as your address and phone or your name and title (e.g. Kate Good | Director of Operations).
- Use relevant hyperlinks. If you can hyperlink text in the signature, such as the community's name to a website, then do so. However, you can consider adding hyperlinks for additional relevant information if you believe they will be helpful (such as a link to an online video tour of your community.)
- Consider social links wisely. It is great to link to your social channels, but there are two things to keep in mind. One, make sure your social channel is active. There is really nothing worse than linking to a twitter account that was last used three months ago. If you're linking to it, make sure you are using it. And two, Social icons often show up as attachments. If you want to use icons to link to the social channels because it looks cool, be wary. Often these icons will show up as an attachment, not be displayed on many mobile solutions, and increase the likelihood your email will be snagged in a spam filter. One way around it is to copy the style of the social channel and link the words to your pages or profiles (**facebook, twitter, YouTube** – these are not exact matches, but they get the point across and allows you to avoid using the icons). Check with your supervisor and legal team prior to including these in your signature line. The fonts used here are Lucida Sans for Facebook, Picowhite for Twitter (you can download it here - http://www2.wind.ne.jp/maniackers/pico.html) and Malgun Gothic for YouTube.
- Use Images Sparingly. Just as the social icon images would show up as an attachment in many inboxes, images of signatures or any other item is also considered risky. If you

feel you must include images, do so only after careful consideration.

Fair Housing and Email

We've discussed fair housing before, and like any other part of your multifamily business, your email needs to also comply with fair housing laws. We're not here to train you on fair housing; hopefully you've received thorough training. Yet we need to emphasize how critical it is to maintain compliance with your company's policies and the law regarding fair housing when sending emails.

Do not make any statements in your email that you would not make in person because you know they violate fair housing. Some of the common missteps would be bringing up seemingly relevant information that could be construed as a violation of fair housing. Sometimes great intentions can really get you in trouble. For example, don't ask a prospect if they have children because you have a wonderful playground. If a prospect emails you that they are in a wheelchair, do not respond with availability only on the ground floor – provide them the same information you would have had they not mentioned the wheelchair and let them decide. Always keep in mind your protected classes and respond accordingly. As crazy as that sounds, this is the best policy to avoid a possible claim of discrimination.

Follow-up and CRM

CRM is customer relationship management. Basically, that is a fancy way of saying you have a system in place for responding to emails in regular intervals in an attempt to maintain a relationship or close a sale. Eighty percent of potential sales are lost due to lack of follow-up. This is one of the biggest mistakes people make in marketing. Do you want to know how you could increase web conversions and sales by as much as 400%? The secret lies in what you do after you generate a qualified lead. The steps you take next to build a relationship and help your prospect get what they want make all the difference. Most people are so focused on getting qualified leads that they neglect to put their web site marketing and Internet Listing Service follow-up systems in place to convert leads to sales. It's so important that I'll say it again: with better follow-up, you could increase web sales by 400%.

Let's look to another blog post from my website, KateGood.com, to give you some of my best practices for CRM.

> Imagine you were training for the upcoming summer Olympics. You're a runner and want to win gold this year. You get a new pair of shoes to help you in your medal quest. Then you map your workout plan. With your coach at your side, you identify which exercises to do and when to do them. Each day until the coming Olympics you eagerly show up at the weight room and the track. What happens? Each week your strength and speed improve, and you become a stronger competitor increasing your chances of winning a gold medal.
>
> Now imagine a competitor who wants to win but after signing up for the team, didn't show up for practice. Who do you think is going to win? The person who follows up on their commitment with a series of planned activities or the one who neglects these? Web site marketing is like training for the Olympics - but with a whole lot more gold medals available! Start with a lead, regularly follow up, and you can win many more customers.
>
> You could continue marketing the same way and get the same results, or you could discover the lead generation and follow-up activities that can increase your sales by 400% or more. Just as in training for the Olympics, what you do and when is critical. Use these 7 follow up ideas you to increase your sales.
>
> 1. <u>Act Immediately</u> – Old leads are cold leads. Use

automated email responses or voice messages to instantly acknowledge a prospect's interest and give them the information they requested. If you plan to call them, let them know when you'll call. If you've offered something free to entice them to respond, deliver it instantly.

2. Use Curiosity to Motivate
The most powerful motivator in marketing is human curiosity. Tempt your prospects with something they want and pique their interest to prompt them to visit your community or to call you to get the details. I feel it is important to have a contact form on your site that asks questions that give you the clues you need to understand their hot buttons. When you use these hot buttons in your response, you will capture their attention.

3. Create a Sense of Urgency
People are prone to procrastinate; just ask me - I started writing this blog post in June! We put off doing things even when we want and need something. Give them a reason to act immediately, such as a limited time offer.

4. Educate Your Prospects
Customers may not have an immediate perception of their need for what you provide. What makes you unique compared to the competition? This product differential must be front and center in your marketing. Use each contact to help them define a problem or concern and demonstrate that your product or service is the solution.

5. Build a Relationship
The stronger your relationship with your prospects, the more likely they'll be to turn to you when they are ready to make a purchase. Do most men or women propose on their first dates? Of course not! And if they do, it is my personal experience you should RUN! It takes time and repeated contact to establish the basis for a long- lasting, mutually

beneficial relationship.

6. <u>Give Special Attention to Prospects Who Demonstrate an Interest</u>
Let's say you sent out a special $100 discount email offer to your prospect list. Typically, 10-16% of your prospects will open the email, and a much smaller percentage will act on it immediately. Go back with an even stronger call to action to the people that opened your initial email. You'll find that approximately 50% will open it, and you'll sell a lot more of your product and services.

7. <u>Use Automated Systems to Follow-up</u>
Set up your email auto responders to do your follow-up for you. Use each email contact to educate and motivate your prospects and tell them about your limited time offer. Remember that prospects are more likely to buy after six contacts, so use a series of six emails spread out over two weeks. However, this does not excuse the need for human contact. Reach out!

Want to earn gold with your business? Like Olympic athletes, you need more than goals. You need a follow up strategy and system. Put these in place, and you can capture the 80% of potential sales you're missing."

With these tips, you can build your own system of CRM to ensure proper follow-up for all your prospective resident leads. If your company utilizes CRM software, utilize it to its fullest potential. If you do not have a built in follow up tool or CRM in the programs you already use, ask if you can get one. There are free options like Zoho that get the job done and make you a more effective leasing professional.

There are two basic types of CRM – Analytical and Operational. Strong Analytical CRM includes acquiring data, analyzing data, and acting on the results. While most communities lack the software and tools to complete true analytical CRM, you can make some general assumptions based on what results you see in your CRM efforts. Pay attention to what email templates get the best results, look for patterns in open and response rates, keep notes, and share with others so you can brainstorm together to improve your customer relationships and email communication methods.

Operational CRM is something you are already doing and may not realize it. It includes maintaining regularly scheduled and spontaneous contact with current and potential residents, documenting all these touch points and finally following up to ensure satisfaction. Resident surveys are a form of CRM in the operational model, as they ask the simple question, "Are you happy with the service I've provided?" Make sure you act on the results from your surveys and follow-up. There is nothing worse than knowing you have problems in a specific area and not acting on it.

One More Thing

Email messages are not the only form of electronic messages you will receive in the office. Social channels like Facebook, Twitter and Google + are often used by consumers to communicate with businesses. Just as you do with email, you need to check these messages often and respond as soon as you can. In fact, people requesting service via social media expect a faster response time than via email. According to a survey by CONVINCE & CONVERT, "42% of customers complaining in social media expect a 60 minute response time."

If at all possible try to move these conversations out of social and onto email or to the phone. It will make it easier for you to keep track of the conversation and ensure you give the prospect or resident your full attention. But if they insist on continuing the conversation in social, then do so.

The same rules we've discussed for email apply to these messages, as well. Pay attention to grammar, maintain professionalism, and remember to get to the point while focusing on the customer's needs. Social messages are only going to increase as more people move away from email and utilize social apps and sites to reach out. Ask your supervisors about creating a plan for addressing residents and prospective residents in social media.

Wrap It Up

I have been an email crusader of sorts for a long time now. Nothing infuriates me more than emailing a community and not getting a response. There is no excuse for it. Regardless of your experience Onsite or your familiarity with best practices in multifamily, you are probably familiar with email and how you like to be responded to in a timely manner. I'm going to end this chapter with an example of exceptional email marketing. I've written about it before on my blog, so forgive me if you've seen it - it is too good not to share.

My cousin, Andrew, placed an order with 6 Dollar Shirts. This could have been your run of the mill internet transaction until he received a game changer in his email box. He found an

-----Original Message-----
From: Thread Pit Inc [mailto:news@6dollarshirts.com]
Sent: Thursday, August 01, 2013 2:55 PM
To: andrew
Subject: Package Shipped to You

This inbox is not monitored. Please do not reply to this email.

Hey Andrew Miller,

what's up superstar? God you look great today, but of course you knew that. Well Captain Fantastic, take this email and stand in front of a mirror. You there? Now say to yourself, "Congratulations, your order from 6DollarShirts is on its way." Because of your brilliant decision to order from us, you can now celebrate the fact that as of today your sweet tees are on the way!

While we know your ESP-ridden brain doesn't need it (we swear we aren't hitting on you), we still must provide you with this USPS.com tracking number to keep in your records: ■■■■■■■

At your request, we shipped the package to the following address:
Andrew Miller
■■■■■■■

If you are spreading your awesomeness outside of the US, here is a customs ID for you as well: . Please note that full tracking is not available to international locations.

Have we mentioned how great you look today?

Since all of this is happening so fast, we recommend you take a second to celebrate. So why don't we light some candles, throw on that Chaka Khan Greatest Hits album we both know you have, and kick up our heels in a platonic way of course.

If you have any questions, love poems, sultry songs or other heartfelt things you'd like to say, feel free to email us at info@6dollarshirts.com We'll be anxiously waiting to hear from you lover..of t-shirts we mean.

With love, as friends,
The 6DollarShirts Team

email that, among the thousands he receives in a week, was cool enough to send to his cousin Kate. Really people, this had to be an amazing email because I don't get emails from Andrew very often (not that I am upset, Cuz, I know you are a busy guy.).

6 Dollar Shirts had already secured the sale, Andrew's credit card was approved, and the shipment was on its way. Most businesses would stop there. The savvy marketers at this online retailer know there is more business to be earned. A simple, crafty, creatively worded email created a stir. Andrew shared with his friends at his office and now more people are aware of this company. This email tickled my marketing ear, and now I am posting it on my Website blog for hundreds of thousands of people to read (okay, maybe just a few hundred loyal readers.). But really, this means something, because before this email forwarded from my cousin, I had never heard of 6 Dollar Shirts.

Who else has told you that you look good today? Now go on, I dare you to check out www.6dollarshirts.com and buy the "Death before Decaf" tee shirt.

Chapter Review

Studies show that the timeliness of your response could be a determining factor if the customer decides to set an appointment for a visit to see your apartments. That does not mean that you can be lazy and ignore the rules of good writing or proper etiquette. Likewise, you must remember your email is often another step in the leasing process and your e-letter must be well crafted to keep prospective residents flowing into the sales funnel.

As someone responsible for responding to email, you need to understand that emails cannot wait, at all. If you aren't responding to email within hours, you're not doing your job.

Ensure that your emails comply both with CAN-SPAM and the Fair Housing Act.

Avoid confusing a prospective resident with multifamily jargon by taking the time to reread everything you type and imagine how the recipient would interpret it.

When crafting a subject line, regardless of the recipient, keep it on point and avoid using exclamatory words, slang, sales phrases, all caps, and punctuation.

Have pre-crafted messages saved for common requests. This will allow you to quickly respond to requests and do so with a message you know is right. Take a look at your requests for apartment information, create standard emails for all of these, and save them in a location where everyone can find them. However, and this is a necessity, take the time to customize each of the pre-written responses so at the very least you are addressing the recipient by name. If you can add any additional customization based on their original request, go for it, as it will make it even better. The more your email feels like you wrote it with only the prospect in mind, the better it will be in gaining trust and interest.

Your primary goal with any email should be to get a response. You may want to lease the apartment over email and may end up doing so, but first and foremost, get a response is all that matters. Signatures are an important part of an email if they provide relevant information in an expected location.

Do you want to know how you could increase web conversions and sales by as much as 400%? The secret lies in what you do after you generate a qualified lead. The steps you take next to build a relationship and help your prospect get what they want make all the difference. Have a customer relationship management (CRM) system in place for responding to emails in regular intervals in an attempt to maintain a relationship or close a sale: act immediately. Use curiosity to motivate, create a sense of urgency, educate your prospects, build a relationship, give special attention to prospects that demonstrate an interest, and use automated systems to follow-up.

Email messages are not the only form of electronic messages you will receive in the office. Social channels like Facebook, Twitter and Google +, are often used by consumers to communicate with businesses. Just as you do with email, you need to check these messages often and respond as soon as you can. If at all possible try to move these conversations out of social and onto email or to the phone. It will make it easier for you to keep track of the conversation and ensure you give the prospect or resident your full attention.

Resources

The Bureau of Consumer Protection (BCP):
http://www.business.ftc.gov/documents/bus61-can-spam-act-compliance-guide-business

Grammar:
http://litreactor.com/columns/20-common-grammar-mistakes-that-almost-everyone-gets-wrong
http://www.businessinsider.com/11-common-grammatical-mistakes-and-how-to-avoid-them-2013-9
http://www.copyblogger.com/grammar-goofs/

Spam Filter check:
http://www.localnews.biz/subjectLine/ValidateSubjectLine.asp
Jill Konrath: http://www.inc.com/guides/201108/7-tips-for-writing-e-mails-that-wont-get-deleted.html

The fonts we used above for examples of similar fonts used in social media are *Lucinda sans* for facebook, *Picowhite* for twitter (http://www2.wind.ne.jp/maniackers/pico.html) and *Malgun Gothic* for YouTube.

Chapter 12
iPad/Tablet Leasing

By Property Solutions

Tablet computers are changing the way leasing professionals connect with prospects and residents on a daily basis. Savvy property management experts are finding ways to use iPads and similar devices for more effective engagement and increased flexibility. This chapter will cover fundamental uses for iPads in the leasing office and the apps and programs that have been specifically designed with leasing in mind. We'll also dive deeper to suggest innovative ways you can use tablets to improve convenience and accessibility both in and out of the leasing office. You'll learn techniques for keeping tablets secure, both in the office and on the go. Let's get started!

When Apple introduced the iPad in 2010, few could have predicted the impact that it would have on the way people interact with their technology. In a few short years, mobile interfaces like tablets and smartphones are on track to become Americans' tool of choice for connecting to information and other people. While the desktop computer probably isn't going anywhere for a while, its place in the leasing office is diminishing to the supporting role as mobile technology moves to the forefront.

Tablets change the way that we are able to connect with prospects *and* residents. They provide an engaging, hands-on experience and introduce a new level of convenience and accessibility to processes. More than ever, our customers expect information that is organized and immediate. Tablets have also introduced an unprecedented expectation of mobility, and renters are less inclined to tolerate inconvenient or time-consuming processes. If it's not simple and immediate, chances are they'll simply move on.

Recognizing this overwhelming shift, the multifamily industry has created a number of tablet-friendly apps and programs that bring the functionality of property management software to this new interface. New apps and software, combined with a tablet's innate advantages, can help leasing professionals create memorable and positive interactions both inside and out of the leasing office. Add a little creativity, and you've got yourself enough functional and emotional advantages to make a significant difference in lease conversion and resident retention.

Chances are you have an iPad available in your leasing office or at least are considering its potential. How do you and your team use them? Do they work with your primary property management software? What apps do you use the most? Do you lock it in a drawer when you go out on the property or carry it with you? How do you keep the tablets themselves, as well as the information they contain, secure? If Candy Crush Saga or personal Facebook profiles are the default go-to apps in your office, you're missing a big opportunity. Read on! The pages ahead offer proven ideas for putting them to better use:

The Basics

Early naysayers to the iPad argued that the tablet computer was designed primarily for media consumption and entertainment and would never have much to offer on the productivity side of technology. However, the iPad and other tablets have proven that the functionality of a simple touchscreen is much more powerful than anticipated. Leasing agents can harness the multi-media advantages as well as transactional tools of the iPad to build a rapport with prospective renters and facilitate all manner of processes.

Availability, Floor Plans, & Pricing

Printing availability reports & property hot-sheets or scribbling current pricing and specials on a paper brochure is *so* 2009, especially when you can pull updated information onto your screen with the swipe of a finger. Multifamily apps give your leasing agents effective tools that let them spend time building relationships with prospective renters and can actually help close deals.

Imagine this: a prospective renter walks into the leasing office and asks about prices on a 2-bedroom apartment. You can dig up the leasing binder printout of today's availability report; duck behind your computer to check current status numbers, or approach your guest with the iPad to start flipping through gorgeous retina-display images of available units with photos, floor plans, associated pricing, and specials.

Digital Guest Card
Stacks of paper cards and old-school file systems only work so well when it comes to lead management. If you're lucky, you'll find time each day to transfer prospect information into your computer and set up appropriate prompts, for follow-up actions.

The iPad can actually help you capture lead information in the moment. Hand it over to the client to enter their details themselves, or make the notes yourself as you gather information in the course of your conversation. Digital guest cards can sync directly with your lead management system, automating follow-up prompts and making it significantly harder for good leads to get lost in the shuffle.

All Star Tip *Be sensitive to your prospect's comfort level with the tablet. Chances are your renters in the 30-and-under age group will happily take over and work their way around the touchscreen like a champ. Others may prefer to use a Bluetooth keyboard (keep one handy) to enter data, while a few may be uncomfortable handling the tablet at all. As with every customer interaction, pay close attention to verbal and non-verbal cues and offer alternatives if necessary.*

Information Sharing
The average prospective renter will visit your property at least two to three times before making their final decision. If you're on top of things, they'll be able to walk in any time and speak to any leasing

agent without missing a beat. If not, your prospective renter's second or third visit to the property may feel a bit like that Groundhog Day movie which is not a promising way to make a good impression.

Your iPad can sync with your lead management system to help any leasing agent retrieve all relevant notes and preferences the instant your prospect returns. By accessing data quickly, the interactions with the prospect will feel that much more personal, and the prospect will walk away feeling confident and cared for: a very good impression, indeed.

Selling the Neighborhood
Renters aren't just looking for units, amenities, and square feet; they're looking for their next home. This means you need to sell your neighborhood as an extension of your community. Apps like Google Maps make it easy to showcase landmarks in the surrounding area and help a renter imagine their life after the move. You can highlight nearby schools, shops, parks, and restaurants, or quickly look up driving directions to their place of business to help them plan their new commute.

All Star Tip *You don't always need an app for that. Bookmark websites for all the local schools and other important landmarks right on your tablet's browser. These bookmarks can be used as an easy reference guide and help to quickly answer frequently asked questions about the neighborhood.*

Online Leasing
Best case scenario: your guest card app will automatically port to your online application (and then the lease) so dual data entry is unnecessary. However even if your lead management and leasing systems don't sync automatically, an iPad can be a very convenient (and eco-friendly) way to collect online applications, saving you (literally) tons of paper over time, and painlessly moving the prospect along the path to leasing. Many apps provide login credentials that allow prospects to begin an application or lease on

your iPad and finish it later at home from their own computer or tablet. Applicant tracking is automatic.

Payments

Payment processing software lets you collect application fees and deposits (and even rent) right on the spot. And by "on the spot" we mean anywhere you can carry your iPad. Out on tour? No need to walk all the way back to the office to take care of the formalities. Everything you need is at your fingertips.

Ratings and Reviews

Your prospective renters expect you to rave about your community; they know you want to close the lease. But they're more inclined to actually believe what your current and former residents have to say. Pull up current reviews on the iPad and reassure them with actual testimonials that your care and attention will continue long after the lease is signed. Use your property management app's ratings and reviews function or bookmark your property's Yelp and Google pages for quick access.

The Technology Experience

Many of your young renters are walking into your leasing office with a small, bright interactive device already in their hand, and it can sometimes become a challenge to compete for their attention. But when your competition is a smartphone, a smart tablet display can help capture and hold their focus and give you a chance to present the information they want.

Believe it or not, the mere presence of sleek, functional tablet computers in your leasing office can help make your customer's experience more memorable. When you're selling the same walls, roofs, and basic amenities package as the competitor down the street, you do what you can to be memorable. You want them to think back to you and say "Oh yeah, that was the place with the iPads." A few tablet computers and you're suddenly high-tech *and* resident-friendly.

Property management companies have had positive results setting up iPad "lounges" where prospects can take self-guided "tours" of the property and research apartment information and amenities while waiting for a leasing agent to become available. (Residents can use these same kiosks to log into your resident portal to pay rent or submit maintenance requests.) In order to accommodate families who visit the office together, one company even set up a small play area for children with several iPad minis preloaded with simple games and tethered securely to the table.

"We're really focused on making it a better experience for both our residents and our prospects, and a lot of it has to do with infusing technology into our leasing centers." -Tracy Bolton, Dominium.

Training and Administrative Tasks
Tablets don't only come in handy when working with your renters. A multitude of note-taking apps (e.g., Evernote) or task management systems (e.g., Wunderlist, Podio, Asana, etc.) can be used and synced across all the iPads in your office to help facilitate file sharing and communication. iPads can be used in training sessions to listen to and evaluate leasing calls. The possibilities are limited only by your ingenuity.

The Reasons

OK, we admit it. Most of the base functionality described above can be adequately handled by the old trusty leasing office desktop or even a handy laptop computer. You may wonder if the cost to invest in a set of tablets for the leasing office is really necessary. We think the answer to that query is an unequivocal 'yes' and the reason for that answer can be summed up in a single word: **Mobility.**

Strike While the Iron is Hot
Every leasing agent has experienced it at least once; it's almost a cliché; you're out on tour with a prospective client, and they love the model and are happy with the location of the available unit. They're excited about the school district and the handy public

transit hub just down the street. They are ready to sign on the dotted line and even a little impatient to get their application submitted and approved. As you return to the leasing office to get the paperwork started, you cringe to see "that" resident inside, loudly haranguing your colleagues about the ghosts in the heating ducts, the latest government conspiracy, or some other misfortune. He's annoying, but harmless. However, suddenly your prospect is a little less enthusiastic. They decide to take the application paperwork home with them and (dun dun DUN) "think it over."

With tablet leasing, this scenario becomes obsolete. Your prospective renter has already completed their application and paid a security deposit before you leave the model. You can bypass the dramatic scene in the office entirely and even send their email confirmation as you escort your client directly back to their car. You are completely empowered to perform your tasks and exchange all necessary information in the right way and at the right time.

The Leasing Office of the Future

A well-equipped tablet computer can turn any restaurant or coffee shop into a fully functional leasing office. This tool was successfully used at one small, urban infill property in downtown Portland, Oregon whose size and location didn't justify building out office space. During lease-up, a leasing agent would meet their prospective renter at the construction site and use the iPad to review property and amenity information, including photos and floor plans. If all went well, they'd sit down at the cafe across the street and the customer would be able to fill out their application and make a credit card or eCheck deposit on the spot.

Another property with a strong iPad policy sends leasing agents armed with their iPads to community events held at local restaurants. These events are able to function as de-facto open houses, and leasing professionals can collect guest card information from any interested customer on the spot, with leads automatically uploading to their property management software.

The Sustainable Solution
Everyone wants to be "green" but no one wants their eco-consciousness to cost a lot of green. Tablet leasing actually allows you to implement more sustainable, less wasteful practices that save you money on printing, paper, and document storage.

[Tablet leasing] has helped to reinforce our sustainable branding message that we've been trying to promote throughout our portfolio. It has helped to streamline leasing efforts at the site level by going paperless." - Brandy Guthery, Guardian

Digitizing property brochures not only costs less than printing, but they're easier to update and personalize, and can be automatically sent to a prospect's email. Guest cards, application forms, and even leases can all be completed, signed, stored, and searched using available property management apps. Resources are no longer being pumped into banks of filing cabinets; time spent tracking misplaced paperwork, or countless hours of filing and retrieving documentation. Electronically filed leasing documents make it easier for leasing professionals to search and locate information, take infinitely less space, and are significantly harder (but admittedly not impossible) to misplace.

A Bird in the Hand...
...is worth two in the bush - so they say. As far as birds go, we'll have to take their word for it. But for our purposes, it means that -- however much we love our prospective renters -- the value of current residents should not be ignored. Happily, the iPad offers ways to facilitate your resident interactions and offer them superior service and convenience. For example:

- Resident portal enrollment: On move-in day, you can stand in your resident's new home with them and use your tablet to show them how to log in to the resident portal and make online payments, submit work orders, or complete other transactions.

- Site inspections: Don't carry the big old spreadsheet around. Use your iPad to complete the inspection, including adding notes and photos as you go.
- Work orders: Equip your maintenance team with a tablet computer to update the status of maintenance requests as they go. Syncing this portable technology with your work order system lets you work through punch list, respond immediately to urgent requests, and keep track of everything as it happens.
- Ratings & reviews: Your tablet isn't just a handy way to display resident testimonials for prospective renters; it can also help you collect feedback directly from residents. Leasing office kiosks can link directly to review sites, making it easy for them to record their experience.
- Renewals: After all of your hard work to keep your residents happy and comfortable, an iPad can make lease renewal an entirely different experience. Rather than sending a notice via snail mail, or email, why not make the invitation to renew more personal. Visiting residents at their door, with an iPad in-hand, gives you a chance to personally hear their thoughts, address their concerns, and re-sign their lease right on the tablet.

"We go door-to-door and allow residents to renew their leases by signing directly on the iPad. Those in student housing know that students sometimes have a hard time getting motivated, so we make it extremely simple for them." - Del de Windt, Cardinal Group Management

The Advanced Level

Are you already using tablet computers to add efficiency, convenience, and style to your leasing tasks? Then maybe you're looking for fresh ideas or ways to get even more from this remarkable leasing tool. Following are some ideas to consider.

The iPad as Emergency Aid: We strongly recommend spending a little extra to get mobile data or 4G capabilities on your leasing office tablets. Why? One property in Massachusetts experienced repeated power outages during periods of high winds. When the neighborhood went dark, this leasing office didn't have to. Residents would still come in, people still showed up for tours, and even without a working modem the leasing professionals could still pull up all the real-time data they needed on their tablets: from resident ledgers to guest cards. Their property management app even allowed them to input information when completely offline, which was cached and synced with their property management software as soon as the connection was restored.

Finger-signing: Online leasing with an iPad can extend beyond guest cards and applications. With online leasing systems and integrations with online leasing documents services such as Blue Moon, renters can literally sign leases right on the iPad's screen. The executed document can then be safely archived, and a digital copy sent to the resident without printing a single piece of paper.

All Star Tip *Although executing a contract with the tip of your finger may be a delightful novelty for some, many still prefer a more traditional experience. Get the best of both worlds by offering your customer a pen-sized stylus to use while signing the lease on the screen.*

Apple TV: Enhance your iPad's capabilities with a $99 Apple TV. You can attach it to the back of your clubhouse TV with a few pieces of double-sided sticky-tape and set up your tablet to mirror onto the larger screen. This is particularly helpful when you're working with several people at once. Rather than all hunching around a small tablet, you can present information to the group more comfortably.

Security links: Utilize apps on your tablet to link to existing security cameras all over your property. This allows you to easily tap into your security feed from near or far and respond more quickly to emergency situations.

The Best Practices

Software
A tablet is only as powerful as its software. The first step for setting up your iPad is to make sure you've downloaded and set up the apps provided by your property management software provider. This will allow you to access important information more conveniently and keep records of your transactions up-to-date. Depending on your software provider, you may find all the accessibility you need on a single app, or you may need to download and set up several apps for different kinds of leasing transactions.

Remember, tablet-friendly technology is still new; the landscape changes almost daily and functionality varies widely, so take some time to do your research. Ask around, talk to your IT department, contact your service reps, or check out industry message boards like Multifamily Insiders for the latest tips and tricks. A little bit of time and effort invested at the beginning of the process can pay big dividends in time savings and convenience later on. The last thing you want is for your tablet to create more work in the leasing office so be sure to look for the following:

- Property hot sheet: The ability to access current availability and pricing is a must. Bonus points if you can associate lead information with specific units.
- Lead management system: You want to be able to access your CRM from your tablet to easily track the status of prospective renters and help create a memorable, personalized experience each time they visit.
- Property photos and floor-plans: Make the most of all those pixels by flipping through floor plans, property maps, and photos of your property.
- Virtual tours and videos: Don't let your multi-media marketing go to waste. Play relevant presentations for

prospects during their visit. Then email them a link to review at home.
- Property brochure emails: Make it simple to send prospects home to an email with all the details they need to make a decision (and collect their email contact plus save paper all at the same time.)
- Digital guest cards: Let visitors input information directly on the tablet and don't risk losing another card.
- Online applications/leases: Simplify the collection of required documentation. Get all the necessary "paperwork" started anytime, anywhere.
- Payment processing: They're ready to make a deposit right now? Use your iPad to accept credit card or eCheck payments on the spot.
- Automatic syncing: With real-time availability information at your fingertips, you're assured that guest-cards and prospect notes will be instantly transferred to your lead management system.

Settings
When introducing tablets into the leasing office, it's important to have a documented policy in place and communicate it effectively. This could include guidelines on which specific apps are required, as well as suggestions for other apps that may be helpful. If some apps are prohibited, make that clear as well, and spell out rules for security settings like passwords or pins, screen locking, and recovery functions such as "Find my iPad."

If members of your leasing staff are unfamiliar with tablets, offer hands-on training. That $600 iPad isn't going to help anyone if it's always locked in a drawer. Touchscreens are built to be intuitive, but learning curves can be considerably shortened by walking staff through relevant tasks such as creating a guest card, checking unit availability, submitting a payment, attaching a photo to a work order, etc. Role-playing can also help employees practice using the tablet in an engaging way.

We highly recommend using automatic lock screens and passwords on all devices that you carry with you on the property. Tablets that are set up in kiosk displays, on the other hand, are more useful if they remain accessible to prospects and residents during office hours. Some property management apps offer a "kiosk mode" that allow visitors to access all public information, but keep them from getting into administrative screens or settings.

All Star Tip *Whether you're setting up multiple iPads at once or adding a new tablet to your office, the Apple Configurator app makes configuration a breeze. Once you have a primary tablet configured to your liking, you can simply plug the new devices in. The app will detect the new tablet and the desired settings will be automatically duplicated. No muss, no fuss. Once you've figured out the functionality for your tablets, take a moment to focus on presentation. Set up a background image that reflects your community's brand and make it consistent across all the tablets used on-site. Keep links to relevant information neatly arranged on the main screen, and move extra or personal apps to a secondary screen. And, this should go without saying, keep a microfiber cloth handy and make a point to clean smudges and fingerprints off the screen regularly.*

Accessories

There's an entire industry of add-ons and accessories designed specifically to make your tablets easier to use. We recommend:

- Cases/Covers: Look for cases and covers that will provide both protection and ease-of-use. Many cases offer a strap or handle to make it easier to hold the tablet securely and easily while on the go.
- Tethers and table-stands: Absolutely necessary for kiosk-mode iPads, many stands can be bolted into the wall or furniture to allow visitor's access to the functionality of the tablet while keeping the tablet physically secure.
Bluetooth keyboards and stands: Invest in a full-size keyboard to facilitate tasks that are more data-entry intensive.

- A dedicated network: While not technically an accessory, a dedicated, secure WiFi network for your tablets -- distinct from normal or guest WiFi networks -- can mean the difference between a seamless tablet experience and uncomfortable lag times.

Chapter Review

Tablet computers are fast becoming the go-to technology for leasing offices. You might say your iPad contains the future of leasing. You don't have to have a tablet computer to create a memorable leasing experience for your clients, or to find current pricing and availability on the apartment they want, or to collect lead information, but each of these transactions is made infinitely faster and simpler with an iPad in your hand. There is no comparable technology right now that can offer the increased convenience, timeliness, and engagement available with a tablet.

Your renters are already using mobile devices like tablets and phones for most of their technology needs. As of this writing, nearly half of traffic coming to the typical property website is from a tablet or a mobile device. It's not unusual or edgy for them to use mobile apps to complete daily transactions; it's absolutely mundane. They're likely to see paper forms and manual transactions, not as normal, but as outmoded and inefficient. Transitioning your leasing office to tablet technologies helps you meet expectations and can be a way of building efficiency and cost savings into every task you complete.

The world of tablet computing is only a few years old, -- practically speaking -- and like most young things, it is growing fast. We think it's easier to embrace the changes as they happen rather than to hold onto old processes until they're completely obsolete. Will the touchscreen conquer the world and keyboards become obsolete? Will hybrid laptop/tablets like Microsoft's Surface find a solid niche? Is there something else, something that's not even on our radar, poised to turn tablet computing on its head in another few years? Only time will tell.

Resources

Property Management Apps
MRI - Vaultware Leasing Tablet
Occius - My Resident Network Mobile
Property Solutions - SiteTablet, Entrata Tablet - https://itunes.apple.com/us/artist/property-solutions-international/id385850025
RealPage Inc. - Mobile Leasing, Smart Leasing Tablet - https://itunes.apple.com/us/artist/realpage-inc./id664001159
Yardi - LeasingPad, ShowHome, Maintenance Manager - https://itunes.apple.com/us/artist/yardi-systems-inc./id425728804

Social Media Apps
Facebook
LinkedIn
Twitter
Google +
Instagram
Snapseed
Foursquare
Pinterest
Hootsuite
Pandora
Spotify
YouTube

Communications, Productivity & Business Apps
iWork Suite (Pages, Numbers, Keynote)
Google Drive
Gmail
Evernote
Wunderlist
Notability

Asana
Power.ME
Paper by FifthyThree
IFTTT
SignEasy
Skype
BAO
DataVault Password Manager
GroupMe
Dropbox
GoToMeeting
Cisco Webex Meetings

Communications, Productivity & Business Apps, Cont'd
Evite
Viber

Hardware & Accessories
Heckler Design Stands - http://hecklerdesign.com/
Square Credit Card Scanner - http://squareup.com
Pynwheel Multitouch Tables and Panels
http://www.pynwheel.com/
Maglus Magnetic Stylus - http://maglusstylus.com/
Pencil stylus by FiftyThree
Zagg Bluetooth Keyboard
Apple Wireless Keyboard - http://store.apple.com
Apple TV - http://www.apple.com/appletv/
Lightning HDMI Adapter
Moshi Versa case

Chapter 13
Fab-YOU-lous Fundamentals of Follow-up

By Toni Blake

A Philosophy of Follow-up

What is your philosophy for follow-up? Do you have one? How much of your effort, training, and leasing plan is dedicated to follow-up? In this chapter I am going to share with you my philosophy for follow-up along with powerful media, techniques and procedures that will make you more successful in leasing. Follow-up is what separates the good from the great leasing consultants.

I recently saw a negative review based on the fact that the leasing office did not get back with the customer. The lack of follow-up drove the consumer back to the site to leave a negative review. Does the customer care whether you follow-up or not? Let's explore this question and others as we dive into a Fab-YOU-lous follow-up for today's consumer.

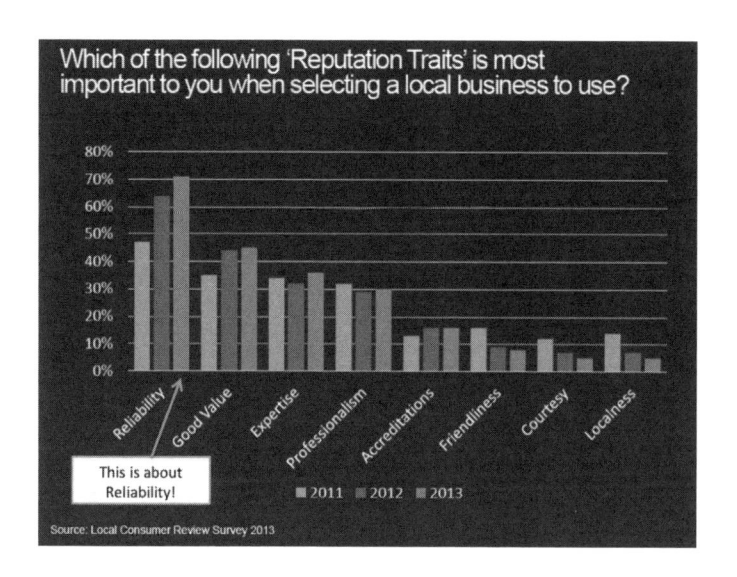

Which of the following 'Reputation Traits' is most important to you when selecting a local business to use?

[Bar chart showing Reliability, Good Value, Expertise, Professionalism, Accreditations, Friendliness, Courtesy, Localness across years 2011, 2012, 2013. Reliability is highest at ~70%. Annotation: "This is about Reliability!"]

Source: Local Consumer Review Survey 2013

BrightLocal, a company that provides a powerful set of local SEO tools, produced a survey with 3 years of data research on the consumer's experience with the rating review sites. When asked: "Which of the following 'Reputation Traits' is most important to you when selecting a local business to use?" the highest rated response was reliability. Reliability ranked 700 times more important than friendliness. Today, people want you to be reliable. This means when the prospective resident asks for information or contacts you to find out about your community, your reliability in delivering information is the MOST important aspect of your role in the beginning stages of the relationship. The first contact a prospect has with your property is an opportunity for you to show reliability. In this chapter, I am going to show you creative and meaningful ways to deliver important relationship-building-information to your customer through follow-up.

In the book "Business @ The Speed of Thought," by Bill Gates, he writes, "The most meaningful way to differentiate your company from your competition … is to do an outstanding job with information. How you gather, manage and use information will determine whether you win or lose." People find great value in the right information. Your customer has so many questions along with problems that need solving before they can make a decision to rent. The more helpful you are in gathering information that provides answers and solves problems, the more you will differentiate yourself from your competition.

Take a moment and put yourself in the shoes of the consumer. Open your internet browser and Google, "questions you should answer before you rent an apartment." You will be amazed at the advice you will find from a variety of sources. Unfortunately, very few of the sources found were representatives of our industry. In the first stage of building meaningful follow-up, I want you to examine the questions your consumer is dealing with and set your intention to be helpful. Gathering information and being prepared to answer your customer's questions carries remarkable persuasive power.

Become a Useful Advisor

In Jay Baer's New York Times bestselling book "YOUtilities," he presents a powerful debate on the need today to be "genuinely and inherently useful." Consumers are inundated with commercial messages today. We compete for their attention with their job, family, relationships, social media, entertainment and everyday life. If the consumer gives you their attention, even if only for a moment, don't blow it by selling! No one likes to be sold. Have you ever answered the phone and recognized it as a pesky sales call? Did you feel your primal inborn response to flee kick in? Let's be real. You're not listening to the caller; you're only trying to figure out how to get off the call -- right? Do you seriously want people to flee from you? Selling and commercial messages are a turn OFF! How many people record shows when they are live and watch them later so they can fast-forward through the commercials? We delete spam, throw away junk mail, and look at our caller ID before answering a call, all to avoid being sold. People are turned ON by useful, helpful advice.

Pinterest's huge popularity speaks to the passion people have for creative ways to problem solve and accomplish life's everyday tasks with style. I love the cooking channel, DYI and educational programs about getting things done. Your customer is about to face moving. Of all stressful events, moving ranks just below a death in the family. What your customer really needs is a helpful advisor with useful, reliable information. Is that you?

Gathering, and having available, useful information will assist your customer in choosing your apartment community to call home. Below is a list of questions most prospective residents are looking to answer:

- Is this the neighborhood I am looking for?
- Is this a safe area?
- How are the schools?
- What kind of shopping is around here?
- Are there nice restaurants in the area?
- Are there any trails, parks, bike or walking paths?
- Is there reliable maintenance service?
- Are the people nice?
- Do I fit in?
- Is there a fitness center?
- Is there a pool?
- Where is the closest Wal-Mart or grocery store?
- Is this apartment in the area and community I am looking for?
- How far do I have to walk to park my vehicle?
- Where are the trash receptacles?
- Is there an on-site laundry facility?
- Where is my apartment within the community?
- Does the apartment accommodate my lifestyle & belongings?
- What is the average cost of utilities?

- How much are pet fees?
- What move-in costs will I incur?
- What do I need to qualify?
- How is the cell signal from my apartment?

Rather than share your opinion, locate helpful resources that provide reliable data and area information. You will find great neighborhood information at Walkscore.com and City-data.com. Area demographics can speak to the "safe" question. City-data.com provides graphs of the latest real estate prices and sales trends, hundreds of thousands of maps, satellite photos, geographical data, state profiles, crime data, cost of living, housing, businesses, hospitals, schools, libraries, airports, radio and TV stations, zip codes, area codes and professionally written city guides.

Schooldigger.com shows test scores, rankings, school and district boundaries, student/teacher ratios, ethnic makeup, scores of other useful metrics and information for over 120,000 elementary, middle, and high schools in the United States!

With a little digging, you are sure to find useful information that will convey reliability to your prospective residents. Be cautious because the quality of the content you share will play a key role in the value your customer finds in your efforts. Take the time to sift through the information and create an easy to read summary to share with your customer. Perhaps you could produce a helpful PDF to attach to a follow-up email as a "10 Important Reasons Why People Love Living at Our Apartment Community." Screen shot a map showing retail, restaurants, and parks and recreation around your community.

A crucial element of follow-up is being prepared to help your customer. Successful follow-up begins by building a plan and then being prepared to quickly share great information when interacting with your prospective resident.

This first step of gathering and sharing reliable information will insure your own personal confidence in creating effective follow-up.

Building a Fab-YOU-lous Follow-up Plan

Building your plan will involve providing great decision making information throughout the prospect's entire apartment search. At the beginning of the search process there are so many unanswered questions and your first contact with a prospect should result in having your property make "the short list."Most prospects will be searching a wide range of apartments. Following up in creative ways, and sharing reliable information will draw attention to your community as a viable choice and will naturally cause the prospect to focus on your community.

Initiate a series of different types of follow-up techniques on first contact that include a telephone, email and video. Prospects are full of questions – be full of answers! Give your customer several unique looks at your community that will show them why they should choose you. There are leasing consultants that don't follow-up at all, and this is a total disservice to the consumer. As property management professionals, we help people find new homes each day and we should be seen as experts in this process. Your role should be to help people along the decision path to selecting a great new apartment home – at your community. When the prospect connects with you by telephone, email or online lead, your first contact with a prospect should establish your expertise, reliability and confidence By taking the time to build reliable information, you will build confidence into the decision making process for your customer.

Develop a Fab-YOU-lous Company Standard for Follow-up

Before I begin sharing my techniques I want to address your success standard and commitment to follow-up. I find many companies do not have clear goals and performance standards for follow-up. It is neither expected nor inspected.

Regardless if you are in leasing or part of the management team if you want to move forward in your career, follow my plan. Do not let a lack of company vision regarding follow-up distract you from developing successful habits in this area. I am confident that on your guest card and within your management software that there are places that will allow you to document and record your follow-up efforts. Set your own standard for success and be committed to being a useful part of the decision making process for your customer with providing creative and useful follow-up.

Property management executives, have you ever heard of the executive law of gravity? The focus, vision and direction of your company are impacted by where you place your attention. If you suddenly look at service, it improves. If you send out a memo to make the grounds cleaner, trash disappears from the properties. I hope to inspire you with a vision for follow-up. Your interest and direction in proper follow-up techniques will help your teams develop fab-YOU-lous follow-up fundamentals. Delegate a group of team members to research follow-up options, media and techniques shared in this chapter. Then, build a reliable follow-up program rich with decision-making information and problem solving advice for your firm. Find out what data fields are already in place for documentation. Develop management habits that expect and inspect your follow-up standards. Help your teams to become committed to being a useful part of the decision making process for your customer with a meaningful follow-up plan. As Bill Gates said, "The most meaningful way to differentiate your company from your competition … is to do an outstanding job with information. How you gather, manage and use information will determine whether you win or lose."

On Your Mark, Get Set - Follow-up

PRINT ME – How to Get Information in Their Hands NOW!

While on a phone call with a customer, you should begin the follow-up process! Find out if they have a computer in front of them, access to the internet and a printer. If they do, get ready to show up where they are NOW, during the call! No sense in waiting to send them information when you can review it with them personally. Ask them to print your information while you speak! Follow-up begins NOW while we are on the phone.

You can't send your prospect information unless you have it readily available. Here's what you need to do to get prepared:

I want you to explore each on-line location where your property markets and make note of the locations and where there is a printable brochure. Most internet listing services and company websites offer a "print button" to print online brochures, or at least floor plans.

Once you have taken note of the best place to print online brochures and floor plans for your community, build a quick email that you can send the prospect immediately, sharing the link to your website with a printable brochure.

When you create an email, in the subject line type: "For you to review while we talk!"

The body of the email would look something like this:

"Here is a quick link to our company website with images of our community, floor plans and all of our contact information."

Ask the prospect for their email address and send them the prepared email. You could say something like: "Rather than just tell you about it, I would love to show you too. If you have internet access, I can send you a quick email with a link right to the floor plan. I can also show you pictures of the property, area, and a detailed list of amenities both inside the apartment and at the community. What is the best email address for me to send that to right now?

Once your prospect receives the email, you can ask them: "Do you have a printer close by? If yes – perfect hit that print button to print the floor plan so you can take notes while we talk." Be prepared to describe the exact location of the print button on any website where your community advertises.

By sending the prospect an email, while you're on the phone with them, you will be able to walk the prospect through the community and floor plan with fabulous visual aids. Once they have printed your information, you have transformed yourself from virtual to reality! While every other property they looked at disappears into a distant memory, with the next click, you are sitting pretty in the printer tray!

Your next opportunity will be to invite the prospect to view your community in person. Make certain to ask them, "Do you know where we are located? I love MapQuest! I can send you a quick GPS link and even let you know where the best price for gas is on the way." This stages your next follow-up.

Once you make an appointment let them know you will send them a digital appointment card. Be sure to give yourself plenty of reasons to stay in touch! Stage your follow-up in the call by letting the customer know what to expect – then deliver!

Leaving a Fab-YOU-lous Voice Mail

In the past, our number one way to follow-up was to give the prospect a phone call. How many of you know people who simply do not answer their phone? Instead of answering their phone, many people prefer to communicate via text messaging. Text messaging has stepped into our fast-paced world often used as a juggling tool for everyday life. People can respond quickly and then move on with their busy day. Because of the convenience and well received mode of communication, it is important that your company have access to a robust SMS (short message service) B2C (business to consumer) text platform. (Make sure your owner or Management Company allows you to text your prospective residents.)

If you decide to call the prospect, you had better work out how to leave a great voicemail! I like to leave a quick voicemail that says, "You've got mail! I sent you the information you requested and added a cool coupon for this new coffee house around the corner in case you want to try it when you come over. See you soon, and I look forward to meeting you!" The combination of voice and email work to bring a personal touch to your follow-up. In this chapter, I am going to show you a ton of great new tools using audio/voice that are not voice mail!

Toni's 5 Fab-YOU-lous Rules for Phone Messages

- Be quick! A 12 to 16 second message and you are OUT OF THERE!!!!!!If you are always quick and to the point with your messages, your prospect will be much more likely to listen to your messages in the future!
- Start with who you are and why you are calling.
- Give information they requested. Don't ever call without reason; "just because" does not work in this relationship. Respect their life and be useful.
- Offer a bit of useful area information or coupons.
- Finish strong. Have a sign off that is confident, full of personality and your own. Just like in the movie Anchorman he signed of by say "Stay Classy San Diego!" Be unique, show personality and be memorable with your own signature sign off!

Practice makes perfect! Be sure to practice your messages and be certain to make and make call notes. Don't' do distracted dialing!! People can tell if you are focused on them or if you are distracted. Make call notes on the prospect's guest card prior to calling. By doing so, you have a reference and also a record of the call!

Fab-YOU-lous Voice Memo – Email

Today most smart phones have a voice memo or an audio recording feature. If not, there is an app for that! If you already have this feature or app on your personal phone, why not use it for follow-up? Simply follow Toni's rules for phone messages and record a few great follow-up voice memos. The pre-recorded voicemail can be sent via email and will most likely be heard long before a voicemail will be retrieved. Unlike the pressure of leaving a voice mail that you can't change, the great thing about recording a message is that if you mess up you just delete it and start over. Also, you can record some generic messages with themes that can be used over and over again. Simply email the messages to your business email and download them into a file on your computer for easy access. (Please make sure your owner or Management Company allows you to use your smartphone to leave messages for prospective residents.)

Fab-YOU-lous E-card Resources

If you are pulling up an email on your business program and typing the prospect a simple message, YOU LOSE!!! Seriously, how boring are you? Below I have listed several websites that will assist you in sharing creative, colorful, musical, animated messages that will help you stand out from the leasing crowd. I also have a Pinterest board where I will continue to post ideas! Follow me at www.Pinterest.com/totallytoni.

Please be certain to test every site before using it to communicate with prospects. Simply send yourself a note or e-card from each website. Make sure the websites haven't added commercials. Also be certain to check the amount of time it takes to load each card.

Discuss a budget for beautiful e-cards and establish accounts so you can be creative and share unforgettable follow-up with your customers. The art and sound of these great cards are worth the investment. Test out the websites and find a look and style the matches your community and invest the small fee to increase your leasing success.

BlueMountain.com – Review the cards and see if this is a site you want to include in your follow-up plan. A free trial is available. To use the service regularly, the service costs approximately $3.99 per month.

Ojolie.com – Here you will find beautiful artist's cards with animation accompanied by music. Your customer will be sent a link to the card and must come to the Ojolie.com website to view it. This site is affordable and cost not much more than a few Starbucks a year.
Hallmark.com – I love Hoops & YoYo as well as many of the thank you cards at Hallmark. Be sure to take a look and see if this is a site you want to use.

MOMA.org – The Museum of Modern Art has some really cool free e-cards with a series for special occasions using art from Any Warhol, Fernand Leger, Mac Chagall and more! The email sent to the customer is plain text that directs them to the MOMA.org website. This site is cool and worth the trip. Send one to yourself, visit the site and then decide. If you have a fun, artsy, future resident, you might keep this one site in mind! The prospect that appreciates beautiful art will surely appreciate your efforts in supporting the arts. You might just gain some extra bonus points!

FleetingGreeting.com – This website is easy, fun and shows up in the email you send without requiring the recipient to click away to the site! This is one of my favorites. Design a series of ideas from this site and you will be ready to send great follow-up FAST!

GoAnimate.com – Offers a way to send video and animation but requires a monthly subscription. This is the perfect tool for a leasing team looking to separate themselves from the competition. You can set up a company account and divide the cost between regions or portfolios to make it more affordable. Don't go look if you don't have the money in your budget because you're going to WANT THIS!

Americangreetings.com – Has talking cards! Pick an image, a voice and then type the message you want shared. It sounds like an avatar, but it is cute and fun! You can pick the voice from male, female, child, UK or US accents and more. People will remember your message plus you'll have fun putting them together.

Smilebox.com – A great website that offers a fun way to send messages with great photos and music.

Jibjab.com – Greetings that are sure to get a laugh! For just a few dollars per month, your staff can create both fun and unforgettable follow-up e-cards. Simply upload pictures of your staff and make cards that your prospects will remember. Be sure to check out the thank you cards and videos! The cards can also be posted to Facebook! Please note: There is some questionable content on this site that is not appropriate for business. Be smart and have all your selections approved by a supervisor.

Picmonkey.com – Free basic service is offered but for a just a few dollars a month you can use all the features available on this fun site. I use this site to build tons of the tools for my power point slides, and it works great for building follow-up messages.

Building a Fab-YOU-lous Follow-up message

Choose Your Theme
When you choose a theme, it makes the follow-up more eye-catching and memorable. Here is a list of some of my favorite themes.

- Noisy Neighbors with images of birds
- It's all here with an area map from Walkscore.com showing what's close-by.
- Coupons – Live where you want – save money on shoping!
- Link List – supply a list of helpful links to online moving resources.

Fab-YOU-lous Pictures Are Worth a Thousand Words
Try to say as much of your message in pictures as you can. Make messages quick to read and easy to understand. Let the prospect SEE the value or humor as fast as possible. Try using an inexpensive source for images such as 123RF.com. If these themes are going to be used by many properties, you might think about buying something cool that was built for marketing use online. For a small investment, you can own some great images to add to your texts and make the look of your follow-up custom and unique. Once you own the picture you can also upload it into picmonkey.com and use the photoshop tools to custom build individual messages. Remember, you should only use photos that you have purchased for professional use and are royalty free.

Write Your Message
All too often we write a message like it is an advertisement and not a note from a friend. Todays consumer is overloaded with commercial messages that they fast-forward and delete. Don't sound like an advertisement, sound like a friend. Be sure you always add advice, helpful resources, and tips they can use. Feel free to use casual language rather than sales copy. For fun, read your note out loud with a radio announcer voice to make sure your copy doesn't

sound like a commercial. If it sounds good, change it. If it sounds bad, you got it right! The voice of a friend would not sound right when spoken in a radio DJ's voice.

Here are a few examples of messages that I like to use:

- Thanks for stopping by today. Below is a list of helpful links found online with great tips for moving, plus a few coupons to save you some money. I know moving can be stressful. I sure hope this can make things a little bit easier.
- When you stop for a minute on our property you can hear, the birds sing. There are so many trees here you don't need a smartphone to get a tweet! After a long day, it's nice to come home to a little twitter!
- I know it is important to make sure all the great things you need in life are close-by. I built this map for you at Walkscore.com to show the retail, restaurants, parks, grocery stores and schools right around your new apartment.

<u>Fab-YOU-lous Digital follow-up</u>

Being digital allows you to find and connect your future resident to helpful advice and links that you can share in an email. There are national tips that can be shared by everyone, but, people like to check out local resources too. Do some searching in your local area for:
- Moving tips
- Moving Coupons
- Local Coupons

Here is an example built by a client in Ohio.

"Open-Me-First" Box
Packing for a move can be a stressful process, one that can often have you asking, "Where do I start?" An often overlooked but

vitally important detail is preparing an "Open-Me-First" box. This handy box will include basic necessities you'll need to get settled into your new place. This box should be on top of your list of priorities before moving day. Here is a step-by-step guide that will help you prepare and asscmble your "Open-Me-First" box.
http://designmymove.com/packing-an-open-me-first-box/

Change Your Address Online For Free
Changing your address can be a pain! Be careful not to share your information on any scam websites! I found a great online source to change your address with a 100% safe rating! Here are both the safe site and the scamadviser.com site.

http://www.changeofaddressform.com
http://www.scamadviser.com/is-changeofaddressform.com-a-fake-site.html

Moving Can Be Expensive!
Don't forget to use great online coupons! This is one of my favorite sites: http://www.retailmenot.com/coupons/moving
Stop for a Treat & Get One Free!
Great deals on restaurants, entertainment, and retail stores plus much more, all near your new home!
http://www.valpak.com/coupons/savings/Restaurants/Columbus/OH

MapQuest Rocks!
Use your prospect's current address and build a great follow-up tool on MapQuest that brings them right to your door. MapQuest allows you to text it to their phone, send it as a message on Facebook, or email it to their phone. You can even send them the cheapest place to buy gas on the way!

Image/Hyperlinks
Be sure to have your property logo image as a hyperlink to the community website as well as social media icons with links too.

Professional Head-shot
Consider adding your photo to your signature line! Have a great photo of yourself taken in your office and add it to your signature block in your email.

Design a Hand-Made Signature Leasing Card

Your Signature Leasing Brand
Follow-up is simply not an option if you plan to excel in this field. You will want to make sure you can build a plan for follow-up that includes voice, digital and print.

In the book "Me 2.0," Dan Schawbel writes, "The same rules that apply to corporate brands apply to personal brands. The successful brand you marketing model has the proper mix of confidence, passion, likeability, determination, and focus." Creating a signature leasing style all your own will allow you to execute a follow-up plan that will increase leases and establish confident relationships with your customers.

Have you ever asked the customer if they remember what they have seen? They will often gaze off and then say "No!" This means they actually spent time with a leasing consultant, toured a property and then promptly forgot them completely! One of my biggest goals is to be unforgettable. I want to help you design a look to your presentation that is memorable. Make choices in the way you use your property collateral that adds your own signature leasing style thereby developing memory associations that reinforce you and your property! Your signature style should be fun and unique.

The Value of a Personal Touch - Hand-made Cards
Sending a personal note puts your follow-up in the "read first" pile of mail we receive. Bills are separated out along with coupons, but hand-written cards are the first to be read! I recommend that you do not use any traditional business materials.

By purchasing items used by wedding planners, the look and feel of your message communicates friend and not business. Finding a home is difficult and stressful. The more you can present yourself as a friendly advisor, the more positive results you will experience with your follow-up. What good is a marketing postcard with a picture of your model, if they throw it away as junk mail? I recommend that you build an inventory of hand-made cards ready to add a quick, personal note and then send. Make it easy on yourself. Build a marketing fun box with your entire personal signature leasing tools including trim scissors, stamps and stickers. Use color coordinating gel pens that match your properties print marketing materials. When you are ready to build cards, go ahead and make a stack of 50 at a time.

Fab-YOU-lous Linen Card and Envelops
Order or purchase blank cards with envelopes in white or ivory linen stock. These cards are 80 lb. cover and envelopes are 80 lb. text. Cards are size 5" × 6-7/8," with matching envelopes. Starting with a blank allows you to custom build your follow-up to match your signature.

Get the EDGE on Your Competition!
Fun trimming scissors are sold at the hobby shops. Using trimming scissors will leave a unique edge on any piece of paper. Choose one that follows the style and look of your brochures and start trimming. By cutting the right side edge of your business card and the side of your floor plan or brochure, your marketing collateral will stand out and be unique. Designs include scallop, deckle, ripple, pinking, imperial, and corkscrew. The deckle edge resembles the irregular edges of some vintage photographs. What an easy way to add your personal touch to follow-up. Pick a design and use it consistently as a memory association.

Stamped With Approval!
There are beautiful "Thank You" stamps that allow you to add an artistic consistent look to your messages. Stamps are easy to use and are if the design is simple, they can even be added to any note or

message. A stamp that reads "Thank You" can be placed on the bottom right hand corner of a blank card to produce a simple elegant thank you note in second!

Make Your Mark!
I love to sign my emails, notes and other messages with a happy face! This is my signature mark. It is easy to find a fun line drawing artistic doodle, flower or image that you can cut and paste into your messages. It also works great if you know how to draw. You could draw your own signature mark and then make a photo of it and add it to your digital messages. People associate me with happy face stickers. I show them when I speak, share them when people leave and post them on my Facebook. Take some time and develop your own signature mark for leasing and use it on your business card, floor plans, follow-up messages and personalized notes.

Fab-YOU-lous Face Stickers
Nothing is more powerful in your signature than your smiling face! One of my favorite, fun ways to be unique is to add my face on my business card, floor plans and any form of follow-up! Create your own face stickers to use for marketing. Save the image as a Jpeg and add it digitally in your email signature. Stickers can be purchased that are dishwasher safe and can be added to property mugs, cups, pens and other marketing logo tools you use in the office. Have fun and use them to "stick" around! The flexibility of the sticker immediately turns anything into a leasing/marketing tool. At the end of your note when you add your signature and mark don't forget to add your face sticker for the final touch! Talk about a memory association! An amazing fact about human memory: most people remember images better than verbal or written information. Using your face boosts your memory for two main reasons. First, images are easier to remember than facts. Second, reviewing your face reinforces their memory of their experience at your property. Be sure to introduce your face sticker at the property by adding one to a floor plan, note, business card or brochure. Be sure they associate the sticker with you and the property.

A Fab-YOU-lous Digital Close: The 24-Hour Reservation Guarantee

Be sure to have tools that are designed for closing in a digital follow-up format. If the prospect left your property without writing a check to hold an apartment, send them a 24-Hour Reservation Guarantee! The 24-Hour Reservation Guarantee is a word document that can be personalized with individual leasing contact information and allows the agent to add a logo to customize it for their property. Screen shot the actual reservation filled out into a digital follow-up to let them know you would like to offer them first right of refusal on the apartment they liked. Share with the prospect that: "There is no need for you to risk losing the apartment you want while you decide. We would like to extend to you a 24-Hour Reservation Guarantee as a courtesy to you while you decide." Add the prospects name, apartment address, date and time that the reservation expires. This can be just the tool to help tip the scales in your favor.

Fab-YOU-lous Video Follow-up

YouTube Apartment Tour Video

Today many communities have phones and tablets that include a video recorder. I love the idea of recording a casual video tour through each apartment as it comes available. Take some staging decorations to make it look great and share an enthusiastic look at their new address on YouTube. YouTube channels are free to set up, and each property should have one ready to go. Use the complete street address and zip code as the video name. Be sure to add the keyword as tags and a great description. This is a wonderful link to send to people that they can then share with their friends, roommate, parents, or spouse!

YouTube – We Miss You Already!

Get your team together and make a few signs on copy paper. One says, "Turn around!" "We Miss You Already!" "Get back in here!" "Don't leave!" Have your staff record a quick video to send to people while they walk to their car. Tell them to turn around, you miss them already, don't leave because someone else will rent your apartment while you are gone and we are all going to be so sad! Get back in here! Once recorded, upload it to YouTube and send it to everyone who does not rent as they leave. The first time we tested this we had two people come back in the first day!

YouTube – Where Are You Now?
Here comes the second message to "We miss you already." Set an alarm to give notice about 20 minutes after the prospect leaves and send them this message: "Where are you now? You're not looking at another apartment are you? No way! You already found your home. Come on back. We're attaching a coupon for buy one get one free sub sandwich. You guys go have a bite and come back here and open your present!" This technique does use a small amount of guilt, however; it is real and shows how much you want them to be a resident. People love to be wanted, and it's funny. It will make them smile and think of you while they are with another leasing agent! Note: At the end when I said, "come back here and open your present." I use a technique in my office called a "Celebration Station." This is a small house-warming party we stage with wrapped gifts to celebrate with each new resident. We believe that finding a home is a moment worth celebrating, and we like to be the first ones to give them a house-warming gift!

Powerful Points in Follow-up: Slideshare.net
Images of your property can be imported into PowerPoint. Add a few extra slides including the floor plan, property tour images, area features, businesses and more. Upload the PowerPoint to Slideshare.net for a great way to share a customized brochure! Tie in your theme and add a link in an email to bring them to Slideshare for more information. You can even add a YouTube video to Slideshare and make your follow-up come to life!

Fab-YOU-lous Animoto.com Follow-up
This great site allows you to add photos and text then turn it into a music video. The video can then be uploaded to YouTube and added to Slideshare.net.

Build Your Plan

<u>Following up a Phone Call</u>
We have discussed a variety of ways you can follow-up: it's time to build your plan. When are you going to follow-up and how?

- Day ONE: Print NOW – have them print down an online brochure.
- Day ONE: Email in 5 minutes – send link list with helpful tips and advice.
- Day ONE: Call end of the day – leave a message or voice memo email "Hope the rest of your day was productive; just checking in to see _____."
- Day ONE: Put a signature series handmade card in the mail – to arrive in a few days. Enclose your card and an area coupon for a treat for on the way.
- Day ONE: Send packet of marketing collateral with a Walkscore.com map.
- Day TWO: Send a FleetingGreeting.com "looking forward to seeing you" confirm the appointment time with a link to directions on MapQuest.

<u>Following up to a Leasing Tour</u>
We have discussed a variety of ways you can follow-up, it's time to build your plan. When are you going to follow-up and how?

- Day ONE: YouTube We miss you already
- Day ONE: YouTube Where are you now?
- Day ONE: Call end of the day – leave a message or voice memo email "Hope the rest of your day was productive; just checking in to see _____."
- Day ONE: Put a signature series handmade card in the mail – to arrive in a few days. Enclose your card and an area coupon for a treat on the way back to your property.

- Day ONE: Send packet of marketing collateral with a Walkscore.com map.
- Day ONE: Send a 24-Hour Reservation Guarantee.
- Day TWO: Send a FleetingGreeting.com that says: "Thank you for visiting! We miss you already."
- Day THREE: Send a slideshare.net with YouTube video built on Animoto.com.

Fab-YOU-lous Follow-up – After They Lease
A great way to use Animoto.com is to build a file for a "Music Video Change of Address Card." Follow-up to the leasing decision by sending them a personalized Music Video Change of Address Card. Take a picture with them in their apartment or near the property sign before they leave and let them know you will be sending them a special change of address card. Animoto.com allows you to "make a copy" of any video once it is built, and then you can make changes and save it by a new name. Build a basic video that includes the community pictures, floor plans, area features, and businesses. Simply make a copy and add their name, address, personal photo and save! TADA! Another way to use Animoto.com is to send a video of a new construction apartment during the make-ready process. Tami Siewruk, Imagination Officer of Multifamilypro, built a video showing carpet being cleaned, a mirror being washed, and maintenance installing an air filter. She then sent the new resident a music video message to confirm that their home was ready and gave them their move-in day appointment. BRILLANT!

The Final Fab-YOU-lous Follow-up – After They Move
When a resident has to move it is stressful, and everyone hopes to be "missed." This is a great opportunity to request a review of their stay at your community and thank them for being residents. This follow-up could be a video message with the whole team! You could take pictures of the team holding these messages and make an Animoto.com music video! Have fun and leave them with happy thoughts of your community!

- Miss you already!
- Thanks for being a great resident!
- Good luck in your new home!
- Please let others know about our great community! Add the link to the apartment review site.

I really enjoyed building this chapter full of Fab-YOU-lous follow-up for you. I believe this plan will increase your leasing, add value to the process and improve reliability in your relationship with your residents. If you like the ideas I have shared be sure to follow me on Facebook: Apartment Leasing Ideas Fab-YOU-lous Fundamentals, and on Pinterest. Thanks for letting me be a part of your success.

Notes

Notes

Notes

Notes

Notes

Notes

Notes

Notes

Notes

Notes

Notes